Materializing the Nation

Materializing the Nation

Commodities, Consumption, and Media in Papua New Guinea

Robert J. Foster

INDIANA
University Press
Bloomington & Indianapolis

This book is a publication of

Indiana University Press
601 North Morton Street
Bloomington, IN 47404-3797 USA

http://iupress.indiana.edu

Telephone orders   800-842-6796
Fax orders   812-855-7931
Orders by e-mail   iuporder@indiana.edu

The paper used in this publication meets the minimum
requirements of American National Standard for Information
Sciences—Permanence of Paper for Printed Library Materials,
ANSI Z39.48-1984.

Manufactured in the United States of America

Library of Congress Cataloging-in-Publication Data

Foster, Robert John, date
   Materializing the nation : commodities, consumption, and media
in Papua New Guinea / Robert J. Foster.
      p.   cm.
Includes bibliographical references and index.
   ISBN 0-253-34147-7 (cloth : alk. paper) — ISBN 0-253-21549-8
(pbk. : alk. paper)
   1. Anthropology—Papua New Guinea. 2. Ethnopsychology—Papua
New Guinea. 3. Nationalism—Papua New Guinea. 4. Consumption
(Economics)—Papua New Guinea. 5. Materialism—Social
aspects—Papua New Guinea. I. Title.
   GN671.N5 F67 2002
   305.8' 009953—dc21

                                        2002001480

1 2 3 4 5   07 06 05 04 03 02

For Andrew M. and Gregory R.

Contents

Acknowledgments

ALMOST ALL THE chapters in this book originated as conference papers; the last chapter began as a seminar given to the Department of Anthropology at the University of Chicago and subsequently given at other universities. I thank the audiences at these various presentations for their interest and comments. I also thank the individual organizers who generously invited me to participate in their conferences, especially Patricia Spyer and Anders Linde-Laursen. Martha Kaplan and John Kelly, old friends and supportive colleagues, invited me to present the paper that became chapter 6 in a plenary session organized by Marshall Sahlins and sponsored by the Wenner-Gren Foundation for Anthropological Research at the annual meeting of the American Society for Ethnohistory (London, Ontario) in October 2000.

In previously publishing some of these chapters, I have benefited from the careful suggestions of several journal editors and anonymous reviewers and from the thoughtful remarks of James Carrier, Nicholas Thomas, Andrew Strathern, Orvar Löfgren, Scott MacWilliam, Dan Jorgensen, John MacAloon, Mark Busse, and Claudia Gross. Deborah Gewertz deserves special thanks for her incisive comments on many occasions.

Mark Busse and Claudia Gross provided me with not only important insights, but also friendship and a home during two visits to Port Moresby. I have similarly enjoyed, in Papua New Guinea (PNG) and Australia, the lively conversation and gracious hospitality of Deborah Gewertz and Frederick Errington, Scott MacWilliam, Margaret Jolly, Nicholas Thomas, Andrew Lattas, Lise McKean, Richard Eves, and Roe Sybylla.

I am grateful to all the people working in commercial media and advertising in PNG who gave me their time and consideration, especially Andrew Johnston and his staff at Pacific View Productions, and John Taylor, former chief executive of EM TV. I also thank Anna Solomon, Phil Sawyer, Steve Landon, Richard Dellman, and Sorariba Nash for sharing their views with me.

For institutional support, I owe a debt of gratitude to both the Institute of Papua New Guinea Studies and the PNG National Research Institute for making my research possible. Wari Iamo, Don Niles, Colin Filer, and Michael Laki have been particularly helpful. I also thank the resourceful and welcoming staff of the Department of Anthropology at the Research School of Pacific and Asian Studies, Australian National University, where I have twice been a visiting fellow. David Robie, former head of the journalism program at the University of Papua New Guinea (UPNG), and a group of students in that program assisted my research in crucial ways. Linus digim'Rina, head of the Department of Anthropology and Sociology at UPNG, and Baulon Maibala have also offered generous support, which I gratefully acknowledge.

For material aid, I thank the Center for International Studies, University of Chicago; the Australian-American Educational Foundation; the American Council of Learned Societies; the University of Rochester; and the Spencer Foundation. I especially thank the National Endowment for the Humanities, which has been a stalwart supporter of my research projects over the last ten years.

In preparing this book, I have received superb editorial guidance from Rebecca Tolen of Indiana University Press, whose confidence and encouragement I greatly appreciate. For permission to reproduce illustrations and photographs, I thank the PNG Department of Education; the Bank of PNG; PepsiCo, Inc.; Coca-Cola Holdings (Overseas) Limited; The Coca-Cola Company; (PNG) *Post-Courier*; Anna Solomon and Word Publishing Company; the late Maslyn Williams; Michael O'Hanlon; and Holly Wardlow. Throughout the book, I have italicized the registered trademarks of PepsiCo, Inc. and The Coca-Cola Company as per agreement with their owners.

Five of the chapters in this book were previously published elsewhere:

Chapter 1, "Take Care of Public Telephones: Moral Education and Nation-State Formation in Papua New Guinea." *Public Culture* 4(2):31–45, 1992. Reproduced by permission of Duke University Press.

Chapter 2, "Your Money, Our Money, the Government's Money: Finance and Fetishism in Melanesia." In *Border Fetishisms: Material Objects in Unstable Places,* edited by Patricia Spyer, 60–90. New York: Routledge, 1998. Reproduced by permission of Routledge Inc./Taylor & Francis.

Chapter 3, "Nation Making and Print Advertisements in Metropolitan Papua New Guinea." In *Nation Making: Emergent Identities in Postcolonial Melanesia,* edited by Robert J. Foster, 151–81. Ann Arbor: University of Michigan Press, 1995. Reproduced by permission of the University of Michigan Press.

Chapter 4, "Commercial Mass Media in Papua New Guinea: Notes on Agency, Bodies, and Commodity Consumption." *Visual Anthropology Review* 12(2):1–17, 1996–1997. Reproduced by permission of the American Anthropological Association.

Chapter 5, "The Commercial Construction of 'New' Nations." *Journal of Material Culture* 4(3):263–82, 1999. Reproduced by permission of Sage Publications.

Finally, I thank Nancy Foster for her many gifts, which include countless contributions to this book in matters of style and substance, patience and love.

Materializing the Nation

Introduction
Everyday Nation Making:
The Case of Papua New Guinea

ACROSS THE HUMANITIES and social sciences, over the last twenty years, scholars have rekindled their interest in the subject of nations and nationalism. Their motivation springs not only from the new exigencies of post–cold war politics, but also from a spate of new responses to Ernest Renan's old question: What is a nation? Anthropologists, in particular, have welcomed fresh opportunities for treating nations as cultural artifacts, contingent outcomes of social and historical processes variously characterized as imagination, invention, or narration. At the same time, renewed interest in nation making has converged with growing concern inside and outside the academy over globalization, a term loosely used to name the rapid circulation of people and money, images and ideas, through complicated networks of almost planetary scope (see Foster 1991 for a review). Two related questions thus continue to attract broad attention. By what ways and means, agents and agencies, have nations been made, remade, and unmade? And what possibilities for making nations have been opened up and shut down by the shifting and uneven effects of intensifying globalization?

This book ought to be read against the background of these questions. Because each chapter derives from ethnographic and historical research focused on Papua New Guinea (PNG)—a place associated more with the anthropology of gift exchange and esoteric ritual than of nations and nationalism—other, narrower questions naturally arise. Nevertheless, I orient the analysis of ethnographic and historical details toward a more general inquiry. What might be learned about how nation making works—and does not work—by studying its particular and emergent manifestations on the margins of both the international state and world capitalist systems? Why, in a globalizing world, do people anywhere come to see themselves, for better or worse, as deeply implicated in a nation that they may or may not want?

In this book, I consider how state officials and corporate executives, university students and office workers, among others, struggle over and use commodity consumption and commercial media in defining and promoting political community and collective identity in national (and sometimes trans-national) terms. "Commodity consumption" here refers to a variety of every-day practices that include chewing betel nut and adding sugar to instant cof-fee. "Commercial media" here refers mainly to the mass media of newspaper and television, especially advertisements, and secondarily to other forms of media, including state-issued money and state-sponsored public cultural per-formances such as the Olympic Torch Relay. The chapters together demon-strate how nation making unfolds not only (perhaps not even primarily) through organized programs of political socialization, but also through mun-dane engagements with radio talk show programs and commodities ranging from locally made tinned meat to globally marketed soft drinks. In other words, the book demonstrates how "the nation" materializes in the form of media images and consumer goods, and thus how national culture in PNG takes shape, to the extent that it does, in conjunction with the spread of both new media technologies and new arenas for commodity consumption. In so doing, I argue, the book says something about the nature of everyday nation making, now and in the past, in PNG and elsewhere.

Besides looking at commodity consumption and commercial media as techniques and practices of nation making—the question of how—the chap-ters in this book also broach the larger and more elusive question of why: Why does "the nation" still (sometimes) loom large in the imagination of (some) people? The questions of how and why are not, of course, always separable. That is, the persistent relevance of "the nation" as a frame of reference for social life derives in part from the insinuation of "the nation" into a host of contexts, some quite banal (Billig 1995), including contexts of commodity and media consumption. In certain instances, such as drinking a can of *Coca-Cola* stamped "PNG Made," it becomes obvious that, despite tendencies to the con-trary, global capitalism plays an active part in sponsoring "the nation" (see Dávila 1998, Guss 1996).

In any case, all responses to the question of why "the nation" remains relevant must begin by granting that nation making is a now thoroughly glo-balized activity, spread worldwide by dint of the modularity of the nation form (Anderson 1991). The institution of "the nation" as a global structure of common difference (Wilk 1995), however, reduces the possibility for creat-ing alternative identities that are equally legible and legitimate. The force of this reduction is felt most acutely in places where political, cultural, and economic visibility on the world stage requires dressing up in the garb be-queathed, or, rather, imposed, by powerful outsiders—first colonial rulers, now inter(national)-state regulatory agencies (and transnational nongovernmental organizations, too). In these circumstances, the continuing relevance of "the nation" is a reflex of the pressing need of a variety of subalterns—whether minority ethnic groups within territorial states or poor and weak states themselves—to make themselves and their claims comprehensible in the ruling language. Such translations inevitably carry a risk; "having a nation" might in these circumstances mean supplying a desti-nation for foreign tourists. Accordingly, the chapters in this book illustrate both the successes and failures of particular people negotiating the limits that a dominant form of political community puts on the imaginations of people everywhere. In doing so, they illustrate an inescapable feature of contemporary social life.

NATION MAKING IN WEAK STATES

Writing a book about "the nation" in PNG might seem implausible on a long list of counts. Most lists would begin—too quickly, I think—with PNG's famous ethnolinguistic pluralism: over seven hundred different languages spoken by culturally diverse people inhabiting radically different physical environments. But every list would include, sooner or later, the notorious weakness of the state to which "the nation" is allegedly coupled.

In contemporary Melanesia, there are no panoptical regimes expeditiously disciplining, surveying, and producing national citizens—*Homo nationalis,* to use Balibar's (1990) name for the species—through pervasive social regulation. In PNG, as elsewhere in the region, the national state succeeded a financially strapped colonial state, the administrative and ideological apparatus of which did not reach very far into the territory or lives of its subjects. A hasty decolonization process unfolded more in response to international pressure and Australian domestic politics than to popular anticolonial protest (see Nelson 2000 for a recent review). Subsequent "official nationalism"—state-sponsored attempts to define a national culture—has generated shallow, contradictory, and often empty effects (Lindstrom 1998, Wanek 1995).

Many scholars would push these observations further, arguing that the institutions of the national state itself have been effectively colonized and subverted by the homegrown interests and agents of numerous localized societies (Strathern 1993, Jacobsen 1995, Dinnen 2001; see also Filer 1992, Standish 1994). Even more than casual observers could therefore be forgiven for seeing PNG as another example of a peripheral postcolony in which "the nation" is "little more than a rhetorical figure of speech, the color of a soccer stripe, an airline without aircraft, a university rarely open" (Comaroff and Comaroff 2000:325). In this unflattering light, PNG appears as an unimagined community, a failed imitation of more established, more homogeneous Western nations, or alternatively, as an early sign of the coming postnational condition.

As if all that were not enough to render talk of "the nation" moot, nation-states everywhere—not just in postcolonial Melanesia—now seem to be in crisis, their political sovereignty and cultural integrity put at risk by movements of people, capital, and technologies insensitive to territorial borders. It might not be only in PNG, where the state of late gives scattered attention to fashioning a national community and instead directs its regulatory gaze outward, that projects of "health, environmental management, and commerce are, to an increasing degree, appropriated by supranational entities which become increasingly powerful" (Thomas 1997:216). Thus the fiscal policies of interstate regulatory agencies such as the World Bank and IMF have provoked widespread anxiety from Seattle to Prague as well as in the streets of Port Moresby, PNG's capital city. Put differently, in this era of economic globalization, the prospects of nation-state formation seem dim, if not irrelevant. Whether capitalism requires the existence of states is debatable, but that capitalism can make do without nations is not. This brute fact seems to register in suggestions that some sort of shift is underway, "from citizenship to shopping" (Thomas 1997), in which consumers replace citizens (see Ewen 1992). That is, instead of political agency linking citizens to the nation-state, consumption practices link autonomous individuals to a global market; indeed, consumption becomes the dominant means for defining personal and collective identities of all kinds.[1]

Given these circumstances, the most recondite fact about PNG is that—despite a twelve-year secessionist war in Bougainville, recurrent crises of law and order, and a steadily deteriorating material infrastructure—a polity resembling nothing if not a nation-state continues to exist more than twenty-five years after formal independence. PNG hardly qualifies as a "strong state," capable of coercing its citizen-subjects through persuasion and/or violence (Migdal 1988, Larmour 1996). But it would be also wrong to characterize PNG as some "intimate tyranny" exercised through grotesque spectacles of power (Mbembe 1991). Indeed, the political analyst Benjamin Reilly has called attention to the way in which procedural democracy in PNG appears to operate relatively smoothly: elections are held regularly and governments changed peacefully. Reilly attributes this outcome to the same impressive diversity that many other commentators see as an inevitable impediment to nationhood, on the grounds that "ethnic fragmentation may actually help consolidate democracy and that PNG's extreme ethnic fragmentation may be the overriding factor in its democratic success to date" (2000–2001:168). Similarly, though I hesitate to gauge its depths, I refuse to dismiss national consciousness in PNG as chimerical—as if nothing less than passionate Nuremberg-style flag-waving indicates "true" national consciousness. "The nation" is clearly present in PNG —not only as a rhetorical figure of speech (the significance of which I likewise hesitate to dismiss), but also as a frame of reference for staging a whole range of collective and personal identities. This book seeks first of all to support this assertion.

What general questions, then, can a discussion of "the nation" in PNG—

like the one carried on across these chapters—address? Kelly (1995), in an insightful epilogue to an earlier volume on nation making in Melanesia, poses two questions well worth posing again. First, he asks, what makes a nation if not a state (or in addition to a state)? That is, what can we learn from studying the ways in which nation making in the areas of education, law, and public ritual proceeds in the absence of strong states? Where else, furthermore, ought we look besides the machinery of governmentality for instances of how "the nation" materializes? These questions should be of special interest if the weakness of the state in PNG anticipates the future of stronger states managing the disjunctures of the global cultural economy (Appadurai 1990, 1993).

Second, and more fundamentally, Kelly asks how are we to think of "the nation" at all. That is, how can we conceive of "the nation" in such a way as to recognize the plain reality that an extreme case like PNG impresses on us, namely, that "the nation" is not singular, either in its form or force, notwithstanding the cogent claim that "nation-ness is the most universally legitimate value in the political life of our time" (Anderson 1991:3)? How can we conceive of "the nation" so as to further an understanding that is both ethnographic and comparative?

IMAGINING AND NARRATING NATIONS

Kelly answers his more fundamental question by suggesting that we think of "the nation" as a narrative—that is, a narrative "constituted dialogically and useful and important politically, for a state trying to regulate a capitalist market or for a people to contest politically within and against the institutional framework of a state" (1995:257). This definition follows on the now-familiar work of Anderson (1991), Bhabha (1990), and Hobsbawm and Ranger (1983), which treats the nation (and hereafter I drop the quotation marks) as a collective representation and asks, accordingly, about the social requirements for imagining the nation and making such imaginings persuasive and compelling. Such a definition also calls attention to the ways in which the nation, as narrative, is always in process, often contested by multiple agents with competing agendas. It is precisely the imaginative aspect of the nation that I emphasize in this book, tracing the ways in which multiple constructs circulate in heterogeneous forms, both discursive and nondiscursive: official policy documents, letters to the editor, school textbooks, state ceremonies, lyrics, advertisements, product logos, coin and currency.[2] These constructs are promulgated through a variety of channels and by a variety of agents, not all equipped with equal resources to make their version of the nation stick (cf. Fox 1990).

Kelly's definition of nation as narrative deflects the argument that the nation has definite and essential content—that the nation form, in other words, is singular: a bounded, "horizontal" community of equal and similar individuals. The great virtue of this move is that it obviates invidious comparisons by which versions of the nation that do not match the paradigm are regarded as inauthentic or unrealized; it therefore makes the nation amenable to ethnographic variation. The metaphorical equation of nation and narrative also informs Kelly's response to the question of what makes a nation if not a state, for clearly, states, no matter how strong, enjoy no monopoly on the production of narratives. Accordingly, Kelly encourages us to look beyond the agencies of the state for sites where the nation as imaginative construct or narrative is made and made real—sound advice on which the remainder of this introduction expands.

The chapters in this book put in the background pronouncements of nation-states living or dying, flourishing or withering. I tell here a different story, of how the complicated and uneven impact of the nation-state is felt "in the everyday contexts of work and labor, of domesticity and consumption, of street life and media-gazing" (Comaroff and Comaroff 2000:325). While I acknowledge (of course) the role of the state—colonial as well as postcolonial—in promoting images and ideals of the nation, I look elsewhere for processes that materialize the nation, especially to mass-mediated commercial culture. I suggest that this strategy is relevant not only in PNG today, but in other places and at other times. Indeed, it becomes possible to compare historically the extent to which states as opposed, say, to markets and media have conditioned nation making. Orvar Löfgren (1993)—from whom I have borrowed the title of this book—has contrasted the United States and Sweden in this way, arguing that mass consumption and commercial media played an earlier and more important role than U.S. state institutions in creating a frame of reference and associations for narratives of the nation. From the perspective I adopt in this book, PNG therefore looks more like the United States than Sweden—despite the obvious difference in strength between the U.S. and PNG states.

Paying attention to mass-mediated commercial culture also makes sense to me because, unlike Kelly, I give more prominence to one particular construct or narrative of the nation in this book, for two reasons. First, a paradigmatic nation form—that of a political community of discrete, equal, and similar individuals who comprise a distinctive collective individual—underwrites a host of commonplace modern institutions, from newspapers to elections to censuses. All these institutions assume and effect "seriality" (Anderson 1998); they construe individuals (Papua New Guineans or Greeks) and collectivities (PNG or Greece) as aggregable components of a single category series (nationals and nations). This logic of seriality also resonates well with the commodity form, even if there is no necessary relation between the two. I have argued elsewhere and I argue here that this resonance is epistemological, an effect of the expansion of practices and discourses of possessive individualism through capitalist markets (Foster 1995b; see LiPuma 2000). Possessive individualism privileges a certain way of conceiving both personal and collective identity—in terms of attributes or characteristics uniquely possessed. Inasmuch as the paradigmatic form of the nation posits a collective individual, nationality becomes a common possession of each individual subject, tangibly in the form of the set of commodities and other material objects that constitute "the national culture." Thus, even if capitalism can in principle make do without the nation, in practice, one often facilitates the interests of the other.

Second, nation making in PNG, or anywhere else for that matter, now happens with reference to this paradigm of the nation-state as a definite kind of political community possessed of a distinctive national culture. This paradigm is built into a variety of global institutions ranging from the United Nations to the International Olympic Committee. Put otherwise, and in terms I will pursue presently, "the nation" might well be pirated, as Anderson says, but it is a dominant definition of "the nation" with which the pirates must contend. Even in Fiji, where, as Kelly suggests, a version of the nation as "vertical" (or hierarchical)—in which all people are neither equal nor the same (cf. Kapferer 1988)—captures the imagination of many Fijians, acknowledgment of the paradigm is made in its very rejection.

MAKING PNG: CHRISTIANITY, CUSTOM, AND CONSUMER GOODS

What does close attention to mass-mediated commercial culture reveal about how the nation materializes in PNG? Three themes, which characterize the practices of Melanesian nation making in general, immediately become visible: Christianity, custom, and consumer goods. These three themes can be twisted into complicated knots—as when definitions of PNG as a Christian nation entail the validation of some customs and the denigration of others (e.g., polygamy; see Strathern and Stewart 2000); or as when advertisements for the consumer products of transnational corporations appeal to the value of local custom (chapter 7). The chapters in this book focus more on custom and commodities than they do on Christianity. I therefore pause here to underline the importance of Christianity to processes of nation making in PNG. Michael Young (1997:91–92) goes so far as to claim that the modern Pacific nation "rides on Christianity's back," and that "in every national celebration . . . a Christian sub-text can be found" (and sometimes vice versa). Indeed, the presence of Christianity in national narrative clearly materializes in the constitution of PNG, where both "Christian principles" and "worthy customs and traditional wisdom" merit equal mention (see Lātūkefu 1988).

While such a juxtaposition might puzzle scholars who see the emergence of national communities as a break from religious ones, it comes as no surprise to anyone familiar with colonial history in Melanesia. During the period of Australian rule from after World War I to independence in 1975, it was Christian missions that effectively served as the welfare arm of the colonial state, providing health and education services throughout the Trust Territory of Papua and New Guinea.[3] Mission activities had both intended and unintended effects on the formation of a nation-state in PNG (Hassall 1990). For example, mission education produced a clerisy that conveyed Christian values to all social strata and a pool of literate candidates for civil service positions as medics, teachers, and bureaucrats. Missions also reinforced supraethnic identities by orienting people to relatively standardized, uniform supralocal worldviews. This orientation involved, from the 1950s onward, increasing, if grudging, acceptance of the use of Tok Pisin (pidgin English) in church services instead of either English or select vernaculars, including the codification of Tok Pisin in the form of Fr. Frank Mihalic's *Jacaranda Dictionary and Grammar of Melanesian Pidgin* (1971).[4] In the 1970s, the mainstream Christian churches launched *Wantok,* a weekly Tok Pisin–language newspaper directed at sixth-grade school leavers. (The mainstream Christian churches also own Word Publishing, which produces the weekly English-language newspaper, *The Independent;* see my discussion of figures 3.4 and 3.5 in chapter 3). Cass (2000:263) has drawn the connection to Anderson's discussion of the nation as an imaginative construct, noting that "the unwitting promotion of Tok Pisin as a language of national unity" by the churches parallels the appearance in nineteenth-century Europe of dictionaries and formalized orthographies for some vernacular languages (at the expense of others), vehicles for the emergence of the nation as a new frame of reference for social life.

What insights, then, does a focus on the instrumental effects of commodities, custom, and Christianity in producing the nation yield? First of all, such a focus has the virtue of taking seriously certain mundane activities—watching television, drinking a *Coke,* reading a newspaper—that are of increasingly global scope as more people are drawn into capitalist markets and networks of commercial media. However, such a focus also makes clear how precisely some of the features often associated with accelerating globalization—commercial media, ubiquitous brands, fundamentalist religions—provide in PNG resources for making the nation an aspect of ordinary people's everyday experience. Commodity consumption and mass media link Papua New Guineans to global flows of objects and images, but they by no means institute a monolithic and homogeneous global culture. Globally distributed commercial culture, however, is subject to more than nationalization. Like Christianity, it is subject to local appropriation and transformation. That is, it can link individuals to an imagined transnational community of fellow consumers, but it can also provide the raw material for pursuing highly localized projects of social and cultural significance. Thus, the implication of consumption and media in imagining the nation is always unstable, potentially dissolvable into specificities of local concern or generalities of global proportion. The hyphen in consumer-citizen, like the hyphen in nation-state, both conjoins and separates at once.

There is another reason to pay special attention to consumption in PNG apart from any epochal transformation of citizens into shoppers. In the wake of decolonization, the independent nation-state was widely regarded as the means and guarantor of long-awaited "development," often measured in terms of increased commodity consumption. Commodity consumption, or the decline thereof for many people, has thus become a politically charged arena in which frustrations about the nation-state are often expressed.[5] Looking at this arena helps explain how "the nation" in PNG takes shape against the state, namely, as "the people" whom the state has betrayed. For example, it might well be that popular protests of the current government's IMF/World Bank–supported privatization programs make visible a nation pitted against not other nations or nation-states, but, rather, the very state to which it is illegitimately yoked.

The incessant discourse of "corruption" in PNG lends some credence to this claim, for talk about reforming corruption has the effect of legitimating the nation-state in principle as it delegitimizes the practice of the current government (see Gupta 1995). Corruption talk also illustrates another way in which Christianity shapes nation making. Consider, for example, the recent letter to the editor of the *Post-Courier* (26 July 2001) from Jacob Kewa of Madang. Kewa cites the book of Proverbs to answer the question of what exalts a nation: "It is righteousness that exalts a nation but sin is a reproach to any people." In so doing, Kewa echoed the prominent billboard that sits a stone's throw from the national parliament building in Port Moresby: "I warn you when evil forces rule the nation the people will hide and mourn but when the righteous forces rule, they will rejoice." Opposition leader Bill Skate quoted the billboard/Bible scripture to roaring applause in his address at the funeral of three university students shot dead by government forces in the aftermath of an antiprivatization protest. Skate—himself once an object of corruption discourse—claimed that "Today, after 25 years [of independence], we have lost innocent lives courtesy of the leadership crisis and ignorance and not accepting Jesus Christ as Prime Minister of this nation" (*National,* 5 July 2001). By contrast, parliament speaker Bernard Narokobi was shouted down by mourners when, after noting that the dead students had stood for their rights and freedoms as stipulated in the constitution he helped draft twenty-six years ago, he added that "there is no place for guns in the campus but only intellectual discourse" (*National,* 5 July 2001).

In this book, I pay attention to routine and familiar forms that the nation takes in PNG as elsewhere, forms often associated with commodity consumption: the iconography of paper currency or the flags used as logos for T-shirts.

That is, I pay attention to forms and practices in which the nation often assumes a "natural" existence mainly because they go unnoticed—forms and practices of unremarked-on banality (Billig 1995). Encountering these forms and practices in the social context of PNG potentially heightens a sense of just how unnatural they are, especially for Western (specifically American) commentators like me; for in PNG, not only are they remarked on, but they are also actively resisted and rejected. Looking at how various agents shape and reshape these forms and practices, moreover, highlights their malleability, and so recalls another general characteristic of the nation in addition to its banality—namely, its modularity (Anderson 1991). In PNG, it is manifestly possible to see how what Löfgren calls the international grammar of nationhood—its familiar panoply of flags, anthems, airlines, and so forth—is uneasily inflected by novel circumstances. Put differently, a discussion of how "the nation" materializes or becomes visible in the everyday lives of people in contemporary PNG exposes two related social processes of more general significance for an historical and anthropological understanding of the nation: modularity and banality. A dual focus on banality and modularity, in turn, advances the prospects of a comparative, historical, and ethnographic approach to that "hyphenated modernist polity," the nation-state (Comaroff and Comaroff 2000:318).

MODULAR BANALITY: AFTER THE LAST WAVE

Benedict Anderson's *Imagined Communities,* a book that has inspired much interdisciplinary scholarship since its publication in 1983, offers a wave theory of the "origin and spread" of nationalism. Anderson argues that the eighteenth-century creole nationalism of the new American states was succeeded by first the vernacular (or popular) nationalism and then the official nationalism of European states. The "last wave" of nationalism took the form of twentieth-century anticolonial struggles in mainly Africa and Asia. Each variety of nationalism, Anderson emphasizes, was able to draw on previously forged instruments for imagining (or narrating) the nation—that is, for defining and disseminating the nation as an imaginative construct. In other words, the nation, once created, "became 'modular,' capable of being transplanted, with varying degrees of self-consciousness, to a great variety of social terrains, to merge and be merged with a correspondingly wide variety of political and ideological constellations" (Anderson 1991:4).

In this chronology, the nation making of the new states of the southwestern Pacific comes into being after the last wave had broken. Fiji, PNG, Solomon Islands, and Vanuatu (the former New Hebrides) all attained formal political independence in the years between 1970 and 1980 in a process more like decolonization from above than anticolonial struggle from below.[6] All discussions of nation making in PNG must therefore begin with the recognition that by the time of independence, not only had nation-ness become globally established as a natural and proper form of political community, but also a whole set of techniques for making nations was available for export—indeed, was required to be put in place before any claim to nationhood be considered legitimate. What does such a recognition entail?

First, right from the start, PNG ("the nation") was made with reference to an "international community." Of course, nations by definition have an international dimension. Nationality and internationality are coeval, a fact illustrated by Jeremy Bentham's timely invention of the English word "international" in 1789 (Billig 1995:84). Opposing the national to the global does not, therefore, always imply antagonism. Nation making often occurs most spectacularly in markedly international contexts, such as the Olympic Games—or the torch relay leading up to the Olympic Games that I discuss in chapter 6. More generally, nation making proceeds with heightened self-consciousness of how things are done in and by other nations, especially powerful ones—models to be emulated or rejected, but rarely ignored. It is precisely such self-consciousness that is revealed in the public discussions over betel nut chewing that I review in chapters 1 and 4, in which concern over spitting in public is bound up with views about public behavior befitting citizens of modern nation-states.

Second, and more specifically, such recognition requires us to see nation making in/of PNG as happening in terms of an international symbolic language—or code or grammar—already firmly in place. Narrating or making PNG requires for the narrators and makers recourse to what Löfgren (1989a) has called a "do-it-yourself kit" for expressing nationhood, a checklist of items and ingredients necessary for all nations—anthem, flag, landscape, heritage institutions such as museums and archives, sports teams, and so forth. What I want to emphasize is that in many ways, this checklist is an inventory of banalities, a toolbox of devices that serve unobtrusively to "flag" the nation in everyday life (Billig 1995). The nation—in PNG as elsewhere—materializes more often in these banal and unremarkable forms than in the spectacular and emotion-charged displays often associated with Nationalism, with a capital N. The nation is thus in many respects on the surface of everyday life, but as I argue in these chapters, that does not warrant dismissal of the nation as superficial.

Third, and relatedly, nation making in PNG got underway in the context of a revolution in communications and media technologies. Anderson is well known for the attention he gives to the nineteenth-century revolution in promoting versions of the nation through print capitalism—the spread of vernacular language texts through which people could imagine their connections to each other (and disconnection from speakers of other vernaculars). Billig

(1995) similarly gives attention to the importance of newspapers, especially the sports pages, in flagging the nation as an aspect of everyday life in the United Kingdom. He notes that the international code of banalities includes very precise conventions about the layout of newspapers—from the separation of "home" (national) news from "foreign" (world) news to the reporting of weather with reference to silhouettes of "the country." (As if, for readers of U.S. newspapers, there were no weather in Canada or Mexico.) It is worth noting that these conventions are equally a part of newspapers in PNG. But it is perhaps more important to note that in PNG, where newspapers reach a small portion of the population as compared with Britain, other mass media such as radio and television follow similar conventions—flagging the nation in thirty-second "signature pieces" for EM TV, the one broadcast television station; in pop songs played on commercial FM stations; or in radio talk show discussions of the sort discussed in chapter 4. Indeed, it is in and through such mass media that the nation materializes both as an unnoticed banality *and* as an object of explicit interest and contest.

Anderson's wave theory, then, emphasizes the mimetic quality of nation making, the way in which a particular style of imagined community was continually exported and reproduced. Reproduction is not always replication, as Anderson duly recognizes; importation of the nation must involve a "merger" with already existing forms of life, social as well as ideological. This process of merging or importation can be and has been looked at analytically in a variety of ways, describing a variety of comparisons, beginning with the invidious kind.

The least generous way of looking at what happens when the nation appears in novel circumstances conjures up "specters of inauthenticity" (see Jolly 1992). Löfgren (1989a:9) has noted that latecomers to the work of nation making "have to live with the ironic comments of the pioneers," whose own imaginative construct had by then become a given, natural fact. To the "pioneers," the new nations seem pale imitations of "real" nations—too small to be sovereign or too arbitrary in their territorial borders, too tribal in their ideal of ethnic purity, or too incoherent in their ethnic heterogeneity. While there is something solid and substantial about Air France or British Airways, the name "Air Vanuatu" can only signal mimetic failure—"an airline without aircraft," to quote Comaroff and Comaroff again. There is a more general question of timing here. Certain strategies of nation making that once seemed plausible and legitimate now appear comical and unpersuasive. Thus, for example, Bruce Grant (2001) has shown how new state-sponsored monuments in Moscow, the folklore and fairy tale motifs of which evoke an innocent and simple Russian childhood, have become targets of loud derision. The monuments, instead of working quietly as banal reminders of both the nation and state power, have become focal points of criticism for an economically embattled and politically disenchanted population.[7]

The question of timing points to a more generous way of regarding variations in nation making across time and space. Rather than deeming some instances of nation making as spurious, this way assumes both that nation making is always and everywhere an ongoing concern and that it proceeds with different emphases at different times. Put differently, the nation as foreign import is domesticated in terms of unevenly distributed local interests and institutions which themselves periodically shift. Thus, as Löfgren's (1993) comparison of Sweden and the United States demonstrates, state agencies may play different roles at different times relative to market or church agencies. So, in PNG, as in much of Melanesia, Christianity has been absorbed as "traditional"—that is, as an element comprising the national cultural heritage that includes ancestral customs. This process has entailed conscious reflection about which customs can be retained and which must be rejected (as incompatible with Christian modernity). While this sort of reflection often preoccupies a segment of the elite (such as parliament speaker Bernard Narokobi; see Otto 1997), it is equally a matter of concern to many ordinary Papua New Guineans. Gewertz and Errington (1996; see also Errington and Gewertz 1996) have thus shown how Chambri elders have embraced the spectacle of cultural tradition offered in the form of music videos and commercial advertisements for biscuits while rejecting the forms of individualism and autonomy promoted by Christian evangelists to Chambri youth as disrespectful of tradition.

Processes of domestication—of putting foreign imports in the service of domestic agendas—have been well studied by anthropologists, perhaps most notably by Marshall Sahlins in his accounts of early encounters between Pacific Islanders and Europeans. Much of this work focuses on how consumer goods (such as cloth) and ritual performances (such as the game of cricket) acquire new meanings as users integrate them into old cultural contexts (Gregory 1980, Thomas 1991, O'Hanlon 1993, 1995; see also Tobin 1992, Hansen 1994).[8] Most studies illustrate the semantic malleability of material items that cross cultural borders. Yet when applied to the nation, one wonders whether there are limits to the malleability of the import. Are there no constraints on how the nation, as imaginative construct, can be shaped in the encounter with various social and cultural terrains?

As Kelly insists, we ought to be mindful of assuming that nations can be imagined in only one way—the paradigm of political communities of equal and like citizens. Nevertheless, it is clearly the case that the international grammar or code of nation making organizes differences among nations in uniform ways. From this perspective, the malleability of the nation does seem limited. Richard Wilk's (1995) comments about global structures of common difference are directly apposite. If there is an emerging global culture, Wilk argues, then its main feature is not bland homogeneity, but rather organized diversity (see Hannerz 1992b). The new global cultural system actually promotes difference, but difference expressed in a standardized vocabulary that renders "wildly disparate groups of people intelligible to each other" (Wilk 1995:130). Like certain versions of contemporary American multiculturalism, difference gains legitimacy precisely because of its uniform manifestations. That is, the celebration of particular kinds of (often commodified) difference —say, in food, dress or music—entails the suppression of other kinds—say, in moral values or notions of personhood.

By this account, "the national"—not to mention "the local" or "the ethnic"—constitutes rather than resists global culture. Nations generated by the international grammar of nationhood express their differences in terms of content instead of form. This sort of expression is apparent, as Wilk points out, in the performance of competitions and pageants, whether beauty contests, sporting events, or cultural festivals. Competitions and pageants define differences as formally equivalent and commensurable, glossing over but not wholly concealing the gross inequities involved when Miss Belize competes for the title of Miss Universe or a Papua New Guinean sprinter loses in the (televised) preliminary heats of the Olympic Games. Competitions and pageants are thus favored practical vehicles for nationalist advocates of "unity in diversity"; they respond to the same logic of seriality that aggregates individuals into collective individuals—a logic that comfortably integrates units within a series of "levels," from local to regional to national to global.[9]

The competition/pageant format is visible across the social landscape of PNG, and not only in the relatively urbane contexts of the annual Miss PNG contest or organized, commercially sponsored rugby leagues (see chapter 4 for other examples). Errington and Gewertz (1995c), for example, describe a choir competition that took place as part of a jubilee celebration of the arrival of Methodist missionary George Brown and the end of the "time of darkness" among the Duke of York Islanders. The competition, which included men and women of other denominations besides Methodist, enacted the "existence of a Papua New Guinea nation composed of equally cultured (or decultured) groups united through Christianity" (Errington and Gewertz 1995c:101)—a perfect example of a Christian celebration with a national subtext. Similarly, Knauft (2002) describes the annual festivities held by different ethnic groups to mark Independence Day in the remote Nomad area of PNG. There, the competitions and pageants include not only sporting events and dance contests (disco and traditional), but also farcical skits in which people depict the oafishness of their own primitive pasts through, for example, renditions of the ignorant villager who attempts to open a can of tinned fish with his teeth.

These skits and the choirs in the Duke of York Islands assert the distance of modern Papua New Guineans from their backward precontact traditions. But both competitions bespeak the self-consciousness and worry that their performance engenders—the recognition that such competitions enforce a putatively universal and natural standard which the participants find difficult to meet (see Foster 2002). Are we Papua New Guineans modern? Is PNG a modern nation? Thus the local organizer of the Miss Universe pageant in Belize asserts that "we [Belizeans] *can* compete with the rest of the world." But, as Wilk notes (1995:126), "that competition also highlights the subordinate position of Belize in a global hierarchy"—and the recognition that local standards of beauty, gender, and sexuality are just that: local.

Wilk's notion of structures of common difference provides an attractive alternative to mistaken reports of global monoculture. Indeed, transnational entities such as The Coca-Cola Company and PepsiCo, Inc.—icons of world consumerism—have successfully integrated structures of common difference into their marketing activities, thereby bringing the logic of branding for both corporations and nation-states in line with each other (see chapter 7). Similarly, this notion dispels any specters of inauthenticity raised by the invidious comparison of national cultures. There is no question that beauty pageants in Belize or cultural festivals in PNG are experiences entangled in local circumstances and motivated by homegrown interests (see Cohen et al. 1996); the replication of homogeneity thus dialectically produces heterogeneity. But neither is Wilk's notion an unqualified celebration of local appropriation or the domestication of the foreign. Such processes cannot, I repeat, be denied; beauty contests and cultural festivals merge, as Anderson suggests, with local political and ideological constellations. But, and this is Wilk's point, the work of appropriation and domestication is channeled in some directions and not others, expended in some forms and formats at the expense of others. So, too, I argue in these chapters, the work of nation making. In their various attempts to narrate or imagine themselves as a distinct but legible nation, Papua New Guineans and their interlocutors use and reuse resources not of their own making. Many of these resources are, as I have already suggested, mundane to the point of banality.

BANAL NATIONALISM, OR EVERYDAY NATION MAKING

In building the claim that nation making in PNG proceeds through contingent encounters with generic forms for expressing nationhood, I have borrowed from not only Anderson's *Imagined Communities* but also Michael Billig's *Banal Nationalism* (1995). Billig makes the good point that nationalism need not only refer to spectacular displays of passion associated with the creation of new states and/or right-wing political movements; indeed, Billig points out, such a view tends to locate nationalism on the periphery, that is, outside Euro-America or "the West." Billig instead calls attention to the ideological habits—assumptions and practices—that serve to make nationhood an uncontested, even unnoticed aspect of everyday existence. This complex of habits is what Billig calls "banal nationalism."

Billig's rhetorical stance against the smug attitude that "we are patriots, they are nationalists" leads him to accept unnecessarily that banal nationalism —apparently unlike the extraordinary variety—is characteristic only of the established nation-states of the West, thereby reproducing the very center/ periphery dichotomy he had originally questioned. I prefer to see banal nationalism as potentially a feature of all nation-states—that is, as an aspect of the work of nation making that occurs in all nation-states, whether "established" or "new." This is true because, as I have already proposed, the ideological habits and practices comprising banal nationalism are part and parcel of what has been exported in the worldwide spread of the nation-state form. The United States of America has a National Gallery; so does PNG. France has a national airline; so does Vanuatu. Every credible nation-state, and not a few incredible ones, has postage stamps. And so on.

What does vary, as Billig notes, and what can be studied comparatively, are the social processes by which modular banalities are made visible and open to question. It is in these processes that PNG, the nation, materializes. Put differently, paying attention to the banal aspects of nation making demonstrates how the nation emerges—not as a particular narrative or particular imaginative construct, but as a frame of reference available for defining and communicating identities. That agents invoke a national frame of reference does not mean it is in every or any context the dominant frame of reference. On the contrary, the national frame of reference rubs uneasily against other frames—as when jubilee commemorations of Christian missionaries align the coming of Christianity with the achievement of political independence (Errington and Gewertz 1995c; see also Young 1997), or when an ancestral Gogodala story about the bird of paradise, PNG's national emblem, effectively encompasses the nation within a highly restricted idiom of clanship (Dundon 1998). Nor does a shared frame of reference imply any definite emotional attachment to the nation(al), let alone a singularly positive one. As Robbins (1998) has effectively shown for the Urapmin (see chapter 6), the national frame of reference might be evoked for the sole purpose of rejecting the nation, an assertion of nonbelonging that betokens an intensely "negative nationalism."

Paying attention to the social life of modular banalities therefore reveals how a national frame of reference becomes engaged with and transformed by local interests and concerns, such that nation making and the production of locality unfold dialectically. A quick look at several interpretations and uses of the national flag in PNG—courtesy of Strathern and Stewart (2000)—makes this point, as well as my previous point about the plurality of emotional correlates to the nation. Strathern and Stewart (following Clark 1997) note that young men in Pangia (Southern Highlands) interpret the PNG flag not as a sign of national sovereignty per se, but as a sign of relationship—the ideally reciprocal encompassment of black people and white, PNG and Australia. The red/European (Europeans are known as "redmen" in Pangia) part of the flag contains the bird of paradise/PNG, while the black/Papua New Guinean part of the flag contains the Southern Cross/Australia. Not too far away, in the Nebilyer Valley of the Western Highlands, members of the Kulka tribe's women's club carried a PNG national flag onto a battlefield. Their intervention marked a truce and initiated a distribution to the men on opposing sides of soft drinks, cigarettes, and small amounts of currency (see Merlan and Rumsey 1991).

These two apparently positive evaluations of the flag contrast starkly with the grim interpretation of a man from Bougainville Island, where a secessionist war continued at varying levels of intensity through most of the 1990s:

> For this man, the red part referred to mainlanders ("redskins" to him) and the black part to Bougainvilleans (dark-skinned), and he indicated that the two parts might fall apart. . . . For him, then, the flag was an icon of his own ethnic view of a fragmenting nation, rather than a symbol of unity. (Strathern and Stewart 2000:26)

These are three very different readings of the flag, to be sure, but all within, against, or at least in dialogue with the nation understood as a salient frame of reference for delineating personal and collective identities. And to these examples, which indicate serious thoughtfulness about a symbol that many see without observing, add one more: the PNG national flags draped over the coffins of the students killed on the University of Papua New Guinea campus in the hours after an antiprivatization protest—tokens of the nation explicitly constructed and contested by both the funeral orators and their audience.

In sum, I am proposing a way of thinking about the emergence of the nation in PNG neither as the gradual acculturation of people to a set of shared, univocal symbols nor as the coming into being of a project in Us/Them contrasts between political communities—though both of these ways of thinking have their uses in PNG, as elsewhere. Indeed, the most obvious project of contrasts in PNG, as I have suggested, pits the nation against a doubly weak state —unable both to coerce its citizens to enact its will and to redeem for those same citizens the promise of national development.[10] Instead, what I am arguing for is recognition of the various means by which the nation enters into the daily lives of ordinary people as a frame of reference for thinking and acting reflexively. These means include state-sponsored and state-organized images, objects, and events—from efforts such as National Law Week (chapter 1) to the designs of official coin and currency (chapter 2). But they also include a range of images, objects, and events that originate elsewhere: in global flows of commodities such as *Coca-Cola* (chapter 7) or long-standing indigenous practices such as chewing betel nut (chapter 4). Appreciating both the modularity and banality of the nation—not only in PNG—requires paying attention to all these means.

NATIONALITY AND TRIVIALITY

Anders Linde-Laursen (1993) tells a story about an unpleasant experience he had while washing up after dinner at some Swedish friends' home in Lund. Linde-Laursen, a Dane, began putting the unrinsed dishes in the drainer prior to drying them with a towel. His host accused Linde-Laursen of not "washing up properly," of washing up "the Danish way," and proceeded to instruct him on how to rinse off the dishes and air-dry them in the drainer. Linde-Laursen observes:

> There was no doubt that my host was unpleasantly affected by my way of washing up, so I let myself be taught . . . As I continued to wash up, I felt that I was being singled out for being Danish. It was perfectly clear that I had breached the local Swedish code of decent dishwashing. (1993:277)

I draw two lessons from this modest account of domestic discord. First, it demonstrates again how the national frame of reference can impinge on the most trivial and mundane of material activities. These activities often involve bodily practices, such that nationality acquires a habitual corporeal dimension (see chapter 4), manifest in pledging allegiance to the flag, daily exercise (Frykman 1993), eating lunch, or even dishwashing. While it would be untrue to say that the material dimension of nationality has been ignored (unlike that of American Christianity; see McDannell 1995), it is fair to say that these everyday or banal activities have been given less attention than more striking materializations of the nation such as public monuments or heritage sites or bicentennial celebrations of one sort or another. The study of nation making is thereby diminished.

Why? The second lesson of Linde-Laursen's story lies in its confession of emotional discomfort. For his host, the experience of seeing unrinsed dishes felt unpleasant; for Linde-Laursen, the experience of being singled out felt likewise. Clearly, belonging—feeling that one belongs—was at stake, just as in the story I recount in chapter 5, of a young immigrant girl whose school lunch of newspaper-wrapped fried food painfully betrayed her Eastern European origins and alien status to her sandwich-eating American peers. Everyday or banal activities can serve just as well as extraordinary occasions—holidays, pilgrimages to national shrines, political party conventions, major sports competitions—to define contexts for feeling the nation, for grounding the nation as narrative or imaginative construct in personal, affective experience. I once asked a young man from Gulf Province, a high school graduate living and working in Port Moresby, when he most felt like a Papua New Guinean. After a brief pause, he responded, "When I watch television and see the station promotions for EM TV."

The disjunction in places like PNG between the banalities of chewing betel nut and consuming a particular brand of tinned meat on the one hand, and more blatant expressions of deeply felt national belonging on the other, has prompted Otto and Thomas (1997) to pronounce the failure of nationalism in the South Pacific. Otto and Thomas concede that perhaps there is nationality —collective affinity or imagining—but not nationalism or affirmative patriotism (see chapter 5). Yet the separation, like that between patriotism and nationalism, is not so easy.[11] Billig would be the first to argue that it is precisely because of the unmarked everyday work of banal nationalism—the insinuation of a national frame of reference into daily activities and contexts—that populations are easily mobilized at times of crisis into the more marked forms of nationalism. Indeed, Billig's strenuous critique of American nationalism rests on precisely this point. The response of citizens to the call of the state at the time of the Gulf War, for instance, presupposes an infinite number of banal rehearsals, daily iterations of the nation which now demands unqualified support and sacrifice. Hysterical nationalism presupposes forgettable nationalism; mind-boggling proposals for missile defense systems presume, if nothing else, the everyday reality of the nation to be defended, however narrated or imagined.

It would be as equally ridiculous to expect the citizens of PNG to heed automatically the call of "their" state as to assert that there is a Papua New Guinean way of dishwashing. As I have argued, perhaps the most dramatic manifestations of the nation in PNG have thus far materialized *against* the state. In these manifestations—large and public protests against actions taken by the national government—citizens have spoken and now died in the name of the nation. While there is a tendency among scholars to say such expressions of nationality are confined to a small urban elite, I suggest here otherwise. The production of a national frame of reference, to the extent that it occurs, happens through commodity consumption and commercial media that cross boundaries between town and village, elites and masses. It is this process of production that the various chapters in this volume address. Nation making so defined takes a distinctive form in PNG, obviously, but nation making so defined is everywhere, I submit, an inescapable aspect of the nation's banal modularity.

THE CHAPTERS IN BRIEF

The chapters in this book were written during the ten years from 1991 to 2000. This period in PNG saw hopeful visions of national self-sufficiency and economic development, common at the time of independence, finally eclipsed by fear and anxiety over violent crime and political corruption; foreign debt and structural adjustment; tribal fighting and a secessionist war; and, not least, the new millennium. By April 2001, Sir Julius Chan, former prime minister and one of the so-called founding fathers of PNG, could easily materialize the nation in anything but glowing terms: "We are no longer a nation seeking to be independent. We've become a nation of beggars" (*National,* 24 April 2001).

Chan's laments are not unusual (see, e.g., Standish 2000). The demise of the nation in PNG is daily news. Yet such talk is, from the perspective adopted here, an instance, albeit cruel, of nation making—a narrative, an imaginative construct. However desperate the circumstances in which many Papua New Guineans find themselves, the nation continues to be made—invoked in everything from public prayer sessions to television advertisements for tinned meat. The chapters in this volume document these invocations; they ground general questions about nation making in the ethnographic particulars of diverse material forms. Taken together, they argue for recognizing the importance of commodity consumption and commercial media in bringing a national frame of reference to bear on the lives of people—every day, in ordinary settings—in PNG and elsewhere.

I have organized the chapters into three parts. Part I looks at two different state-sponsored projects of nation making through moral education and the ways in which these projects were received, resisted, and, in some cases, subverted. Chapter 1 describes the events of National Law Week in 1984, a multifaceted educational program that coincided with public expressions of outrage over growing violent crime in PNG, especially in Port Moresby. This chapter foregrounds the dilemmas facing the state in trying to reconcile national cultural symbols such as betel nut with international definitions of modern citizenship. Chapter 2 similarly addresses this dilemma, discussing how first the colonial state and then the independent state attempted to use state-issued money as the practical vehicle for imagining a community in national terms—political, economic, and cultural. This chapter in particular demonstrates the contingent and dialectical process by which national and local frames of reference—in this case, frames of reference for articulating and creating value—mutually transform each other.

Part II looks at the ways in which the nation is constructed in and through advertising. The chapters consider both print advertisements from national newspapers and television advertisements from the one commercial television

ving and judging, an experience of seeing oneself through the eyes of oth-
to whom one is now connected via commodities and mass media. Accord-
ly, I conclude chapter 7 and the book as a whole with brief reflections
the nature of ethnographic practice in an era of globalization. How are
thropologists being challenged to study, for example, the vast commodity
ains that link consumers in Port Moresby with corporate executives in New
rk? What happens to "the field" when, like "the nation," we recognize it as
imaginative construct, more and more subject to the effects of forces origi-
ting elsewhere?

station in PNG. Chapter 3 develops the argument tha
sessive individualism underlies dominant or paradi
both nations and consumers. In other words, I sugg
capitalist consumerism provide mutually reinforcing
personal and collective identities. In chapter 4, I dev
ther by looking specifically at how commercial adver
course of health that targets bodies. I demonstrate h
mulgate a rhetoric of individuated, autonomous selves
instances of how some Papua New Guineans engage ar
ric. Chapter 5 rounds off this part of the book by cons
the instrumental role of commodity marketing and mas
ducing nationality as a dimension of personal and col
chapter puts case materials from PNG into a wider co
guing that the construction of the nation as a communi
sumption has a history that includes, for example, the s
grants to the United States in the early twentieth centu

The two chapters in part III explicitly consider natio
text of contemporary globalization. Chapter 6 looks at h
eans variously attempt to imagine themselves as cosm
scend, even if only temporarily, provincial national identi
in global social movements. I look closely at two cases. I
lagers in a remote area of PNG embrace a version of mil
ity imported from the United States as a way of assertin
transnational community destined to better fortunes than
despised PNG nation. In the second case, a diverse cast of
eans and Australians struggle over the opportunities for na
casing the nation—Australia as well as PNG—presented
Torch Relay leading up to the 2000 Games in Sydney. This c
how contests over the nation take place within a transnatio
in which resources and capacities are unequally distributed
1990, 1991).

Chapter 7 further pursues questions of how Papua N
themselves and are seen by others as located in a global co
that is, how a national frame of reference articulates with a m
It briefly discusses the way *Coca-Cola* and *Pepsi-Cola* soft
keted and advertised in PNG and the role of such activity
public culture. In so doing, it demonstrates how global comm
material for defining national identities and how the meanin
modities is subject to negotiation by marketers and consumer

Both chapters in part III emphasize how the network of p
ated by contemporary globalization conditions nation making
is, nation making involves an intense self-awareness that other

PART I

State-Sponsored Nation Making

1

Take Care of Public Telephones
Moral Education and Nation-State Formation

INTRODUCTION: MORAL EDUCATION AND
NATION-STATE FORMATION

The title of this chapter came to me in the mail. It is one of several exhortations that served as cancellation marks on the envelopes of letters that I received from Papua New Guinea (PNG) during the late 1980s. Here are some of the others: Address Mail to Private Box No.—It Expedites Delivery; Good Scouts Make Better Men; Mekim Pren Wantaim Lo ("Law is Your Friend" in Tok Pisin); and Make National Law Week Work. The last two of these messages refer to what has become an annual occurrence in PNG, the proclamation and performance of National Law Week. Other messages circulated as cancellation marks during the initial National Law Week in 1984 included these: Help Maintain Law and Order; National Law Week is for Everyone; and National Law Week is for You. On the cover of the record of events and activities published the following year by the National Law Week Committee (Wallace 1985), there is a drawing of an envelope addressed to "All the people of the Highlands of Papua New Guinea"; the envelope's cancellation mark asserts: Your Family Needs Law and Order.

The admonitions issued by the Post and Telecommunications Corporation were only one element in a wide array of undertakings sponsored by the National Law Week Committee, a group composed of members of parliament, government officials, and university faculty. Commemorative postage stamps were planned; advertisements were taken out in the national daily newspaper and a jingle was composed for radio; public lectures and seminars were held at the main campus of the University of Papua New Guinea as well as at selected centers for extension studies; bumper stickers and street banners were distributed. Much of the committee's effort was concentrated on the captive population of school students in both urban and rural areas, upon whom were visited a variety of magistrates, legal officers, and law enforcement representatives, as well as a traveling theater group. Students from four national high schools publicly debated topics such as "In Papua New Guinea, there is too much law and too little order." In addition, grade school students in several provinces were enlisted in poster and essay competitions. Detainees at several corrective institutions also participated in the essay competition.

All of this coordinated activity unfolded amid proliferating newspaper accounts of increased violent crime in the national capital of Port Moresby, where the gang rape of a New Zealand woman and her daughter in October 1984 sparked mass protests of outrage. Reports of resurgent tribal fighting in the Highlands and the appearance of two major studies of the government's policy on law and order also contributed to the perception—shared by prominent politicians and ordinary residents—of rampant lawlessness and social disorder. Public pressure on the government continued to build at home and from abroad into 1985, the tenth anniversary of PNG's independence. In response to unabated concern over violent crime, the government declared a state of emergency in the National Capital District from 17 June to 4 November. The emergency provisions extended police powers; allowed the use of military personnel in policing; prohibited demonstrations; and imposed a curfew (see Morauta 1986a for details and discussion).

The purpose of National Law Week 1984 was expressed by Paias Wingti (quoted in Wallace 1985:1), then deputy prime minister and a patron of National Law Week, in a statement to the national parliament:

> Our principal aim is to bring to grass root levels a greater understanding of "what the law is all about." For proper maintenance of law and order in the country, it is very important that the people are aware of their legal rights, their legal obligations to society, and that they obey and abide by the laws of the land.
>
> In other words, the main thrust of our committee is to educate the people of this nation about what law and order can do for them providing they, the people, see "the law," as our slogan so clearly states, "as their friend."

In speaking so, Wingti did no more than highlight the agency of the state in a project of moral regulation, of rendering natural and taken for granted a set of particular and historical premises about social life (Corrigan and Sayer 1985:4). Durkheim's characterization of the state as "the organ of moral discipline" is relevant here (cited in Corrigan and Sayer 1985:5). For Durkheim, the state consists in "a group of individuals *sui generis,* within which representations and acts of volition involving the collectivity are worked out" (Giddens 1986:40). That is, the state produces and disseminates, in relatively self-conscious fashion, collective representations—images and ideals of the collectivity and of the persons who comprise the collectivity.[1] Education, as Wingti noted, is the practical means by which the state promotes awareness ("a greater understanding") of the collective ideas and sentiments it defines.

The original National Law Week was very much an attempt to educate people into a well-defined sense of collective *and* personal identity—indeed, to constitute these identities. Consider the twin slogans: National Law Week is for *Everyone*/National Law Week is for *You*. To accept these claims is to accept both that there is an "everyone," and that "you" are one of the everyones; the nation is defined at the same time as one is defined as a national citizen. The totality of which one is a member and one's identity as an individual imply each other. Thus, the numerous competitions and contests mounted during National Law Week functioned much like Foucault's examination to individualize and differentiate student-citizens while at the same time placing them within a whole field of contenders. In this way, too, the campaign for National Law Week illustrates well the coextensiveness of moral regulation and nation-state formation (Corrigan and Sayer 1985); for the successful naturalization of an individual's acquiescence in the "laws of the land" marks not only the effectiveness of state control, but also the internalization of a definite representation of one's self and one's relation to other selves. The apparent goal of the National Law Week Committee was to communicate and inculcate these representations as much as to secure outward compliance with the law.

In this chapter, I identify two of the ways in which the national citizen— and by implication, the nation—were created in and through the discourse of National Law Week. First, I examine campaign materials that formulate the "rights and obligations" of individuals toward each other. Second, I examine campaign materials that present ideals of socially approved behavior or propriety. My goal is to disclose how these discursive products import a particular definition of personhood into an alien social context and how different agents variously construe this importation in terms of an encounter between tradition and modernity. By exploring one exemplary discussion of betel nut chewing, I outline some of the paradoxes that such contested constructions pose for the state in regulating multivalent collective representations and practices. My goal in this regard is to demonstrate how the creation of a national citizen inevitably appeals to prevailing international definitions of civility.

RIGHTS AND OBLIGATIONS: INDIVIDUALS WITHIN THE COLLECTIVE INDIVIDUAL

One of the most pronounced themes of the 1984 National Law Week concerned respect for the law or "Obligations of Citizens and Others as Regards Law," the title of a public lecture presented by then ombudswoman Jean Kekedo. In her talk, Kekedo (quoted in Wallace 1985:13) urged that historic legal sensibilities, such as respect for leadership and proper legal authority, be used as the basis for developing similar sensibilities in changed circumstances:

> We can use [these sensibilities] to also develop an appreciation of the obligations the citizen has in the modern community, and in the kind of democratic and ordered society we live in. We must end the remoteness of law from the people.

In other words, Kekedo stressed the continuity between the traditional and modern community.

By contrast, the remarks of then minister for justice, A. L. Bais, in his address on "What Benefits Are Gained by Proper Respect for the Law?", suggested that traditional sensibilities posed an obstacle to the rule of modern law: "They [children] are taught to obey customs of a traditional society but they are not taught to obey laws of the land." Bais argued that this deficiency in domestic education stemmed from the limited social applicability of traditional custom:

> "They [children] are taught to respect the rights of their kinsmen but they are not taught to obey laws of the land. . . . " Parents with strong traditional backgrounds did not teach the children that they should not steal from or assault strangers, he said. (*Post-Courier*, 7 September 1984)

In other words, Bais claimed that in order to become law-abiding citizens, children must be taught to interact with other people—stranger-citizens—in accordance with principles defined in terms other than those of kinship. What are these principles?

Elsewhere in his lecture, Bais claimed that democracy was the model chosen for the modernization of PNG because "it gives people the greatest amount of freedom for the development of individuals." The constitution of PNG, according to Bais, explicitly set out the rights and freedoms of individuals:

> Legally there is no country in the world in which citizens and non-citizens have more safeguards to ensure that their freedoms are not curtailed: freedom of speech, freedom of movement, freedom from improper search and improper arrest and freedom from improper imprisonment or detention.

Other participants in National Law Week spoke of such freedoms as "fundamental rights" or "human rights," rights vested in all individuals by virtue of their humanity. Taken together, these rights and freedoms defined for one participant the liberty referred to by John F. Kennedy in a statement used as part of a full-page newspaper ad for National Law Week: "Observance of the law is the eternal safeguard of liberty and defiance of the law is the surest road to tyranny."

The principles necessary to guide social interaction in the modern world therefore involve recognition of universal rights and obligations that attach to all individuals. In this sense, then, the modern world consists of a population of individuals essentially alike in their humanity, whereas the traditional world consists of a population of persons differentiated with regard to contingent local criteria such as kinship.[2] What is the relationship between this conception of modern individuals and nation-state formation, especially given the manifest contradiction between the universalism of modern individualism and the sometimes strident particularism of nationalism?

Richard Handler (1988:7), following Dumont, has argued that ideologies of nationalism and individualism share the same "epistemology of 'entivity,' " the presupposition that entities can be bounded by attributes or characteristics that each "possesses." That is, both ideologies presuppose the existence of entities—individuals or nations—distinguishable by their uniquely possessed characteristics. Nationalism, from this perspective, posits the nation as a collective individual, an individuated being rather than a differentiated constituent of some encompassing order. The nation, in turn, is composed of similar individuated beings related to each other by their likeness, their shared possession of some certain characteristic or attribute. Each and every individual (an American) thus replicates the collective individual (America).

Whether or not these presuppositions are definitive and necessary features of nationalism and nationalist ideology is not my concern here (see Kapferer 1988). Rather, I want only to point out their operation, however muted, in the discursive context of National Law Week. At the same time that the National Law Week supporters issued calls for the recognition of rights common to all human beings, they emphasized the role of the national constitution and national law as the safeguard of these rights. In other words, the nation was constructed as a collection of individuals each of whose basic humanity is protected by a commonly held constitution or law. This common possession at once defines the nation as a community and distinguishes it from other national communities that possess other constitutions and laws. Indeed, as Bais's remarks show, nations can be compared with regard to the degree that their laws safeguard basic human rights. Accordingly, there is no contradiction between *national* law and *human* rights; on the contrary, the former is the guarantor of the latter.

NO SPITTING: PROPRIETY AND RESPECTABILITY

The definition of the nation as a collection of individuated beings with basic rights underpins certain diagnoses of the law and order problem in PNG as a problem of "uncaring attitudes." Consider this newspaper account of Paias Wingti's speech opening National Law Week in Port Moresby (*Post-Courier,* 11 September 1984):

> There was an atmosphere of disquiet in the society because of the "lack of consideration for one's fellow man."
> There was a natural tendency for people to throw bottles out of moving vehicles, damage trees, and public property, leave betelnut stains on the streets, and to light fires without thinking or caring, Mr. Wingti said.
> Such an [*sic*] anti-social behavior was "seemingly endless."

"Such thoughtless behavior was so widespread that it could be called an epidemic of the uncaring mind," Mr. Wingti said.

Wingti went on to characterize this "epidemic" as the product of rapid social change and to attribute it to a movement away from the discipline of traditional societies. The problem here is not the inappropriateness of traditional values, as Minister for Justice Bais would have it, but rather the erosion of traditional values ("discipline") in the face of modernization. Nonetheless, the practical result is identical: people were incapable of recognizing their "fellow man" and thus interacting on the basis of fellowship. Consequently, Wingti argued, there was a need for teaching young people in particular to change their "uncaring attitudes."

Quite clearly, part of the mission of National Law Week was directed toward this task of moral education, of educating the public to an ideal of generalized caring.[3] Among the advertisements taken out in the national daily newspaper (*Post-Courier*) in connection with the National Law Awareness Campaign were a series of notices informing readers of offenses punishable by fine. Many of these notices concerned traffic violations:

> It Is an Offence to Exceed the Speed Limit, 50 kph in Towns or 65 kph Outside Towns.

But others specifically concerned the sort of antisocial behavior identified by Wingti:

> It Is an Offence to Lean Out of the Car to Spit on the Road.

This latter message referred to the practice of staining the streets red with expectorated betel nut juice. Along with public drinking, such spitting and littering typify the sort of behavior indicative of disrespect for one's fellow citizen. Thus the 4 January 1986 issue of the weekly *Times of Papua New Guinea* contained two full-page-size handbills placed by the National Capital District Interim Commission. While one of the posters queried "Drinking in Public Places?", the other pointedly asked "Are You a Litter Bug?" "Litter bug" was defined as

> one of those uncaring, untidy and bad mannered people who throw litter or spit betelnut on to the streets and not in a proper dustbin or litter bin. . . . Nobody likes litter bugs.

The discourse of basic individual rights slides easily into the discourse of propriety and socially acceptable behavior. "Respect for the laws of the country" and "respect for one's fellow citizens" become entangled in a discussion of respectability in general. To this extent, state agency in projects such as National Law Week not only communicates representations of generic human individuals, but also cultivates a whole set of behavioral expectations about how such individuals ought to act toward ("care for") each other; in short, a whole set of *manners*. State activity perforce functions to promote moral discipline by licensing "the range of what are the proper ways of public performance" (Corrigan 1981:327). That is, such state activity seeks to form national citizens by securing conformity to the permissible parameters of individual identity, parameters that define normal morality.

In PNG, the state project of morally educating the citizenry often takes the discursive form of a modernizing, if not a civilizing, process. For the normal morality endorsed by the state, particularly in regard to bodily conduct—sexuality, hygiene, and consumption, for example—is implicitly legitimated as that which is appropriate to the modern (Christian) world. But to the extent that the PNG state responds to external pressures exerted by dominant definitions of normal morality, it potentially contradicts local definitions of normal morality, and hence local ideals and images of the collectivity and persons comprising the collectivity. In particular, to the extent that the state imports definitions of moral order from "the West" (or indeed from non-Western exemplars of modernity such as Japan and Singapore), it exposes itself to charges of misrepresenting the collectivity. That is, the state no longer—to resume Durkheim's argument—simply re-presents the collectivity with a relatively high degree of self-consciousness, but instead disseminates collective representations that originate beyond the collectivity.

This contradiction within state activity informs contests over moral regulation in PNG and numbers these contests among the ongoing and increasingly open challenges to the legitimacy and consensual authority of the state (Morauta 1986b:15–16, Dinnen 1986). Dissent and controversy over moral regulation of the social environment become a focal point for contests over the definition of behavior befitting a national citizen. In PNG, the practice of betel nut chewing provides ample grounds for just such a contest.

BETEL NUT: AN AMBIVALENT SYMBOL

On 31 July 1973, two years before PNG became independent, an article titled "Betel Nut Course?" appeared in the *Post-Courier*. It reported the following:

> A speaker at a Rabaul meeting of the Constitutional Planning Committee has said non-indigenous people seeking PNG citizenship should be required to have some knowledge of the customs of the native people.
> "I think they should be made to learn to chew betel nut," Mr. Singut Kapun said. "If they can't do this then they should not be granted citizenship."

The suggestion was not taken up by the committee, but it might as well have been.[4] Betel nut chewing is a virtually universal practice in PNG; its consumption has spread since World War II into areas such as the Highlands, where the areca palm that generates betel nut cannot be grown but where local entrepreneurs struggle to satisfy an unlimited demand (Connell 1984, Hirsch 1990). Betel nut is one of the 124 items in the basket of goods and services used to determine the national consumer price index. Given an index weighting of 7.6 percent in 1984, betel nut dramatically inflates the overall consumer price index with its periodic upward fluctuations in price (Connell 1984).

Despite its pervasiveness, though, betel nut chewing is an ambivalent practice in the eyes of state officials and ordinary citizens alike. Betel nut can indeed be represented as "native custom." As one anthropologists has pointed out, betel nut is unlike other stimulants regularly consumed in PNG in that it is the only one

> grown, marketed and consumed by Papua New Guineans. It has no association with the norms or values introduced by Europeans. It is quite the opposite with a stimulant such as beer, whose ethos and effect is often contrasted with that of betelnut. . . . Many writers have commented on the socially disruptive effects of beer consumption and have likened the behaviour it elicits to that associated with Europeans either as they have been observed or as portrayed in films. (Hirsch 1990:25)

Betel nut thus potentially connotes an indigenous identity delineated in opposition to a European identity—unsurprising, perhaps, inasmuch as until 1962, alcohol consumption was illegal for the native population in the Trust Territory of Papua and New Guinea. Significantly, this opposition of betel nut to beer effectively marks a distinction between restrained behavior and peaceful social relations on the one hand, and uncontrolled aggression and belligerence on the other (Lepowsky 1982). That is, betel nut consumption comes to stand for "civilized" behavior in the traditional mode, while beer symbolizes the pathology of externally imposed "modernization."

However, betel nut chewing is equally susceptible to being represented in a negative light. Consider the following letter to the editor of the *Post-Courier,* which appeared under the heading of "Chuck out chewers!" (29 November 1988):

> In this province, . . . one cannot help but notice so-called public servants, from junior ranks to senior, chewing betelnut during working hours.
> As a businessman and villager I often wonder whether there is any control at all in the system over this practice. It appears to me that the Department head . . . is either slack or lacks management and control experience. . . .
> I believe at this time of development in Milne Bay we, the grass roots,

THE CHEWING OF

BETEL NUT

IN WORKING HOURS IS

STRICTLY

PROHIBITED

FAILURE TO OBSERVE THIS

RULE COULD RESULT IN

INSTANT DISMISSAL

Figure 1.1. Sign posted in PNG government office.

would like to see more dedicated and technically qualified public servants. . . .

I think it is high time the government weeded out all these betelnut chewers who waste time and money. There is no place in public offices for such unprofessional behaviour.

The author clearly construes betel nut chewing as incompatible with the goals of modern development and *therefore* a practice that requires increased regulation on the part of the government (see figure 1.1). Rather than a marker of some traditional and indigenous identity, betel nut chewing throws up an obstacle to the achievement of technically and economically efficient self-rule. Moreover, as the campaign against litter attests, betel nut chewing can be construed as offensive to official definitions of health and sanitation. Thus, for example, the PNG Defence Force has banned betel nut "on the grounds that spittle attracted flies and betel rubbish littered every public place" (Connell 1984:58); while in 1984, the premier of Eastern Highlands Province acted for similar reasons to ban betel nut trading and chewing in the main towns of Goroka and Kainantu.[5] This particular construction of betel nut chewing, then, does not oppose the practice to beer drinking; on the contrary, both forms of consumption are classified together (as in the newspaper inserts) as instances of bad and improper manners.

The ambivalence of betel nut as a national symbol is well captured in a news report that members of parliament were presented with an invitation to join a "Parliamentary Betel Nut Club":

> The idea was put forward by the Deputy Prime Minister, Akoka Doi.
> He told Parliament during Grievance Debate that such a club would sponsor a campaign to educate people on how to chew betelnut, and to conduct research into the possibility of establishing a permanent betelnut industry. (*Pacific Islands Monthly,* January 1990)

While betel nut chewing qualifies for the official endorsement of parliament, and even merits consideration as a potential national commodity, the practice also requires state regulation. The reach of the state extends to public conduct. People must be educated how to chew betel nut, which presumably means that people must be educated in both the proper disposal of betel nut juice and the proper sense of when and where to chew betel nut. Most importantly, people must be educated to regard improper behavior on the part of others as a *personal* offense.

CONCLUDING REMARKS: IMAGINING THE NATION

Benedict Anderson (1991) has made the point that since its inception, "the nation" has been modular—a model of an imagined community eminently capable of being copied and introduced into circumstances wholly unlike those in which it originated. This model today enjoys global currency; internationally recognized conformity to the model is a prerequisite for staking legitimate claims to collective existence. Thus it is possible to devise an "international cultural grammar of nationhood" (Löfgren 1989a), the approved checklist of ingredients necessary to form a nation. Such ingredients include not only the familiar repertoire of flag, crest, and anthem, but also definite ideas about national history (time) and landscape (space), and institutions such as national museums and educational systems (see Foster 1991).

The National Law Week campaign illustrates in two related ways how one state agency, the National Law Week Committee, drew on this checklist in promoting identities for both the collectivity of PNG and the persons of its constituent citizens. At least one sponsored speaker appealed explicitly to "universal concepts of human rights," codified in "international documents," in order to stimulate consciousness of a community of fellow citizens—jurally defined persons in possession of inalienable rights and obligations (Wallace 1985:18). Less explicitly, but in similar fashion, the committee's campaign against bad manners appealed to international standards of civility. Surely the abstruse notion of "litterbug" is as much a foreign import as the idea of National Law Week itself.[6] In both instances, then, ready-made definitions of collectivity and personhood were invoked as part of the process of representing the nation. The wider circulation of such ready-mades is starkly illustrated by the following news service dispatch from Jakarta (*Weekend Australian,* 9–10 November 1991):

INDONESIANS TOLD BALDLY HOW TO BEHAVE

Soldiers have been issued with an unusual weapon for fighting crime on the city streets—shaving kits.

Jakarta's military commander, Major-General Harseno, wants Indonesia's chaotic capital to become as clean and orderly as Singapore or Tokyo and he believes shaving heads for a range of "public nuisance" offences will encourage better behaviour.

So the 150 soldiers who daily join the city's police to maintain public discipline are armed with shaving kits,

Originally, Operation Strengthening National Discipline was aimed at students.

But General Harseno believes it is so good, he has extended it to delinquent drivers.

"We focus on trivial things like teaching the public to throw garbage in dust bins, to cross the streets at appropriate crossings or by asking them to stand in orderly lines," he said.

In PNG, as in other former colonial states throughout the South Pacific, agents promoting imported models of collectivity and personhood identify these models with modernity and juxtapose them to some version or another of tradition or custom. The perceived relationship between modernity and tradition is, of course, not singular (see Lindstrom 1998). "Tradition" might be advanced as a heritage to build on, as values that are weakened, or as outmoded customs to reject out of hand; all of these possibilities emerged in the discourse of National Law Week 1984. In any case, however, the discursive exercise of reconciling tradition and modernity signals the practical problem confronting the state in its task of producing and disseminating ideals and images of the nation. On the one hand, the state must produce representations in conformity with models of nation and citizen already in place; on the other, it must produce images and ideals that represent a distinctive and unique identity for the nation and its citizens. It is this conflicted project, carried out through various strategies of moral education, that ultimately conjures up such improbably hybrid images as that of the well-mannered citizen of PNG delicately disposing his or her betel nut quid in a proper dustbin.

2

Your Money, Our Money, the Government's Money
Finance and Fetishism in Melanesia

In Memory of Jeffrey Clark

INTRODUCTION: CARGO AND FETISH

Talk about fetishism in Melanesia sooner or later leads to the subject of cargo cults.[1] Lindstrom (1993)—doing for "cargo cult" something like what Pietz (1985, 1987, 1988) did for "fetish"—has traced the genealogy of the term while trying to account for its continuing currency within and beyond anthropological circles. He asks:

> Could it be, then, that we are entranced by cargo cults because we are, at heart, commodity fetishists? That cargo cults are so titillating and seductive because we imagine the natives to be exercised by our own secret desires? We want cargo but we know also, at heart, that the moral connections that dominant capitalist rhetoric narrates between hard work and material success are fraudulent and ultimately illusory. (Lindstrom 1993:9)

Lindstrom's questions point to how the construction of and delight in cargo discourse tentatively reveals a range of otherwise hidden doubts, fears, and desires: doubts about the connections between labor and wealth; fears of an unsatisfied "endless yearning" (1993:9); and desires for a world of instant and unlimited abundance delivered without the necessity of labor. In this view, the attraction of cargo cult lies in the projection of Our secret fantasy onto Them.

Pietz's work suggests a related way in which cargo cult discourse sustains an uneasy separation between Us and Them—namely, by indulging Our lingering Enlightenment fantasy of a world without fetishes. Cargo cult discourse validates the conceit of a critical acuity acquired from living in a world where the real and true value of material things is self evident and irrefutable. It is this conceit, I suggest, that organized official cargo cult discourse in the context of post–World War II Australian colonialism in Papua and New

Guinea. And it was this conceit that, in the context of Australia's role as administrator of a United Nations Trust Territory, inevitably prompted a campaign of native education, a process whereby They would learn the truth and so become like Us.

I begin this chapter by first examining some of the means used by the postwar Australian Administration to educate the people of Papua and New Guinea about money and wealth. I go on to look at other subsequent instances of discourse about money in postcolonial Papua New Guinea (PNG), focusing on the way in which constructions of money become entailed in constructions of both nation and state. I ask: How did the fetish discourse identified by Pietz as originating in the intercultural space-time of fifteenth-century West Africa erupt in the intercultural space-time of late twentieth-century Melanesia? What specific forms did "the problem of the fetish" (Pietz 1985) come to assume for various agents encountering each other along the final frontiers of European expansion?

My reply rehearses the themes of fetish discourse singled out by Pietz: the irreducible materiality of objects; the composite fabrication of heterogeneous elements; the nonuniversality (and hence social constructedness) of value; and the power of fetishes over human bodies. My aim is to show how the moral educational projects of first the Australian colonial state and then the national state of PNG effectively, though differently, sustained a fetish discourse through explicit teachings about money and wealth. I demonstrate how the peculiar difference between money as an abstract medium of exchange on the one hand, and metal coins and paper notes as gross matter on the other, defined an arena for contesting and conjoining disparate conceptions of "the nature and origin of the social value of material objects" (Pietz 1988:109). In conclusion, I propose how some indigenous Melanesian understandings of money might furnish a critique of both commodity and state fetishism while at the same time construing money and indigenous wealth objects as material media that articulate diverse value codes.

YOUR MONEY: FEAR OF FETISHISM AND COLONIAL EDUCATION

Lindstrom traces the first written appearances of the term "cargo cult" to the pages of the news magazine *Pacific Islands Monthly*—more specifically, to a three-sided debate among expatriate planters, colonial administrators, and Christian missionaries over the future of the natives in Papua and New Guinea after World War II. Norris Mervyn Bird, described by *Pacific Islands Monthly* as an "old Territories resident," initiated the debate in print with a 1945 article that invoked the government anthropologist's authority to argue that " 'ill-digested' religious teaching" was the main cause of cargo cult. The following year, Bird responded to the letters of several missionaries that criticized the labor practices of the planters. His letter exposes the underbelly of cargo talk in Melanesia during the immediate postwar years in all its ugliness:

> My views on the acceptance of primitive natives into a civilised society are well known, but as Mr. Inselmann [an American Lutheran missionary] has raised the subject, in his letter, I challenge him with one question: Is he prepared to accept, as an equal in civilised society, the New Guinea native in his present state of development? Would, in fact, Mr. Inselmann be prepared to allow the average New Guinea native to marry his daughter or sister? I have asked other would-be reformers this question and the stock answers are:
> • Having neither sisters nor daughters the question does not apply. But would have no objection to these savages marrying other people's sisters or daughters.
> • Would not try to influence the women either way, but would rely on their good taste and innate decency to prevent their making a decision that they may later regret.
> • A long and pointless dissertation on the equality of man in the sight of God.
> • Ditto on the inadvisability of mixing the races (i.e., the "colour line" with reservations supported by quotations from the Bible). (quoted in Lindstrom 1993:21)

Lindstrom's observation is worth underscoring: "Breakouts of cargo cults and miscegenation are both directly predicted if comfortable structures of colonial inequality are permitted to decay" (1993:21).

Here, surely, is fear of fetishism. For like the offspring of a "mixed race" union, the fetish is composite: a novel identity of "articulated relations between otherwise heterogeneous things" (Pietz 1985:8). Cargo cult and miscegenation are elided inasmuch as both are taken to be cognate forms of confusion, of radical heterogeneity and unacceptable coupling.

If miscegenation described the unacceptable mixture of racially distinct bodies, then cargo cult described, at bottom, the transgression of hierarchically distinct statuses. It is this sort of social confusion against which educational campaigns about cargo cult were directed, even though these campaigns often presented themselves as targeting an *intellectual* confusion—the presumed incapacity of the native mentality to sort out cause from effect and so to unite promiscuously different value codes. Hence, for example, "How You Get It," a column that appeared in the *Papua and New Guinea Villager,* a newsletter produced in English by the Australian Administration during the 1950s for the small population of literate natives. Each month, the column took it upon itself to answer questions like these:

> When you go to the store and buy a packet of tea, do you ever wonder how the tea got into the packet?

Most of us eat rice. We like to go to the store and buy a bag and take it home
... How does the rice get into the store?

Having posed the question, the column would go on to describe the processes
of production that got the tea or rice from India to Australia and, finally, to
Papua and New Guinea. The column apparently presumed that what required
explaining to the natives was the unseen production of things rather than
their manifestly unequal distribution. So, for example, the "How You Get It"
column dealing with money explained the procedures for designing and mint-
ing metal coins and printing paper notes. The implicit concern of the whole
exercise was thus to dispel the dangerous idea that things, including money,
were *not* produced, but rather somehow delivered ready made—say, by be-
nevolent ancestors or by potent magic.

The unarticulated assumptions of this educational effort became explicit
in later joint attempts by the Administration and the Reserve Bank of Australia (RBA) to provide the natives in the Territory "with an understanding of
the management of money" (Australia 1962:34). In June 1961, "financial
booklets" were produced by the Bank in English, Pidgin (Tok Pisin), and
Motu; they were distributed throughout the Territory, mainly to secondary
school students. The titles included the following: "Prices," "Savings Clubs,"
"What Is Wealth?", and "Your Money." Film versions of the last two booklets
were also commissioned by the RBA for showing to native audiences (RBA
1962a, 1962b). Audiences in Australia were informed of the project by a brief
notice in the government publication *Australian Territories.* Here is how the
notice describes the first booklet, "Your Money":

> This explains the use of notes and coins in everyday transactions, and lays
> stress on the value of the individual's personal savings in planning a well-
> ordered and productive life. It also stresses the need for the health and growth
> of the co-operative enterprises so widespread now throughout Papua and
> New Guinea. (Australia 1962:34)

It is in the attempt of "Your Money" to explain money to the natives that
one can glimpse the colonial strategy for preventing fetishistic couplings,
namely, the strategy of assimilation—of replacing the old with the new, the
primitive with the modern:

> In this country, metal coins and paper notes are replacing things such as
> shells, clay pots, feathers and pigs, which earlier were used to buy things
> which men and women needed. This change has occurred in other countries
> in the past and is still taking place in parts of the world other than Papua
> and New Guinea. (RBA 1961a)

This strategy begins by identifying "money" (notes and coins) with specific
wealth items such as shells and pigs; but having done so, it then discounts these

wealth items as inferior forms of money due to their irreducible materiality and localized or nonuniversal recognition as valuable.

The irreducible materiality of wealth items impedes their capacity to discharge the function of money as means of payment: "Can you imagine the difficulty of exchanging at a shop or a store a pig for a radio set or guitar? Even if you could bring the pig to the shop or store which had the radio set or guitar for sale, the shopkeeper might not want a pig." (The film version of "Your Money" includes a protracted scene of a man futilely trying to exchange shell valuables in a trade store.) Money, by contrast, is "small and easy to carry" and, moreover, allows one to get what one desires in a single exchange, whenever one so desires. Money therefore reduces the materiality of the pig into that of the guitar, just as its own reducibility from note into coin allows it to measure differences between the values of material items (such as pigs and guitars). Thus, the shopkeeper would always accept money.

Not only would that shopkeeper accept money; *any* shopkeeper *anywhere* in the country would accept money: "Money can be used in all parts of a country for buying and selling, but other things can not always be conveniently used." In other words, money is recognized translocally; the social recognition of it as acceptable extends beyond the localized society of the village, the archipelago, or the valley system. The portability and spatial extensiveness of money are of a piece.

In the same way, the essential and translocal immateriality of money makes it a superior standard and store of value. Yes, the booklet does point out how "money does not decay or go bad like such things as taro, sugar or tobacco." But this is somewhat beside the point that money transcends its materiality, and not only with respect to the convertibility of paper notes and metal coins: "Even when notes become soiled or worn, they can always be exchanged at a bank for clean and fresh ones." Thus, money's spatial extensiveness is paralleled by a deep temporal extensiveness. (It is the space-time defined by money that practically defines "the country" of Papua and New Guinea, a silhouette of which graces the covers of both "Your Money" and "What Is Wealth." But this definition is problematic, inasmuch as the money in question is *Australian* money, which was also used in the Territory from after World War II until independence in 1975; see below.)

Both materiality and locality of wealth items, then, make them less convenient than "money," and it is convenience above all that accounts for the replacement of wealth items by money (a point also argued by Adam Smith): "Money, then, has come to replace most of the older ways of making payments, because it is much more convenient to use." The evolution toward "money" is thus imagined as inexorable and natural, a consequence of the search for more efficient ways of discharging the presumably universal functions of money. The replacement of wealth items by money is an index of Papua and

New Guinea's inevitable participation in this unilinear evolutionary progress toward a life of greater efficiency and convenience—"a well ordered and productive life."

The problem in and for this strategy of colonial education lay in communicating to the natives that the matter of money does not matter (Pietz 1985:15). In other words, the challenge of colonial education lay in teaching a mode of symbolization in which money could be apprehended as a signifier referring beyond itself (Pietz 1985:15). To what? Work. Accordingly, the explanation of the "properties" of money in "Your Money" gives way to a section called "How We Get Money." It is here that one can sense the fear of cargo cult/fetishism emerging anew—the fear that the natives will embrace money not as a signifier that transcends its materiality, but as a substance whose intrinsic material properties underpin its efficacy:

> You have been told that the coins and notes are issued for the Government. You may wonder why much more is not issued and given to us so that we need not have to work, grow crops, or perform a service for it. (RBA 1961 I)

The answer to this hypothesized puzzle involves revealing what money "really" represents: work.

> When people buy things with money they have earned, they are really paying with their work or their goods or services which are stored up in the money they have earned.
> People who are paid with money are really paid with work and, as we have said before, money can be either metal or paper, but it still represents the value of the work or goods which people bring into existence by their efforts. (RBA 1961a)

Accordingly, education about money required teaching the double lesson that money is *a form* of wealth and all wealth is not (in the form of) money.

Both the booklet and the film titled "What Is Wealth?" are lessons in a labor theory of value and an ethics of industry and frugality that seem drawn directly—like the stuff about money's convenience—from *The Wealth of Nations*. The film version opens with a staged scene of natives lined up on a beach, bowing and waving leaf wands toward the sea in an apparent attempt to summon the cargo. Ismael ToMata, vice president of the Gazelle Peninsula Local Government Council, announces an anticargo message: "This is ignorance and foolishness." He goes on to assert that wealth comes from work, and explains how he went to Australia and saw that people there have more wealth because of their work. Thus, in a stroke, this particular labor theory of value takes care of the problems of production *and* distribution. The booklet asks: How does a man get wealth? Answer: Wealth can only be created by someone's work. The booklet asks: Why are some people richer than others? Answer:

Some people in Papua and New Guinea will never be very wealthy but every person can, by hard work and saving, become better off than he is now. The man who wastes all the money he earns will always be poor. The man who saves money whenever he earns some, will gradually improve his standard of living. (RBA 1961b)

And so the booklet catechizes along the lines of what Lindstrom (1993:9) refers to as the "dominant capitalist rhetoric," narrating "the moral connections . . . between hard work and material success." Why cannot we be given motor cars, etc.? Answer: You will see that it costs a lot of money to make a motor car, and the people who buy cars must pay a big enough price for each one so that the people who own the factories can get back all the money they have spent (paying for work and materials). Note that "profits" here means "reward" and payment for "risk." Why cannot we make such things as motor cars, radios, and refrigerators in the Territory? Answer: People in Papua and New Guinea do not yet have enough money to buy machines and materials to set up factories. And so forth.

I will return presently to the implications of the RBA's program in moral education for enforcing a particular notion of personhood—that of the modern individual. For the moment, however, I would like to concentrate on a tension in the program surrounding the attempt to dematerialize money—that is, to render money as no object. This tension derives, I suggest, from the dissonance between the ideological explanation of money on the one hand, and the immediate practical goal of the Administration on the other. That goal was to get natives to put their money in one of the four Australian trading banks operating in the Territory and thereby to accumulate capital locally for financing the development of the Territory. Accordingly, the educational campaign emphasized the virtues of saving, of "growing" money in a savings bank (see *Papua and New Guinea Villager,* September 1954). At the same time, the booklets and films raise the specter of losing money, especially paper money, not through improper consumption, but through its material dissolution: "Paper money not put into a BANK may be eaten by rats or other pests, or, if there is a fire, it can be burned." Even ordinary conditions might prove disastrous for notes, which "might be spoilt over a long period because the paper can deteriorate in hot and humid climates." In other words, in order to motivate natives to deposit their money in a bank, the educational campaign emphasized the fragile materiality of money. This emphasis, I suggest, potentially fanned the flames of fetishism by making out of money not a signifier that referred beyond itself, but a material object that was intrinsically mysterious and potent.

The clearest evidence of this potential is *The Luluai's Dream*, commissioned by the RBA as one of three films made for showing to native audiences. *The Luluai's Dream*, however, is distinctive in that it presents its case in the form of a dramatic narrative enacted entirely by New Guinea natives. (There is anecdotal evidence that New Guineans also collaborated with the film's producer, Maslyn Williams, in writing the script; for more on Williams's films, see Foster 2001.) The story revolves around the attempt of John, a sophisticated young agricultural officer, to persuade Tengen, an old untutored rustic and the government-appointed "chief" (*luluai*) of his area, to stop keeping his money in an old tobacco tin and instead to put it in a bank. Tengen is depicted as a man who, rather like Dobbs in *The Treasure of Sierra Madre,* is obsessed with his money—that is, his actual notes and coins. Tengen inspects his tin frequently; he counts out his money again and again; and he lies with his money at night.

The climax of the film is a dream sequence in which Tengen's spirit leaves his sleeping body. This immaterial Tengen runs to a burning village. An ethereal voice urges him to hurry or his money will be cooked. But Tengen arrives too late and discovers his house and money on fire. Waking suddenly, Tengen reports his dream to John and vows to change his ways. John accompanies Tengen to a bank in Rabaul, the district headquarters, where Tengen deposits his money and receives in exchange a bank book, the use of which the narrator then explains. The end.

The Luluai's Dream precisely depicts Tengen's money as his fetish, in the specific sense that Tengen surrenders his autonomy, his self-control, to the force of his money objects. Here we encounter one more of Pietz's themes of fetishism: the subjection of the human body to the irreducible materiality of the object. The film represents Tengen's struggle as one of overcoming the influence or control over his body exerted by a powerful external organ: his money.

Perhaps we can characterize this film as strategic fetishism. In order to compel the natives to use banks, the film draws on the power of the fetish—even if this means suggesting that the matter of money does, after all, matter. (Likewise, the film depicts banks primarily as secure places in which to store money, physical repositories of money objects.) In the end, though, Tengen does manage to establish his autonomy by bringing his money fetish under control, indeed, by reducing the materiality of the money objects into that of a bank book. This is the trade-off that the film makes: money's fetishization facilitates projecting the image of a progressive, self-disciplined individual—an image that returns us to the sort of moral education implied in the RBA's program.

Who is the "you" addressed in "Your Money"? It is, first of all, a singular "you," a "you" that presupposes a certain kind of individuated, self-contained person—in short, an individual externally related to his (always his, if implicitly) possessions. It is this modern individual whom the RBA's educational campaign at once presupposed and naturalized in claiming that each individual's security and status depend on his relation to money, not to other people. Consider this parable from an article in the *Papua and New Guinea Villager* (September 1954), titled "Wise People Save Money":

> Let us imagine a young man who has just got a job. He works at that job until he is 50 years old, but he never saves any money. He spends it all on himself. The time comes when he cannot work. His family have to look after him. That is very hard on the family, and not very fair.

And consider this advice from the booklet "Your Money": "A man with money in a BANK is a more important man. People know he is a sensible man and respect him." Both of these declarations presuppose a world of individuals defined not through their relations to each other, but prior to and independent of those relations and hence definable only in terms of a common external standard: the standard of wealth in the form of money. Indeed, there is a surprising openness—almost crassness—about this state of affairs in the RBA's campaign. In the booklet "What Is Wealth?", it is suggested that if a man "puts most of his money in a bank, he can show his friends how wealthy he is by letting them see his bank book." And so at the end of *The Luluai's Dream*, Tengen can be seen displaying his bank book to some interested onlookers, advertising thereby his identity measured in pounds and pence. But the outcome is indeterminate: does not the irreducibly material bank book itself take the place of Tengen's notes and coins as his new fetish?

OUR MONEY: FROM COLONY TO NATION

The bank book–cum–identity card marks one of two moments in a single strategy of moral education fitfully pursued by agents of Christian colonialism in Papua and New Guinea. It indexes the moment of individuation, the creation of individuated persons (individuals) as the primordial units of modern society. The second moment, then, is that of aggregation, the bringing together of individuals to form a society or "community." This community in turn is imagined as a collective individual, the corporation formed out of many singular individuals—some of whom might be unknown to each other. It is in this second moment of the educational process that one sees the connection between the Administration's talk about money and wealth and its United Nations–mandated program for nation building.

The RBA's effort to explain the nature of money and wealth was bound up with its concern to accumulate capital in the Territory. Discussions of hard and efficient work as the source of an individual's wealth often merged into discussions of "community wealth": "The wealth of any community includes the total of all the wealth owned by individuals in the community, together with a great many other things which are owned by the community or the country as a whole" (RBA 1961b). Such things include schools, aid posts, roads, airstrips, and wharfs. The acquisition of these things was beyond the means of any one individual and therefore required an association of individuals, each member of which would contribute a small amount of money. Of course, the most usual way of building up community wealth was through paying taxes to the government (or Native Local Government Council; RBA 1961b). But other sorts of novel voluntary associations, such as women's clubs and cooperative societies, were also vehicles for accumulation. As the narrator of the film "What Is Wealth?" puts it: "Small amounts of money collected together make it possible for a group of people like yourselves to do big and important things."

My point here is that colonial education conjured not only the singular "you" in "your money," but a collective "you" as well. This collective "you" was imagined as a community of ownership composed of discrete individual owners, such as "a village." But at the highest level, this community designated the country: "Beyond the village, we think of the wealth of a country—things which belong to all the people of the country. They all share in the ownership of these things, even though they may never have seen them" (RBA 1961b). This country is the collective "you" imagined by the colonial state. When such imaginings become those of the colonized themselves—a process that Anderson (1991) has deftly outlined—assertions of Your Money become nationalist counterassertions of Our Money. And it is in the context of such counterassertions that fetish discourse about money and wealth items—pigs, pearlshells, and clay pots—becomes transformed.

In the Territory of Papua and New Guinea, Australian notes and coins (first pounds, shillings, and pence, then dollars and cents) circulated in the post–World War II years, replacing the specially minted Territorial coinage and printed currency in use in New Guinea during the interwar years. After the proclamation of internal self-government in 1973, planning began for the name and design of the future coinage and paper currency of PNG. The then minister for finance (later prime minister), Mr. (now Sir) Julius Chan, announced that the new currency would be distinctly Papua New Guinean, with designs that reflect "the spirit and feeling of Papua New Guinea" (quoted in Mira 1986:139). The following year, Chan proposed to the House of Assembly a format for PNG coinage and notes—denominations, size, weight, etc.—that was broadly similar to that of Australian currency, but with significantly new names for the basic monetary units:

> I therefore propose that the name of the dollar equivalent should be *Kina,* and the name of the cent equivalent should be *toea.* The word *Kina* is found in both the Pidgin and Kuanua languages. In pidgin it refers to the valuable pearl shell used widely in the Highlands as a traditional store of wealth. It is probably the source of one of the terms for pearl shell in the Mount Hagen Melpa language, *Kin.* The fact that this shell is traded into the

Highlands from coastal areas far afield makes it an appropriate national name for one of the basic units of our new currency.

The word *toea* is a Motu word meaning valuable arm-shell. The *toea* has had a wide traditional use in coastal Papua for trading and bride-price payments. One bride-price recorded about 70 years ago consisted of 43 *toea*, three pigs, and 100 dogs' teeth. I am not sure whether there has been inflation or deflation since then. The combination of these two names should help to preserve a valuable part of our cultural traditions, drawn from as broad a spectrum as possible of the whole of Papua New Guinea. (Quoted in Mira 1986:140–41)

In April 1975, the new currency was issued. After a year-long "dual currency period," during which PNG became an independent state, the new currency officially supplanted Australian dollars and cents.

Chan's proposal indicates two ways in which state officials constructed the new money, and by the same token (so to speak) the new nation itself, as a fetish—that is, a fetish in the sense of a composite fabrication, a coming together of previously heterogeneous elements. First, the money was to be understood as a synthesis of elements drawn from different locations within the borders of the territorial state, thereby expressing both the unity of the nation as a whole and the parity of its constituent parts. Considerable attention appears to have been given to devising a monetary symbolism that would mediate some of the major cleavages emerging within the new nation, especially cleavages between the Highlands and the Islands, between Papua and New Guinea, and between Motu speakers and Tok Pisin speakers. (Special mention also seems to have been given to Kuanua [Tolai] speakers, an important and potentially secessionist ethnic group during the time of independence.) Not only the names of the major monetary units, but also the iconography of the paper currency was conceived with this mediation in mind. The back of every note of each denomination depicts items of traditional wealth—cowrie shell necklaces, clay pots, and so forth (figures 2.1 and 2.2). Taken together, the notes depict items from all of the administrative districts (now provinces) within the nation.

The second way in which Chan's proposal indicates a familiarly post-colonial sort of fetish discourse for the nation lies in its invocation of "cultural traditions." The following statement of Sir Henry ToRobert, once governor of the Bank of PNG and before that a member of Chan's 1973 Currency Working Group and manager of the Port Moresby Office of the RBA, makes the point concisely:

In preparation for political independence, currency in Papua New Guinea on 19 April 1975 took on its own unique form and emphasis. Physically the needs of a modern world and a desire to maintain the country's heritage came together to give meaning to our notes and coins. (Mira 1986:ix)

The coins and currency of PNG are, in this view, seen as the material embodiment of an encounter between the past and the present, tradition and modernity. But the upshot of this encounter is not, as in the colonialist rhetoric of RBA's booklets, the replacement of the former by the latter. There is no assumption here of a process of total assimilation to the imported but irresistibly superior media of modernity. Rather, what is emphasized is the continuation of the past in the present, the resilience of tradition or heritage in the modern world. Thus, for example, a grade 6 school textbook used throughout PNG as an introduction to the topic of money tells its readers that "Early Papua New Guinean money is shown on our present banknotes. The drawings on our banknotes show valuable traditional things that have always been used as money" (PNG 1987a:4).

The point I wish to make in this regard is that the threatening fetish of colonial times—the irreducibly material and locally restricted wealth item—has been rehabilitated as an emblem of cultural identity. But this rehabilitation (or revaluation) is also a form of domestication, for the wealth items now indicate not an alternative and competing value code, but rather a non-threatening, if apparently different, mode of cultural identity. In other words, what takes the place of assimilation—the replacement of the primitive with the modern—is juxtaposition, a complementarity of differences made viable by a new structural equation: modernity is to tradition as economy is to culture. Let me illustrate how this trope of juxtaposition makes itself present in a range of images, all of which play self-consciously on the visual dissonance of bringing "cultural traditions" within the same frame as the "modern economy."

The pictures that I discuss next are taken from a modest coffee-table book published in 1970 by Maslyn Williams, producer of the RBA films and numerous other documentary films for the Australian government (see Foster 2001). Pictures 1 and 2 form a pair (figure 2.3); they are captioned, respectively, "Housewife—1960" and "Housewife—1970." The message seems to be that a major change has taken place; an old and primitive version of "the housewife" has been replaced by a new and modern one in the short span of ten years. Such, I suggest, is the colonialist reading of the trope, *In One Lifetime*, the title of the book of photographs (compare the subtitle of the popular autobiography of Sir Albert Maori Kiki: *Ten Thousand Years in a Lifetime.*) In this reading, what is emphasized is the process of replacement—that is, the radical difference between the before and after pictures.

Picture 3, however, lends itself to a different reading (figure 2.4). It is captioned, "Highlanders shopping in a self-service supermarket." Here the contrast is not that of before and after, but rather between heterogeneous elements of the same present—a contrast within the now, as it were. It is not a process of replacement that is emphasized, but rather an instance of juxtaposition. From one point of view, the photo can be read as a transitional mo-

The front of a K2 note.

Figure 2.1. Design of PNG two-kina note.
Papua New Guinea 1987a, p. 11. Used by permission of the Bank of PNG.

ment and thus placed after picture 1 as a step on the way to picture 2. But from another point of view, the photograph can be read as depicting what Julius Chan and Henry ToRobert were imagining—namely, the timeless co-existence of cultural tradition and modern economy. In this latter reading, indigenous cultural practices are not replaced but rather repositioned—indeed, reclassified as tradition or heritage—as Culture. These repositioned cultural traditions then become the basis for defining a unique and distinctive national cultural identity in a homogeneous modern world economy.

The ambiguity of picture 3—its intelligibility within both colonialist and

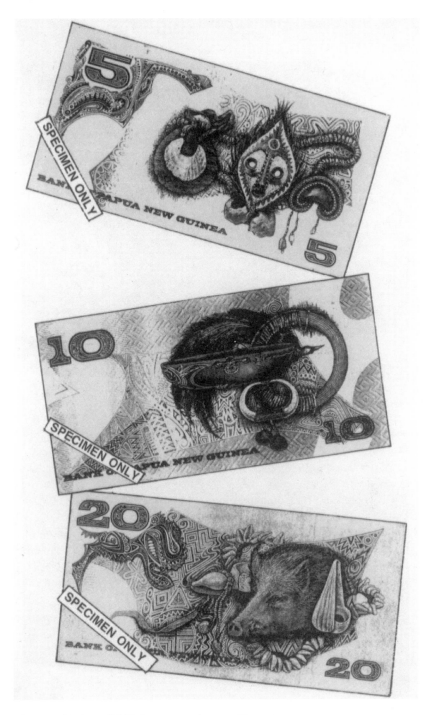

Figure 2.2. Designs of PNG five-, ten-, and twenty-kina notes.
Papua New Guinea 1987a, p. 12. Used by permission of the Bank of PNG.

Figure 2.3. "Housewife—1960" and "Housewife—1970."
Williams 1970:53. Used by permission of Maslyn Williams.

postcolonialist readings—disappears in the self-consciousness of pictures 4 and 5 (and, of course, the PNG paper notes). Picture 4 forms the cover of *Money,* the community life pupil book for grade 6 used in community schools throughout PNG (figure 2.5). A diagonal line bisects the cover. In one section, there is an image of a woman (as usual) paying a cashier at the checkout counter of a supermarket; in the other section is an arrangement of shell wealth items. The cover is a composite, a coupling of tradition and modernity —but *not* a promiscuous mixing: tradition and modernity each occupy discrete domains. It is juxtaposition, not blending, that organizes the image.

The same can be said for picture 5, a 1995 advertisement taken from PNG's daily newspaper, the *Post-Courier* (figure 2.6). Here the text of the ad makes explicit precisely what is at stake in the displacement and juxtaposition of visual markers of local and premodern life: the construction of a new national cultural identity. *Pepsi* is not a threat to PNG national culture, but on the contrary an active supporter of this culture in its sponsorship of the annual Port Moresby Show, a state fair–like event highlighted by its prize competitions in traditional dance and self-decoration among emerging ethnic groups. Indeed, the marriage of *Pepsi* and "cultural heritages" yields a "new generation" for PNG: not the once-feared offspring of "mixed-race" unions, but instead a nation of Papua New Guineans (rather than Trobrianders or

Figure 2.4. "Highlanders shopping in a self-service supermart."
Williams 1970:70. Used by permission of Maslyn Williams.

Tolai) whose identity derives from the ever-present, infinitely repeatable encounter of tradition and modernity. The national Us that crystallizes from
this imagery is indeed a composite one: not so much a composite of diverse
ethnicities—"unity in diversity," Indonesian style—but a composite of past
and present, indigenous and exogenous, traditional and modern. Like its coin
and currency, then, the nation of PNG embodies—now and forever—an encounter between radically heterogeneous elements; the nation form here mim-
ics the fetish form.

THE GOVERNMENT'S MONEY: STATE FETISHISM IN PNG?

The rhetoric of the RBA's financial booklets insisted that the notes and
coins called "money, because they are issued for the Government, . . . are al-

Figure 2.5. Cover of the textbook *Money*, produced for community schools in PNG.
Papua New Guinea 1987a. Used by permission of the PNG Department of Education.

Figure 2.6. *Pepsi* advertisement.
Post-Courier, June 1995.
Pepsi, Pepsi-Cola, the Pepsi Globe design, and *The Choice of a New Generation* are registered trademarks of PepsiCo, Inc. Used by permission.

ways good." In other words, "the Government" is the ultimate source of all the money circulating in the Territory (and Australia, too). Conversely, "the Government" is responsible for collecting a portion of all the money in circulation, through taxes paid by individuals in money, in order to build up "community wealth." Money, then, is the mundane instrument through which "the Government" asserts and legitimates its holistic existence and reality. It is this entity and being—"the Government"—as much as it is work or labor that is the something beyond itself to which the material signifier of money refers. Put otherwise, money is what "the State" designates as its mask, as the material form that gives shape to an insubstantial but powerful fiction (Taussig 1992).

The grade school book "Money" likewise deploys a rhetoric that animates the matter of money with the idea of the independent state of PNG. In its iconography, PNG currency represents the nation-state as the totality holding together the ethnic/cultural diversity of "the country." Thus, the national emblem, a bird of paradise perched on an hourglass drum, appears on the front of almost every coin and every note (figure 2.1). The backs of the coins and notes vary, however (figures 2.1 and 2.2). Coins depict various fauna—crocodiles, a cuscus, and so forth; notes, as already mentioned, depict wealth items that can be associated with different regions of the country—"different kinds of traditional money," as the school book puts it.

The exception is the one-kina coin, the largest of all the coins and the only one with a hole in the center, enhancing its portability by making it easy to carry on a string looped around one's neck. This coin bears instead of the national emblem a "specially designed figure of a Bird of Paradise [which] is the symbol of the Bank of Papua New Guinea" (PNG 1987a:13). The textbook, in a section titled "The Government's Money," explains:

> Every country has its own bank to look after the country's money business. The Bank of Papua New Guinea does this for us. It plans how much money people will need to carry on the country's business.
> All the other banks get banknotes and coins from it.

In this representation, the Bank of Papua New Guinea ("the Government's" bank?) is the ultimate source of all the money in the country. The Bank is also the storehouse of "the nation's wealth" in the form of gold (the textbook thus includes a photograph of dozens of bars of gold stacked in a vault). It is the mother of all banks, the bank to which not only all other banks, but also all individuals who use money are simultaneously and necessarily connected.

In other words, the coinage and currency of PNG—like that of many other states—are inscribed with visible traces of state. Yet coinage and currency "work" efficaciously—in PNG as elsewhere—only when these traces are erased from consciousness—that is, subsumed under an implicit fiction that the coinage and currency as signifiers depend on nothing (whether labor or the state) beyond themselves, on no signified. Or as Taussig (1992:138) puts it, "The fetish absorbs into itself that which it represents, erasing all traces of the represented. A clean job." Under such conditions, the matter of money—including its iconography—really (i.e., practically) does not matter. Under such conditions, the connection between money and the state goes without saying and so goes unsaid.

Do such conditions prevail in PNG? Hardly, I think. But I don't mean to suggest that such conditions prevail elsewhere, either. Take, for example, the much-publicized militia movement in the United States, a complicated discursive field that engages, among other things, attacks on the Federal Reserve banking system. In a pamphlet called "Why a Bankrupt America?", published by Project Liberty (1993), the question of what is money is taken up as part of a critical inquiry into the nature of the Federal Reserve. The pamphlet seeks to establish that the Federal Reserve is a private company and not part of the U.S. government. It also seeks to demonstrate that only gold and silver, not paper, are money (thereby reviving a debate that gripped many Americans in the nineteenth century; see Michaels 1987, Shell 1982):

> Precious metals such as gold and silver have been the most highly prized means of monetary exchange for many centuries. They are honest money. By mining the Earth, one exchanges his God-given talents and resources for wealth. That wealth can, in turn, be exchanged for the goods and services honestly produced by another's talents and resources.

After citing the United States Code at Title 12, Sec. 152, to the effect that lawful money of the United States shall be construed to mean only gold and silver coin, the pamphlet draws its conclusion:

> What we really see from these definitions is that paper cannot be money. What we carry in our pockets—Federal Reserve Notes—are disqualified as money, because they are notes. A note is an IOU—an evidence of debt. It is not money! Why, then, do we call it money? Have we been tricked?

We have been more than tricked, as it turns out; for close scrutiny of the image of the seal on the back of every U.S. one-dollar bill will reveal the motto of the devilish conspiracy in which the Federal Reserve participates: *novus ordo seculorum,* new order of the ages—the New World Order of global government ruled by the United Nations.

My point follows accordingly: if one looks hard at and takes seriously the material form of money—especially the stateish iconography of coin and currency—then one can recover money's erasure and question the connection between one's self and the state. Such inquiry is happening in PNG, where the idea of "the Government's money" is taken very seriously. But in PNG, the main issue is not whether paper currency is somehow less real or less valid than metal coinage. In fact, I doubt that this problem has ever been a problem for most Papua New Guineans, mainly because most Papua New Guineans have historically understood money (coins and paper notes) as the material token of a social relationship, a relationship of power between themselves and some radically alien Other. The first of these Others were the Germans, who were compelled in 1900–1901 to issue ordinances forbidding the use of shell money (*diwara*) in transactions between Europeans and natives. Then came the Australians, who were also compelled in 1920 to issue the Native Currency Ordinance, which stipulated that "no European or any other person having the status of a European and any coloured person in the employ of such European, shall sell, exchange, give or take in payment, or use as a means of barter or exchange any of the earthenware saucepans which are commonly used in currency by the Siassi group of Islands, nor earthenware articles similar in nature to such saucepans" (Mira 1986:29). The Japanese imposed their money during World War II, and the Australians reimposed their money afterward. It is not surprising, then, that I heard men in rural New Ireland narrate a history of colonialism in terms of currency shifts: first we had marks, then shillings, then dollars.

During the last currency shift, around the time of independence, many people, especially in the Highlands, felt uneasy about converting their Australian dollars and cents to PNG kina and toea. The PNG government was compelled twice to extend the deadline for free conversion of Australian money due to the large amounts being withheld in rural areas (Mira 1986:143). This widespread hesitation to convert Australian currency bespoke widespread anxiousness about political independence and the fortunes of PNG apart from Australia. It also bespoke the fate of the newly independent state—namely, to be cast as the latest in a long line of Others with whom diverse indigenous local populations entered into contested relations of power.

Because, then, Papua New Guineans have always understood money as the ambivalent index of both "the Government's" power over them and its ability to supply desired goods to them, criticism of the PNG government today is articulated through criticism of its money. Several New Ireland men complained to me that their money was not as strong as it was before independence; they equated the diminished purchasing power of their money with the weakness and mismanagement of the PNG government compared with that of Australia. Jeffrey Clark (1997:81) reported a similar, but more specific, complaint from Pangia in the Southern Highlands: "It is believed in Pangia that Australian money was made by the Queen, Papua New Guinea currency made by [Sir Michael] Somare [former prime minister] in Port Moresby (people prefer the K2 note because it is most like the one pound note)." Here the invidious comparison of PNG with Australia entails a personification of the state by Somare and an identification of Somare with PNG currency. These equations are not unpersuasive, given that the recently issued K50 note bears the images of both Sir Michael himself and the National Parliament building. The main Parliament building, moreover, was built in the singular shape of a "spirit house" (*haus tamberan*) from the Sepik area, Somare's place of origin (see figure 3.8).

Clark's point is that Pangia people imagine the PNG state as a classic Melanesian "big man" whom they follow *if and only if* the big man remains bound by moral obligations of reciprocity and redistribution. My point is different. I want to stress that people in PNG can accept as eminently plausible the claim that money *is* the government's money. Indeed, they verify the claim with reference to the iconography of the money, thereby uncovering a connection that the fetish power of money ordinarily obscures. But having accepted the claim, Papua New Guineans are then free to develop its implications into a critique of the government, to apprehend the PNG state as an Other with whom nothing less than an egalitarian, reciprocal relationship is morally proper. Hence the consternation of one New Ireland man at the depictions of wealth items on PNG bank notes. When I pointed out to him the image of a masked figure (*dukduk*) from nearby New Britain and southern New Ireland, he immediately observed: "that's not *our* custom (*kastam*)." The PNG state, despite its deliberate efforts, failed to represent (in both senses of the term) him; "the government's money" was not, in this instance, "our money."

CONCLUSION: NEW MONEY, OLD FETISHISMS

There are other ways in which to qualify or subvert the claim that money is the government's money. I conclude by considering two of them. Both ways recall the critical remarks made by New Irelanders and Pangia people about PNG money in that they take the matter of money seriously. That is, they re-evaluate money—notes and coins—and/or wealth items in terms of material properties—in aesthetic terms—and in so doing accomplish what colonial educators sought to prevent: they create material media capable of traversing and articulating diverse value codes.

The first way, which I will call after Nihill (1989:157) "the contextual demonetization of money," is illustrated by the ceremonial uses to which Anganen men (Southern Highlands) put twenty-kina notes. Nihill reports that Anganen liken twenty-kina notes to pearlshells (*kina*) and use the two interchangeably in certain exchange contexts in which men accrue prestige. This perceived similarity does not extend to all money, but rather only to the twenty-kina notes. First of all, Anganen regard paper money as "male" and coins as "female." Moreover, they associate small denominations of paper money (two-kina and five-kina notes) with mundane productive activities (wage labor, coffee selling) on the one hand, and acts of consumption (buying cigarettes and beer, paying taxes) in which money is "lost" on the other. This association also metaphorically links small-denomination paper notes to women, who grow and sell coffee, and, in the eyes of men, "eat" cash by channeling it into wasteful consumption.

By contrast, twenty-kina notes—new, red notes—are unequivocally associated with the masculine realm of exchange. They are, according to Nihill, "like male-oriented groups (clans, subclans)" in their capacity to integrate "power and value into a single entity which should then be directed to purposeful" and socially reproductive ends (1989:153). They are like the intact pearlshell crescents that men esteem and care for, "applying red ochre to renew their 'skin' " (1989:152). Men display these pearlshells in prestations made in respect of bodies—prestations undertaken to alleviate illness, compensate death, or combine a woman's "womb blood" with her husband's semen and thereby create children. And herein lies the analogy that underwrites the spectacular substitutability of pearlshells and twenty-kina notes:

> The stress on presentational excellence also suggests why the Anganen emphasize the newness or crispness of paper money in a manner parallel to the renewing of shells through red colouration. They may even go so far as to swap old notes for new at savings banks in Mendi. Like pearlshells, new notes have an aesthetic quality all their own which gives their display a value that older notes cannot achieve. An analogy with human bodies is not misplaced here: tight, shiny skin or brilliant body decoration, bright red pearlshells and crisp, pristine 20-kina notes are all of inherent merit and beauty. (Nihill 153–54)

The display of money thus has an iconic quality to it; the twenty-kina notes at once evince and ensure the ends of social reproduction: strong and beautiful bodies. Hence, as Nihill points out, the cultural good sense with which one Anganen man named his son and daughter Kina and Toea, the basic units of PNG money.

All this was probably not what the RBA had in mind when it assured the natives that soiled notes could always be exchanged for fresh, clean ones. In fact, the use of twenty-kina notes in Anganen exchanges seemingly realizes the worst fear of the RBA: the (noncommodity) fetishization of money. The fetish power of twenty-kina notes consists in their capacity, like that of pearlshells, to evince the regeneration of social relations and perforce the reproduction of healthy bodies. New money becomes fetishized on old grounds, animated with the life-giving qualities that distinguish pearlshells as wealth items of the highest order. But this fetishization is unstable; for despite their "contextual demonetization," twenty-kina notes are always at risk of remonetization, of being fragmented into smaller denomination notes and coins and "lost" in un(re)productive consumption. The fetish power of crisp, red twenty-kina notes thus depends on sustaining a separation between two realms: the realm of socially reproductive ceremonial exchange among male transactors, and the realm of wasteful and multiple retail transactions where women and lesser men circulate dirty money (see Parry and Bloch 1989).

A similar (though ungendered) dichotomy is entailed in a second way in which indigenous strategies have implicated state-issued money in old fetishisms. In this instance, however, old wealth items become (re)fetishized on new grounds. I am thinking in particular about the famous "shell money" of the people of the Gazelle Peninsula (East New Britain), called *tabu* or *tambu* by Tolai and *diwara* by Duke of York Islanders. This shell money has been the subject of discussion by missionaries, government officials, and anthropologists for more than a hundred years—mainly because it has impressed outsiders as a "true money," that is, a medium of exchange, and a measure and store of value. Its material properties lent themselves well to all these functions:

> Shell money . . . consisted of small cowrie shells (*nassa camelus*) strung onto strips of rattan and counted either individually or measured on the body in standard lengths . . . Continuously spliced, these strips could be arranged in large wrapped and sometimes decorated coils containing hundreds of fathoms. (Errington and Gewertz 1995b:54)

These same outsiders were equally impressed with the sheer pervasiveness and unambiguous centrality of shell money in the life of the Tolai and Duke of York Islanders. Neumann (1992:186) claims that today not only must shell money be used to purchase magic and commission dance performances, but also that "at the village level nearly all other goods that can be bought with kina can also be bought with *tabu*—which makes *tabu* in that sense the 'truer' of the two currencies used on the Gazelle." Errington and Gewertz (1995b:54) add that

> shell money was the single standard by which not only everything but everyone was distinguished. The differences in the amount of shell money that an individual owned and used in public ceremonies distinguished a person of importance from one of mere respectability and the latter from one of no consequence. Shell money was fundamental to the prestige system and to the ordering of social life.

Yet while outside commentators have sought to identify shell money with "real" money—a curious parallel, perhaps, to the Anganen effort to identify twenty-kina notes with pearlshells—inside commentators have sought to maintain a clear contrast. This contrast is drawn in terms that recall the Anganen distinction between twenty-kina notes and other inferior forms of money:

> shell money was frequently described by Duke of York Islanders in terms of an essentialized contrast to money: Shell money was extolled as "heavy" (*mawat*)—as substantial and significant—as capable of generating the ac-

tivities on which both male and female reputations were built and social order rested; money was denigrated as "light" (*biaku*)—as flimsy and inconsequential—as incapable of creating or sustaining personal worth or enduring social relationships. (Errington and Gewertz 1995b:58)

Here again we see the world divided into two realms, one where money flits away in the purchase of "easily broken, imported goods" (Errington and Gewertz 1995b:58), another where shell money circulates indefinitely, generating further exchanges. But in this version of the dichotomy, the difference between the two realms parallels a valenced opposition between Them and Us in which They—Europeans—are construed as being like Their money: morally suspect.

This particular version of the contrast between shell money and money emerged out of the long history of encounters between Tolai/Duke of York Islanders and Europeans. As I have mentioned, German colonial administrators were compelled to ban shell money in certain transactions in order to limit *their* dependence on the natives and force the natives into the cash economy. The official annual report for 1900–1901 noted that

> It was often very difficult for the European firms to obtain the shell required to purchase copra etc. In this respect they were completely dependent on the natives, and at times the exchange rate for shell money was forced up absurdly high. (Translated by Sack and Clark 1979:220; cited in Errington and Gewertz 1995b:58)

But it is also important to note, as do Errington and Gewertz (1995b:64), that this history of encounters includes the exercises in colonial education exemplified by the RBA's financial booklets. These booklets can thus be regarded as instances of what Carrier (1995) is pleased to call "occidentalism," the self-representation of the modern West in terms of an essentialized contrast with some nonmodern Other ("the East," though not necessarily in a geographical sense). Accordingly, contemporary Tolai/Duke of York understandings of money as "light" and inconsequential must be themselves understood as in dialogue with an occidentalism promulgated first by the colonial state and then, in a revised form, by the independent PNG state.

Looked at this way, local understandings of shell money on the Gazelle can be seen, at least potentially, to do two things. First, they designate shell money as a cultural icon. In this way, people accept the official postcolonial evaluation of wealth items as emblems of both "tradition" and "ethnic" identities contained within a unifying national-cultural framework; hence the successful effort of one prominent Tolai government official to stop the export of shell money on the grounds that it is (national) cultural property (see Errington and Gewertz 1995b).

Second, local understandings devalue European money as an inferior form of shell money, thereby inverting the moral of the RBA's teaching. Unlike European money, shell money can be displayed in the form of accumulated coils that are sometimes cut apart and redistributed in mortuary exchanges that enact the reproduction of matrilineal social relations (Epstein 1992). But the devaluation of European money is plausible precisely because shell money has become and continues to be used every day in all contexts as a universal currency. Indeed, Errington and Gewertz (1995b:59) report that in parts of East New Britain, it is now possible to do what the Germans and Australians explicitly outlawed: pay taxes with shell money—a brilliant assertion of how to build up "community wealth." The "culturalization" of shell money as a marker of collective identity has gone hand in hand with its spread as a medium of exchange into new transactional contexts. And it is this duality— its suitability for both short-term commercial (commodity) transactions and long-term kinship (gift) exchanges—that makes shell money superior to European money (as well as both PNG state-issued money *and* the defunct indigenous currencies of other ethnic groups). Thus, one of the underlying objections to the foreign export of shell money for display in European museums and collections was that the exporters were "buying large amounts of shell money in order *not* to use it" (Errington and Gewertz 1995b:68). That is, the exporters threatened to fetishize shell money on the wrong cultural grounds.

*   *   *

The Anganen use of money and the Tolai/Duke of York Islanders' use of shell money articulate different value codes with different forms of one material medium: notes and coins on the one hand, coils and "loose" shells on the other. Anganen reserve new twenty-kina notes for ceremonial exchanges and circulate coins and soiled small denomination notes in mundane transactions. Tolai and Duke of York Islanders reserve their precious coils of shell money for mortuary displays and distributions while they use small strips of cane or unstrung shells for everyday purchases. Anganen money and Tolai/Duke of York shell money, in other words, are two versions of the unacceptable coupling or miscegenation that inhabits the fetish. They bring together what colonial and postcolonial administrations hell-bent on modernization, with or without a nod to local culture, have been at pains to keep apart.

Whether one should regard this articulation of value codes as "resistance" is another question. After all, the Anganen use of twenty-kina notes in ceremonial exchanges puts the whole system of exchange at risk; and the celebration of shell money as a local cultural icon for Tolai/Duke of York Islanders masks the rapidly emerging class lines within those "communities." What is certain, however, is that the colonial encounter not only introduced Marx's fetishism of commodities across the borders of Melanesia, but also cleared new grounds and furnished new means for reenchanting home-grown ideas about the social value of material objects.

PART II

Commercial Nation Making

3

Print Advertisements and
Nation Making

IN MAY 1985, the National Parliament of Papua New Guinea (PNG) passed the Commercial Advertising Act, initiated by Ted Diro.[1] According to this act, all commercial advertising in PNG must be locally produced by local agencies employing local talent—designers, artists, models, and so forth. Infractions are to be treated as criminal rather than civil offenses.

Letters to the weekly *Times of Papua New Guinea* (hereinafter *TPNG*) by two critics of the act, both expatriate advertising managers, provoked responses from Moale Rivu, then executive officer for Diro.[2] In a *TPNG* article on 12 April 1986, Rivu defended the act as a deliberate effort by the government to promote "nationalism" and "nation building." He asked:

> Is it any wonder that we still find it difficult to be self sufficient in such basic foodstuff as rice and peanut butter? When the Markham factory was in operation it had to compete against imported peanut butter whose agents on numerous occasions used ready-made ads from overseas to promote their products. That, in essence, is the bottom line in this debate on the Advertising Act.

Rivu's nationalism was motivated by mainly economic concerns, the famous "bottom line." It is hardly contentious, however, to maintain that advertising and mass consumption in general are inevitably deeply cultural matters. This is not only a question of cultural imperialism, of resisting "Coca-Colonization"—the flow of images and objects emanating from various dominant regional centers. It is equally a question of the instrumental effects of mass-consumption practices in nation making—that is, a question of the potential for advertisements to present constructs of "the nation" and perforce to define the terms of membership in "the nation."

I address this broad question through a consideration of print advertisements taken from several sources: two newspapers, a billboard, and the in-flight magazine of Air Niugini. How do these ads construct "Papua New Guinea" and "Papua New Guineaness"? How do these ads and the consumption practices that they publicize enable (if not exhort) the steadily growing population of school-educated, urban-dwelling, wage-earning citizens to imagine themselves as "Papua New Guineans"? To what extent is an emergent urban consumer culture implicated in the processes of nation making in PNG (see Jourdan 1995)?

ADVERTISING AND "THE NATION"

I use two complementary approaches in considering the relationships between advertisements and "the nation"—"the nation" understood here as an imaginative construct. The first approach emphasizes the sociocultural linkages brought about by the spread of mass-consumption practices. Social historians have long observed, for example, that the formation of an imagined national community in the United States during the late nineteenth century was coeval with the birth of modern consumerism (Boorstin 1973, Bronner 1989, Ewen and Ewen 1982, Fox and Lears 1983). Department stores assembled within their palatial confines thousands of big-city dwellers; chain stores replicated these gatherings on a smaller scale in towns across the country; and mail-order catalogs functioned to connect the most remote farmer's family to this expansive network of consumers. The proliferation of images and objects of mass consumption brought the most diverse audiences, including newly arrived immigrants, into not only a developing marketplace, but also into an emergent set of shared understandings, memories, tastes, and habits.

The growth of an advertising industry figured largely in this process, inasmuch as advertisements mediated the anonymous encounter between buyers and sellers. Advertisements became important vehicles for the imagination of a community of consumers whose shared consumption practices and ideals put them in experiential unison with each other. Orvar Löfgren (1989b: 373) made this point in reviewing a history of American advertising in the 1920s and 1930s:

> Reading the same ads, listening to the same radio personalities, or watching the same movies created a shared frame of reference for those growing up during the interwar years, in the same ways as it does for those growing up today.

Circulated through the mass media of newspapers, radio, television and videos, advertisements continue to expose large numbers of Americans from a cross section of social categories to images of a supralocal world. Put otherwise, shared mass-consumption practices still provide Americans with the means not only for making, remembering, and contesting a common experience, but also for anchoring an imagined national community in ordinary, everyday practice.[3] Benedict Anderson's (1991:35) arresting description of the "mass ceremony" of newspaper reading comes to mind:

At the same time, the newspaper reader, observing exact replicas of his own paper being consumed by his subway, barbershop, or residential neighbors, is continually assured that the imagined world is visibly rooted in everyday life.

From this perspective, then, it is possible to regard nations as imagined communities of consumption, "large-scale, non-intimate collectivities unified by the ritualized fantasies of collective expenditure," to borrow Arjun Appadurai's (n.d.) words. Such fantasies circulate at high velocity through the mass media, most familiarly in the form of advertisements.[4]

The second approach, by contrast, does not focus on the specific content of ads—on the "frames of reference" or "ritualized fantasies" that ads exhibit. Instead, it focuses on what might be called the "ad form." I argue that the general *form* of advertisements, however different their specific content, communicates a particular conception of both "the nation" and its constituent "nationals." Accordingly, I approach advertising as "a discourse about and through objects which bonds together images of persons, products and well being" (Leiss et al. 1990). But I am especially concerned with the general structure of social relations that such a discourse presupposes and naturalizes, a structure of social relations characteristic of commodity consumption in capitalist societies.

More precisely, I am concerned with demonstrating how the ad form at once reflects and constitutes both a definite kind of relationship between subjects and objects (consumers and commodities) and a coordinate relationship between subjects and other subjects (consumers and other consumers) (see Miller 1987). That is, the social relations of commodity consumption implied by ads entail particular definitions of personhood on the one hand, and of community on the other. It is my argument that these definitions of personhood and community potentially supplement, if not displace, definitions of personhood and community grounded in social relations of kinship and locality (LiPuma 2000). More importantly, it is my argument that these definitions of personhood and community mesh with a conception of "the nation" as a community of individuals fundamentally similar in their status as "proprietors" or "owners" of a distinctive reification: "their" national culture (Handler 1985). In this conception, everyone who belongs to a nation is everyone to whom the nation belongs.

My approach, then, follows Anderson (1991) in emphasizing that the generic or paradigmatic imaginative construct called "the nation" is distinctive *in form*. "The nation," whatever its particular characteristics, implies a community that is unambiguously bounded, temporally as well as spatially, and inhabited by people whose manifest diversity belies a latent sameness (Handler 1988:6). This sort of imaginative construct derives from and gives rise to a variety of processes of objectification in which "the nation" takes on a thing-like form, external to the individual (see Keesing 1989, Linnekin 1990). Such objective forms—flags, costumes, dances, foods, monuments, languages—are "possessed" in common by the individuals constituting the nation as markers of their shared subjective identity as "owners" (Handler 1988:6). That is, the proprietors of these forms regard them as elements of a "national culture," as material evidence of an essential national cultural identity. National culture, in other words, emerges as a collection of collectively held things, the discrete, bounded objectivity of which tangibly replicates the conceptual form of the nation itself.

Here I want to consider advertisements as textual vehicles of such objectification. I am not concerned with the intentions of the advertisers themselves —with whether advertisers attempt to enlist nationalist sentiment in the service of selling toothpaste; nor am I concerned with the putative effects of ads on individual purchasing decisions. My primary concern is not with the particular messages of particular ads, but rather with the rhetorical form common to all ads.[5] By rhetoric, I mean two things: the way in which ads transfer meaning to the commodities that they publicize so as to endow these commodities with a set of "objectively" given qualities (Williamson 1978); and the way in which ads involve consumers as participants in constructing the ad's meaning.

The ads that I examine, I argue, qualify commodities as somehow Papua New Guinean, as embodiments and/or possessions of "the nation." They imply, furthermore, that to consume these commodities is to appropriate the quality of Papua New Guineaness as an attribute of one's person. The consumption of national commodities, then, nationalizes the person. At the same time, each ad implicitly construes the nation as a community of consumption, a collectivity of nonintimate people whose shared consumption practices and fantasies express and constitute their nationality. Membership or citizenship in this community is acquired through acts of consumption so qualified, by participation in the "lifestyle" represented in the ad.

When taken together, however, these ads leave open the possibility for consumer-citizens to differentiate themselves from each other on the basis of *unshared* consumption practices. Diversity is (re)construed as differential participation within a single universe of consumer activity. Thus, the national community of consumption is neither mechanically solidary nor even organically cohesive; indeed, differentiation of consumer-citizens constantly threatens to expose and create new cleavages (such as class and status divisions) within the community.

I begin the discussion by demonstrating the semiotic logic by which ads impute qualities or attributes to various commodities (Williamson 1978). The particular quality at issue here is nationality, or Papua New Guineaness, a detachable attribute capable of being attached to commodities as manifestly diverse as sugar and airplanes.[6] This imputation is complemented by a second: namely, the attribution of Papua New Guineaness to the consumer of commodities qualified with nationality. I concentrate in this regard on how ads define the relationship between commodity and consumer as one of "possession" or "having," and I explicate the presuppositions this definition makes about the nature of persons and objects.

The transfer of Papua New Guineaness from commodity to consumer is completed by a third imputation. Consumers are implicitly put into relation with other consumers on the basis of shared *and* unshared consumption practices. Most inclusively, this scheme of social relations defines the nation as a community of fellow consumer-citizens. However, distinctions among consumers are made with reference to a shared understanding of unevenly distributed consumption practices. That is, consumers of specific commodities are constituted as less inclusive totemic groups or "kinds" of people (Williamson 1978; cf. Comaroff 1987). This totemism thereby allows for a diversity of consumer groups within the larger national community of national commodity consumers.

NATIONALIZING COMMODITIES, NATIONALIZING PERSONS

The process of nationalizing commodities in advertising works in more or less subtle ways. Ads for state-owned businesses often render the process explicit. Consider this ad (figure 3.1) for Air Niugini, the state-owned airline, that appeared in a special independence anniversary issue of the *Post-Courier*, a nationally distributed newspaper with a circulation of 30,000 in 1985.[7] The top of the page announces: "We're proud to be your airline, PNG." Beneath this caption are four photographs, each of which pictures an Air Niugini employee (two women, two men) holding or touching some piece of airline equipment—a ticket, a cockpit control switch, a tire on the landing gear, a coffee cup. These employees are not only apparently Papua New Guineans, but also "owners" of Air Niugini. The text continues: "As long as PNG has been independent, we have been the wings for the nation. Because we're the airline owned by all the people of Papua New Guinea." Indeed, the airline's claim to be "*Our* National Airline" (emphasis added) effectively blurs all distinctions among owners, employees, and customers. The ad sets up a closed circuit of signification in which the reader is invited to construct the Papua New Guineaness of the employees with reference to the material objectifications of the airline, and to transfer this quality from these objectifications to

We're proud
to be your airline, PNG.

As long as PNG has been independent, we have
been the wings for the nation. Because we're the
airline owned by all the people of
Papua New Guinea.
And together with everyone in
PNG, Air Niugini is proud to celebrate on this 14th
anniversary of Independence.

Air Niugini
Our National Airline

Figure 3.1. Newspaper advertisement for PNG's state-owned airline.
Post-Courier, 14 September 1989.

the "owners" of the airline, the "people of Papua New Guinea" who purchase the services of the airline. In short, "the people of Papua New Guinea" are assimilated to the ambiguously inclusive "us" implied in the slogan, "Our National Airline."

A similar discourse of collective national ownership is found in ads for Ramu sugar, the product of an industry protected by the state against foreign competition. The text of one such ad (figure 3.2) proclaims, "From the cane-fields of Papua New Guinea comes nature's own energy food. . . . The goodness of Papua New Guinea's natural cane sugar can be enjoyed by everyone." Consumption of Ramu sugar thus promises "everyone" (every individual consumer) access to one of PNG's natural goods. In a related sense, consumption of Ramu sugar implies consumption of PNG itself in the form of one of the land's "natural" products.

Finally, we have two advertisements that apply the argument of national ownership to the one commodity that seems by its abstract nature impossible to nationalize, yet operates as perhaps the most potent and mundane symbol of any national community: money. At the top of an ad for the Papua New Guinea Credit Corporation runs the heading: KEEP OUR MONEY IN OUR COUNTRY. Beneath this advice is a picture of the national flag and a logo of the Credit Corporation. The text reads:

> Credit Corporation is a 100% Nationally owned company. Invest with us— keep our money in our country and help yourself to interest up to 14.50%.

Likewise, an ad for the Papua New Guinea Banking Corporation (figure 3.3) appeared with the slogan, "Our country, our bank, celebrating together." At the center of the ad is a photograph of a female bank employee, proffering money in a gesture that extends beyond the border of the picture. The reader is implicitly positioned as the recipient of this gift, just as the ad for Air Niugini positions the reader as the recipient of the ticket and the cup of coffee.[8]

Currency, the means of consumption, not only objectifies "the nation," whether in the iconographic forms of pigs and pearlshells or of Sir Michael Somare and the Parliament House—the fifty-kina note depicted in the PNG Banking Corporation ad. Currency also symbolizes the nation-state as one entity in a system of such entities. It is entirely appropriate that the notes proffered by the woman in the PNG Banking Corporation ad include samples of U.S. and Japanese money, and that the same ad could appear in the in-flight magazine of Air Niugini (*Paradise,* January 1992), captioned "The First Bank You See in PNG," as information for visitors seeking to convert currency. The use of currency, then, practically affirms the existence of a bounded community of consumers, the borders of which are defined by the extent to which the territorial state authorizes the currency as legal tender.[9]

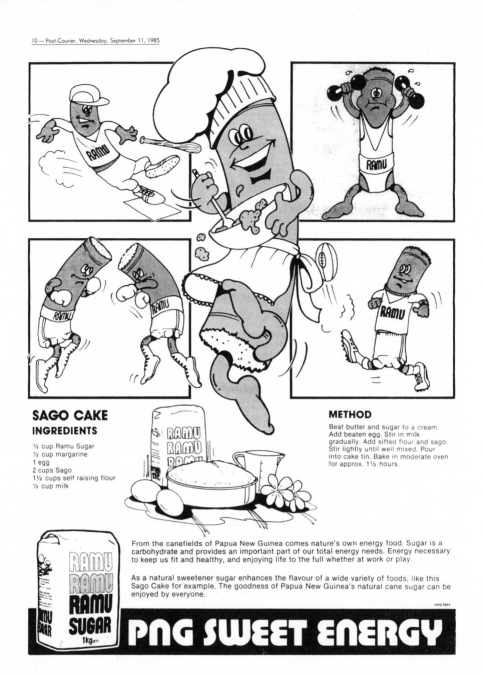

Figure 3.2. Newspaper ad for the state-protected sugar industry.
Post-Courier, 11 September 1985.

Figure 3.3. Newspaper ad for PNG Banking Corporation.
Post-Courier, 14 September 1989.

It is important to recognize, nonetheless, that the nationalization of commodities is by no means monopolized by the state. The rhetoric of national ownership also appears in an advertisement for Word Publishing Company (figure 3.4) that gives an interesting twist to Anderson's observation about the mass ceremony of newspaper reading. The caption asserts, "OUR OWNERS." Underneath are eight snapshots of men and women in urban and rural settings, some dressed in blouses and shorts, others in grass skirts and feathers. The ad claims that Word Publishing is "Proud to be the publisher of Papua New Guinea's first nationally owned newspapers" (*TPNG* and *Wantok*) and informs the reader that Word Publishing is "fully owned by Papua New Guinea's four largest churches: Catholic (750,000 members); Lutheran (550,000 members); United (300,000 members); and Anglican (220,000 members)." It concludes that "Six out of Every Ten Papua New Guineans Have a Stake in the Company's Future."

What this ad does, semiotically speaking, is to reconcile its own depicted diversity of Christian denominations and of traditional rural and modern urban dwellers through an appeal to joint ownership of the newspapers. That is, at the level of collective ownership, the enumerated members of each church are not Catholics or Lutherans but, rather, Papua New Guineans, all of whom have a stake in the company. Thus, reading these particular newspapers does indeed constitute a mass national ceremony, as Anderson observed, but not merely because it is a shared act of consumption. Here, the newspaper itself is presented as the quintessential national commodity.

GENERIC INDIVIDUALS, SPECIFIC CONSUMERS

The rhetoric of national ownership makes certain presuppositions about the nature of objects and persons, presuppositions revealed in a meta-advertisement (figure 3.5) placed by Word Publishing in its *TPNG*. This ad attempts to persuade other advertisers to buy space in Word's Tok Pisin–language (Pidgin) newspaper, the weekly *Wantok*. At the top in big letters reads: "HE LIKES TO EAT RICE and TINFISH." On the left, a large caricature of a man dressed in "traditional" style (grass skirt, feather headdress, and a bone through his nose), carrying a bulging briefcase with several kina notes carelessly sticking out. To the right of this, text:

> OH! and he . . .
> SHOPS at major department stores, buys different FOODS, likes SOFT
> DRINKS, enjoys SMOKING CIGARETTES, has a family to feed and
> CLOTHE, sends his kids to SCHOOL, he owns a CAR, has his own HOME,
> has money invested in a BANK and in his spare time he likes to play SPORT
> and listen to MUSIC

Figure 3.4. Newspaper ad for the paper's publisher.

Times of Papua New Guinea, 11 January 1986. Used by permission of Word Publishing Company.

He likes to eat RICE and TINFISH...

OH! and he...

SHOPS at major department stores, buys different FOODS, likes SOFT DRINKS, enjoys smoking CIGARETTES, has a family to feed and CLOTHE, sends his kids to SCHOOL, he owns a CAR, has his own HOME, has money invested in a BANK and in his spare time he likes to play SPORT and listen to MUSIC

OH!......

and one other thing that advertisers tend to forget — he speaks Pidgin, 90% of the time, as his natural language — unlike English!

Make sure you advertise cost effectively!

There are 2,000,000 Others like him in Papua New Guinea!

Wantok   The only Pidgin newspaper in PNG Ridiculous isn't it?

The Times of Papua New Guinea, Saturday 8 March, 1986

Figure 3.5. Newspaper ad in English-language paper for PNG's only Tok Pisin–language paper. *Times of Papua New Guinea*, 8 March 1986. Used by permission of Word Publishing Company.

OH! . . .
and one other thing that advertisers tend to forget—he speaks Pidgin, 90%
of the time, as his natural language—unlike English!

Make sure you advertise cost effectively!
There are 2,000,000 Others like him in Papua New Guinea!

Alongside the name *Wantok* at the bottom of the ad are the concluding words,
"The only Pidgin newspaper in PNG[.] Ridiculous isn't it?"

Here is a succinct definition of the prototypic consumer-citizen—or, somewhat differently, the essential consumer-citizen (apparently male) who underlies the celebrated manifest diversity of PNG's population. At this level of description, the consumer-citizen is generic and virtual, a potential waiting to be
realized in the specific forms of specific consumption practices and fantasies.
That is, at this level, all consumer-citizens are identical, potential participants
in a national marketplace. I reiterate that this conception of a generic individual is similar to the conception of a generic human being, endowed with
certain inalienable rights, that is promoted by the state in a variety of other
contexts, such as state-sponsored campaigns of civil education, trials, and elections (LiPuma 2000).

Furthermore, the ad implies that generic individuals distinguish themselves from each other through the work of consuming or appropriating particular objects (Carrier 1990a, 1991, Miller 1988). Such work incorporates
these objects into the consumer's definition of his or her social self or personhood. But this implication, in turn, implies a world of anonymous or "neutral"
objects—that is, objects "which could be owned by anybody and identified
with anybody" (Gell 1986:113); in short, a world of personless objects. Of
course, this world is no more than the necessary complement of a world of
objectless persons, the generic and virtual individuals awaiting specification
and realization through acts of consumption that attach objects and persons
to each other. "Ownership" or "having" is the means for attaching specific
qualities to an otherwise generic persona.

Here I would argue that this view of persons and objects, a view communicated by the rhetorical argument of all ads, directly challenges Melanesian
conventions about objects and persons. On the one hand, the conventional
Melanesian person is relational, the precipitate (or node) of numerous and
particular social relations (Strathern 1988). This particularity is irreducible,
such that the concept of generically identical persons is unconventional or extraordinary, if not unimaginable. On the other hand, since Marcel Mauss published *The Gift* in 1925, anthropologists have been aware of the way in which,
for Melanesians, persons and objects generally implicate each other. This is
a matter of neither mysticism nor animism. Rather, it is a correlate of social
practices—most notably, gift exchange—that embed objects in definite social

relations (see Carrier 1990b). That is, there are no unattached or "neutral" objects, objects that could be identified or owned by "anybody."

NATION AND CULTURE AS COMMODITY

One of the effects of the organizing logic of persons and objects in ads is to open up the possibility of rendering the nation as a "neutral" object awaiting attachment via consumption to a "neutral" or generic consumer (see Jourdan 1995 on the "neutrality" of popular culture). An ad for Nestlé products, also in the special 1989 Independence Day issue of the *Post-Courier,* illustrates this possibility (figure 3.6). Although part of a transnational corporation, Food Specialties (PNG) Pty. Ltd. employs the rhetorical strategy of collective ownership and presents itself as a PNG manufacturer. The ad features a drawing of Nescafé Niugini Blend instant coffee, the label of which promises the consumer a beverage made of "100% PNG Coffee." The implication of the ad is that just as the producer and the product are qualified as "100% PNG," likewise will the consumer be qualified.

Perhaps this implication was all the more obvious to an audience already familiar with previously circulated ads that promoted the slogan "PNG Coffee—For PNG People!" Among the ads in this campaign to sell coffee beans grown in the Highlands, there appeared one that illustrated in nine separate steps "How PNG People Make & Enjoy PNG Coffee." The ad functioned as an instruction manual for making a cup of coffee from scratch, depicting in step-by-step fashion a consumption practice ascribed to PNG people in general. By contrast, another ad in the campaign publicized "PNG's Magnificent 5," five different named brands of PNG coffee (No. 1, Goroka, Namasu, Okka, and Koroma) available for PNG people to consume. Uniformity and similarity are thus portrayed with respect to the generic practice of coffee consumption, while singularity and difference are offered through the consumption of particular brands.

Let us return, however, to the Food Specialties ad (figure 3.6). It identifies Food Specialties as a sponsor of the Hiri Moale Festival, an independence weekend event in which the Boera villagers of Port Moresby staged songs and dances for themselves and visitors. The *Post-Courier* of 14 September 1989 described these songs and dances as "some of the oldest . . . in Boera history," and one old Boera man is quoted as saying, "We do not want to see any exaggerated or made-up dances that do not reflect our culture." The juxtaposition of commodity and "culture" in this context valorizes the advertised products as national commodities by associating them with "authentic" native traditions. This valorization occurs despite the fact that the "authentic" tradition in question is not Papua New Guinean, but Boera; for the definition of the national culture implied in the ad is one of a repertoire of diverse "traditions." That is, each tradition is construed as a variable item in the total inventory of

As a sponsor we
are glad to help...

As a Papua New Guinea
manufacturer we are proud
to be involved in...

THE HIRI MOALE FESTIVAL

Food Specialties (PNG) Pty Ltd

Figure 3.6. Newspaper ad for Nestlé products.
Post-Courier, 14 September 1989.

traditions—a brand of tradition. Put otherwise, tradition is itself given the
form of the commodity with which it is juxtaposed: discrete, objectified, and
valuable on account of its intrinsic properties (see Babadzan 1988).

There could be no clearer demonstration of the commodification of tradition than an ad campaign for Benson and Hedges cigarettes from the early
1970s, on the eve of formal political independence in 1975. In one set of ads,
artsy pictures of various locally made artifacts (such as carvings from the
Sepik area) were juxtaposed with a picture of a pack of Benson and Hedges
cigarettes. The caption of the ad announced, "From the Benson and Hedges
collection." At the bottom of the ad ran the rhetorical question: "When only
the best will do . . . and isn't that all of the time?" The symbolic equation
of carving with cigarette pack effects a semantic transfer in which the presumably "traditional" carvings are evaluated as "modern" commodities ("the
best") and thereby rendered as a thing to be possessed or collected.[10] Recip-
rocally, the pack of cigarettes is domesticated and rendered indigenous, an element of local culture.

Precisely this process of metaphorical equation making surfaced in the
overdetermined symbolism of a parallel set of ads for a cigarette called Paradise Gold. Two of these ads appeared in December 1974. The first ad is captioned in large block letters: "I AM PAPUA NEW GUINEA." Beneath this
is a picture of the Rabaul harbor and, further below to the left, a picture of
the product: a pack of cigarettes in a gold box, stamped with a bird of paradise
logo. To the right of the product is the following text:

I am the rugged mountain range
I am the field of waving grass
I am the mighty river that flows to the sea

I am the towns and the people of this proud land
And my cigarette is Paradise Gold

Here, the nation, in a soliloquy that equates natural features of the land and human occupants of the same land, discloses its preference for Paradise Gold. That is, the nation discloses its preference to smoke itself, because Paradise Gold is nothing so much as a material embodiment of the nation.

Another ad for Paradise Gold, which appeared in the 11 December 1974 *Post-Courier,* sounded these same themes in a slightly different key. The ad contains snapshot scenes from a variety of broadly identifiable locales: Rabaul, the Highlands, Port Moresby, Madang, and Lae.[11] Its caption is an invitation, or perhaps a command: "Discover the quality and value of this cigarette made specially for the people of Papua New Guinea." The text continues: "A fine taste of selected high quality tobaccos, presented in a superb personal gold pack. A cigarette to be proud of—a true symbol of Papua New Guinea today." At the bottom of the ad runs the predictable conclusion: "Paradise Gold belongs to Papua New Guinea."

The semiotic form of this particular ad accomplishes what I am arguing that mass-consumption practices have the potential to accomplish more generally: a reconstitution of social geography. A diversity of disjunct locales (communities) are brought into relationship with each other through their shared relationship to some single object of consumption.[12] The "people of Papua New Guinea" emerge as a collectivity—a nation—only in relation to the cigarette made for their consumption. That is, the nation takes the form of a collection of people united by the commodities they jointly possess and consume in common. What are the implications of this definition of collective identity for the definition of personal identity and interpersonal relations? How does a national community of consumption define relations among its citizens?

TOTEMISM: NATIONALIZING THE COMMODITY

To some extent, the answer to these questions follows inevitably from defining the nation as a community of consumption; for when such consumption occurs within the context of a capitalist mode of production, the nation comprises a collectivity of commodity buyers. To advertise a fish-flavored biscuit— perhaps the paradigmatic Papua New Guinean product—as "Number 1 in PNG" or "New to PNG" is to define PNG as, above all, a delimited marketplace. The citizens of PNG, in turn, are defined as consumers, people who affirm their membership in the nation through commodity consumption.

Commodity consumption, as I have argued, attaches specific qualities to generic individuals. It also predicates relations among such individuals by categorizing them as either fellow consumers, and thus alike, or as consumers with unshared consumption practices, and thus different. These alternatives are not exclusive; consumers who share consumption practices with regard to one commodity (say, coffee) might differ with regard to the brand of coffee they consume (Goroka versus Namasu). Likewise, consumers of a common brand of coffee might differ in their consumption of other commodities (such as tobacco). The possibilities of similarity and difference with other consumers are potentially infinite, and it is this infinite potential that makes it possible for consumers to create for themselves a *specific* individuality. By attaching to one's person, in a continuous act of consumerist bricolage, a unique ensemble of qualities, one can aspire to distinction.

Three ads illustrate how commodity consumption introduces new criteria for differentiating and individualizing persons—how commodity consumption can provide the means for producing simultaneously both a national consumption community *and* subcommunities of consumption.

The first ad (figure 3.7) appeared as a billboard on the side of a small shack not far from the government office buildings in Waigani, next to a path that connected these buildings to a Public Motor Vehicle stop on Waigani Drive. Various workers from the surrounding offices, as well as people seeking government services, frequented the shack to buy soft drinks, snacks, and cigarettes. The ad is for a coarse-cut tobacco called Gold. It pictures two hands, apparently a man's, rolling up some tobacco in a patch of newspaper—perhaps a patch of the classifieds from the *Sydney Morning Herald,* sold for this purpose in many rural tradestores. The caption reads, "EM NAU," a multivalent Tok Pisin phrase that here expresses an interjection of satisfaction and a recognition of appropriateness on the order of "That's it" or "Perfect."

This cigarette is a popular item of both urban and bush consumption. The ad thus depicts a consumption fantasy with extremely wide geographical distribution. It is accessible primarily to readers of Tok Pisin, but perhaps to nonliterate viewers as well. Moreover, its elliptical form evokes almost entirely through connotation a shared bodily experience, an element of the habitus characteristic of the community of consumption defined by the ad (see Löfgren 1989a). This community is a community of shared tastes and smells. By articulating these otherwise unobjectified sensations, the ad re-presents to people a particular routine—rolling tobacco in a patch of newspaper—as typical of the collective praxis of Tok Pisin speakers. By associating this routine with Gold tobacco, a commodity produced and distributed in PNG, the ad makes the boundaries of its implicit community of consumption coterminous with the product's market.

The second ad illustrating my purpose and presented earlier (figure 3.2), for Ramu sugar, publicizes a commodity widely, if not universally, available—indeed, the only brand of sugar available in PNG. Ramu Sugar is thus a para-

Figure 3.7. Billboard advertising coarse-cut tobacco sold in
PNG.
Photo by Nancy F. Foster.

digmatic national commodity ("PNG Sweet Energy"), the consumption of
which "can be enjoyed by everyone," and the enjoyment of which constitutes
participation in the PNG community of consumption.[13] But notice the recipe
for sago cake that appears in the ad. Certain ingredients of the cake—milk
and margarine—presume access to a supermarket; it is unlikely that sago
cake will be a popular item of consumption for people who live in the bush.
To what extent, then, is this recipe an index of an emergent set of urban,
middle-class consumption practices? Is this an image of the collective expenditures that unite middle-class urban dwellers into a single community of
consumption (Jourdan 1995)? Apparently, the same commodity consumed
nationwide provides the means for defining a less inclusive community of consumption. This "subcommunity" would be characterized by a relatively different habitus, a differently routinized set of tastes and associations.

That such middle-class consumption practices have taken a discernible enough shape to be parodied is evidenced by a humorous calendar illustration done by Bob Browne, originator of a celebrated comic strip portraying the adventures of an unsophisticated urban PNG Everyman, Grass Roots. The illustration depicts "What All the Young Village Kids are Getting Educated to Become: The Yuppies." These Yuppies synthesize in their consumption practices elements of both a global or transnational marketplace—Walkmans, running shoes, American television programs, instant noodles—and objects with a more local reference—tinned meat and designer-label *laplaps* (sarongs). Likewise, the sago cake is identifiably local but at the same time unattributable to any particular local cuisine (say, Baktaman or Iatmul). Is the sago cake one homely item in an evolving national cuisine—that is, an element in a consumer lifestyle that is neither wholly local nor wholly imported? The question points to one of the tensions inherent in the relationship between mass consumption and national culture: the massive introduction of objects and images produced abroad (Indo-Mie Noodles, Nike jogging shoes, American TV shows) generates a shared experience that transcends local particularity, but which also potentially effaces national particularity. The national community imagined through mass consumption is thus inherently unstable, always threatening either to fragment into subcommunities of consumption or to melt imperceptibly into the transnational flow of commercial images and objects (see Foster 1991).

The third and final ad in this illustration (figure 3.8) similarly presents a consumption fantasy with extremely restricted distribution. The ad appeared in *Paradise,* the in-flight magazine of Air Niugini. It is for POSH (Protocol and Overseas Service Hospitality), an agency that provides, among other things, a personalized service for VIPs, executives, overseas visitors, and business travelers; hotel and air travel bookings; and air-conditioned, chauffeur-driven cars for city and country trips. Presumably, this ad is intended as much, if not more so, for overseas visitors to PNG as for the small number of local business executives who might purchase the service for their clients. Its caption reads: "When you need to arrive in style . . . ," and despite the association with the National Parliament Building (see Rosi 1991), it promotes a rather undemocratic, exclusionary sentiment. Style is available to all who have the means to purchase it, but presumably, if this were everyone, then style would no longer be style.

Clearly, the advertisement for POSH reiterates that consumption practices and fantasies furnish people with the means for distinguishing themselves from other people as well as for establishing an imagined similarity or commonality. "The Yuppies" likewise distinguish themselves from village consumer-citizens in their personal dislikes—items stereotypically consumed by villagers: *kaukau* (sweet potato) and tinned fish. Yet this sort of differen-

When you need to arrive in style...

Figure 3.8. Magazine ad for travel service agency.
Paradise, November 1984.

tiation is no more than the complement of the kind of assimilation represented in ads such as the one for Paradise Gold, ads that subsume different locales under the unifying image of a single commodity. If in one case similarity is achieved through shared consumption practices (see note 11), in the other case, diversity is achieved through the consumption of different commodities. In both instances—and this is my point—personal identity and interpersonal relations are effectively defined in and through relationship to consumer commodities. Otherwise generic consumer-citizens take on various individualized identities through the various consumer commodities possessed or owned. A new mode for constituting personal identities thus accompanies the establishment of a collective national identity in the form of a community of consumption.

CONCLUDING QUESTIONS

Linnekin and Poyer (1990) have made the case that "ethnicity" should be understood to connote a specific ethnotheory of cultural identity rather than some universal feature of social life. This ethnotheory, they explain, rests upon a distinctive ontogeny, or perhaps even ontology—a set of presuppositions about what constitutes a person and what determines collective identities. Its most salient characteristic, in their view, is the privilege given to the "biological inheritance of substance as the determinant of identity" (1990:7). This presupposition can be broadly contrasted with ethnotheories of identity that privilege environment, behavior, and situational flexibility—ethnotheories that Linnekin and Poyer claim underwrite Pacific conceptions of personhood and community.

For my purposes, the more relevant feature of the ethnotheory of ethnicity is its preoccupation with discrete, bounded individuals (persons or groups), the identity of which derives from putatively innate and essential characteristics. Louis Dumont has long identified this preoccupation as indicative of modern egalitarian individualism, an ideology that renders as "given" the existence of bounded, unitary, categorical individuals. Richard Handler (1988) has extended Dumont's observations by noting the logical congruence between nationalism and (possessive) individualism; both define integrated, autonomous units as primordial entities.

My questions, then, are these: Are such ontological presuppositions being communicated as an aspect of nation making in the new Melanesian states? If so, how?

I leave aside here the question of whether presuppositions about bounded, categorical personal and collective identities are a necessary feature of all versions of "the nation"; they are not (Kapferer 1988, Kelly 1995). Instead, I want to suggest that such presuppositions are indeed being communicated in PNG, at least, and communicated in a number of ways. Perhaps the most visible of these ways is the undertaking of the state to expose people through formal schooling and periodic public campaigns to a moral ideal of citizenship based on the inalienable human rights of all individuals. But perhaps the most effective of these communications is one that is more subtle.

I refer here to the way in which the ontological presuppositions of capitalism and nationalism interpenetrate and reinforce each other. As LiPuma (1995:41) points out, "the association of the nation with commodities"—explicitly rendered in some advertisements—"objectifies the nation in such a way as to imbue it with the properties of capitalist commodities": discrete, bounded, intrinsically valuable—a reality apart from and independent of its creators. He continues,

> When linked and likened to a commodity, the nation appears to be "objective" rather than socially constituted; it appears as primordial rather than historical; it appears as "necessary" rather than contingent; and it appears as a unified, autonomous reality.

In this sense, then, participation in mass commodity consumption potentially functions as a practical training ground for the development of a national style of consciousness (as defined in note 6), for such participation conditions one to the presuppositions of categorical identity that define what a nation is and what a national citizen is. Not only is the world of commodities a world of bounded, external objects, but it also is a world in which subjects are related to such objects only externally, by "having" them. One "belongs to" a nation or "possesses" a national culture much as one has or possesses commodities. When such "having" (or "not having") becomes the dominant, taken-for-granted mode in which one relates to the object world, the idea of being a national citizen who "has" and/or "needs" a national culture follows unproblematically.

4

Commercial Mass Media
Notes on Agency, Bodies,
and Commodity Consumption

AS ANTHROPOLOGISTS GRAPPLE with the proliferating forms and effects of globalization, there emerges an unavoidable challenge to integrate "the study of
mass media into . . . analyses of the 'total social fact' of modern life" (Spitulnik 1993:293). Globalization, as Appadurai (1991) notes, enhances the capacity
of people almost everywhere to envision possible lives, and the imaginative
resources for these lives often arrive through mass media. Spitulnik poses several pertinent questions:

> How, for example, do mass media represent and shape cultural values within
> a given society? What is their place in the formation of social relations and
> social identities? How might they structure people's senses of space and
> time? What are their roles in the construction of communities ranging from
> subcultures to nation-states, and in global processes of socioeconomic and
> cultural change? (1993:293–94)

In this chapter, I touch on all these questions from the point of view of contemporary Papua New Guinea (PNG), famous since before Malinowski's day
as anthropology's "land of the archetypally Other" (Battaglia 1992:1003). I
am concerned with the potential implications of consumerism for how metropolitan Papua New Guineans configure personal and collective identities.
While the construction of social identities has long attracted the attention of
Melanesianist anthropologists, inquiry has been given new impetus by the specific historical circumstances of postcolonialism and post-Fordist capitalism.[1]

MASS MEDIA IN PNG: COMMERCE, IDENTITIES,
AND A DISCOURSE OF HEALTH

The neglect of mass media historically shown by anthropologists, Powdermaker (1950) notably excepted, might seem less puzzling in the case of PNG
than elsewhere. But mass media—locally produced, if not always locally owned,
commercial mass media—now assert a vigorous presence in PNG, especially

in urban settings. The *Post-Courier,* part of Rupert Murdoch's global News Corporation, is the largest circulation daily newspaper of the South Pacific (circulation 41,000) (Robie 1995:5). A second daily, the *National* (circulation 11,000), began publishing in late 1993; it is owned by a subsidiary company of the Malaysian logging group, Rimbunan Hijau. In addition, two smaller PNG-owned newspapers, the *Independent* (formerly the *Times of PNG* [circulation 9000]) and *Wantok Niuspepa* (circulation 15,000), are published weekly.

PNG's radio network likewise dwarfs those of other small Pacific Island nation-states. The Kalang FM service is the commercial arm of the National Broadcasting Commission, the only radio broadcasting authority in the country. It consists of fifteen relay stations in towns throughout the country and "sells airtime and operates independently as a business oriented radio station" (Nash 1995:42). The English-speaking DJs of the Kalang service broadcast, among other things, the multilingual pop music of PNG musicians, thus promoting dissemination of *"lokal musik"* ("local music" in Tok Pisin) in the form of audio and video cassette recordings made by commercial studios in PNG (see Webb 1993, Sullivan n.d.).[2]

EM TV ("It's TV" in Tok Pisin), the only broadcast television station currently operating in PNG, has been a commercial enterprise from its initial broadcast in 1987.[3] The station, a wholly owned subsidiary of the Australian Nine Network, has steadily increased the size of the audience it can reach. According to one report: "Before May 1993, EM TV reached 95 per cent of the urban population—an estimated audience of about 500,000. Since then, broadcasting via Indonesia's Palapa B2P satellite has enabled EM TV to reach virtually anywhere in the country where there is a satellite dish" (Robie 1995:59; see Foster 1999a, Sullivan 1993).[4]

The expansion of commercial mass media in PNG has made advertising —both its production and consumption—a matter of concern to various PNG governments and ordinary citizens alike. Not only have government-sponsored reports sought to establish standards for the content of ads, especially ads on radio and television (PNG 1987b, 1993), legislation has also been enacted regulating the production of all commercial advertising (the Commercial Advertising [Protection of Local Industry] Act, passed by the national parliament in 1985).

Despite subsequent modifications—concessions to companies wishing to use readily available foreign-made television ads or to use superior production facilities abroad—the Act seems to have achieved its aims. Even at EM TV, "more than 90 per cent of [the] commercials, station IDs and public service announcements are . . . locally produced" (Robie 1995:59). Advertisers can commission station-trained staff at EM TV to produce an ad or use independent agencies such as Pacific View Productions, which has made television commercials for *Pepsi* (Sullivan n.d.) and, more recently, Ox and Palm tinned beef.[5] Pacific View Productions also used to dominate the production of music videos, brief clips of which ran on EM TV in 1994 as ads for Chin H. Meen and Pacific Gold recording studios.

By the same token, ordinary Papua New Guineans have begun to express concerns about advertising. One pilot study of television viewers in two peri-urban villages near Port Moresby reports that "the majority of families [interviewed] agreed that there were far too many commercials on EM TV" (PNG 1994:11). Individual informants claimed that "commercials make me sick" and that "there are too many commercials and it is always the same ones repeated over and over again" (PNG 1994:11). Government reports (PNG 1987b, 1993) echo these very concerns with recommendations that the amount and timing of television advertising be restricted, for example, to ten minutes of "non-programme material" in any sixty-minute period during prime time (PNG 1993:77).

Families interviewed for the pilot "TV impact study" also criticized a number of television commercials as "too Western," singling out *Coke* and *Pepsi* commercials aired during the two popular music video programs, *Mekim Musik* ("making music" in Tok Pisin) and *Fizz,* sponsored by each company, respectively (see Gewertz and Errington 1996).[6] Related criticisms have been voiced on the Kalang service's call-in show (see below) and in the letters column of PNG's newspapers. Take, for instance, the following letter, signed by Jack Kagoi of Port Moresby, which appeared in 1995 in the *Post-Courier* under the heading, "Shell's television advert portrays PNG wrongly":

> The new Shell television commercial showing a Tari [Southern Highlands] man and his family dressed in traditional gear driving to a Shell station with a pig in the car, is in low taste, and portrays a very primitive PNG society.
>
> In case Shell hasn't noticed, we Papua New Guineans do not walk or drive around in grass skirts carrying pigs with us.
>
> Maybe a small group of people up in the Highlands still do this, but the rest of us don't.
>
> To the expatriate executives of Shell, we Papua New Guineans are working very hard to take our place in the modern world.
>
> Generally we try to speak English, wear clean clothes and most of us make an effort to behave in a civilised and decent manner.
>
> ... Where I come from which is the Momase region, we do not cheapen the value of our traditional clothes by using them to sell petrol.
>
> I have my sense about PNG and the fact that we the people are still lacking in some areas of human development, but I value my culture so much that I do not allow business houses to mock it and use it for their own purposes.
>
> I believe most of us Papua New Guineans want to go forward, whilst preserving our traditions.
>
> We want to take our place in the 21st century.

We want the world to know that we are civilised and decent and can survive anywhere on this planet.

Please Shell, don't keep us down there.

Don't treat us like primitives. You've convinced the poor Tari man that he is still in the Stone Age, and he has never been to a service station, let alone a trade store in a village in Tari.

As for me, I refuse to go to a service station where there are people shopping with pigs.

Kagoi's letter forcefully demonstrates not only how talk about advertisements has itself become an element of commercial mass media in PNG, but also how this talk engages complex issues of identity: cultural, national, regional (ethnic), and personal. Kagoi invokes a collective identity ("we the people") expressed in national terms ("us Papua New Guineans") at the same time that he distinguishes the coastal Mamose region (Madang/Morobe/Sepik areas) from the Highlands. This distinction is invidious, representing the Highlands as a region perhaps "still lacking in some areas of human development." But Kagoi does not wholly embrace "the modern world" signified by the Shell station; instead, he argues for the recognition of the value of "our traditions" and, moreover, for the recognition of tradition (culture) and business as properly separate domains. This recognition serves to distinguish Kagoi and his fellow Papua New Guineans from the "expatriate executives" presumed to have created the Shell ad. Kagoi concludes with an assertion of self-determination: a declaration of his intention ("as for me") as an individual consumer not to shop at Shell service stations.

Put differently, what Kagoi's letter indicates, and what I confirm in this chapter, is that advertising and commentary about advertising—mass mediated through newspapers, radio, and television—constitute a vibrant arena within PNG's emergent public culture.[7] More specifically, my aim is to show how some of the visual imagery and verbal exhortations of commercial advertising constitute what can be called a discourse of health. This discourse targets the body; it communicates ideals of healthy bodies—bodies that are physically strong and morally sound. In so doing, I argue, this discourse invokes the dominant themes of a particular conception of personhood, a conception conventionally associated with modern Western individualism. In this conception, body and person are coterminous—individuated and discrete, the site of autonomous agency (free will, free choice, self-determination). The evocation of persons as consumers is but one construction and validation of this autonomous agency; evocations of persons as citizens and Christians are two more. Commercial mass media thus function as instruments for making an individualist definition of persons and bodies publicly visible in contemporary PNG.

The individuated person/body conjured by the discourse of health clearly recalls the spread of colonialism, capitalism, and Christian evangelism into Melanesia. It would be too simple, however, to regard this discourse as a wholly imported progressivist ideology imposed upon the people of PNG by "the West." First of all, Papua New Guineans are themselves creating this discourse, for example, as commentators on and producers of ads (in accordance with the Commercial Advertising Act). Although the creative directors of almost all advertising agencies in PNG are indeed "expatriate executives," Papua New Guineans do shape the multiauthor process of producing ads.[8] In addition, as I will suggest, some of the ads on EM TV seem to resonate with what several ethnographers have identified as distinctively *Melanesian* conceptions of bodies and persons. From this perspective, the discourse of health appears to be formed of imagery precipitated out of the encounter between indigenous and exogenous conceptions of persons and bodies. This imagery suggests syncretic "tension between rhetorics of an individuated, autonomous self and rhetorics of a collective, relational self" (Battaglia 1995a:7).

Second, Papua New Guineans—such as Jack Kagoi—do not in any case automatically accept the images presented in commercial advertising. As I suggest in discussing the reactions of some radio callers to a television ad for chewing gum, the ideals of healthy persons/bodies promulgated through commercial media are subject to critical reception, if not outright rejection. If the discourse of health offers a view of persons and bodies consistent with modern individualism—and I think it does—it must be remembered that this view is not the only one available to contemporary Papua New Guineans.

A nuanced ethnographic approach to the discourse of health would focus resolutely on both the actual practices of producing and receiving commercial mass media. While this article anticipates such an ethnography, it primarily uses texts and images, especially those of commercial advertisements, to think about agency, bodies, and commodities. My method, influenced by Judith Williamson's *Decoding Advertisements* (1978), consists more in attributing a semiotic logic to these texts and less in documenting particular responses to the texts and images. To this extent, this chapter is a preliminary and partial exercise in determining how commercial mass media may facilitate the ongoing transformation of cultural, national, ethnic, and gender identities in PNG. I return to the question of method—the limitations of textual analysis—in my conclusion.

CONSUMERISM: AGENCY, BODIES, AND COMMODITIES

At the heart of late twentieth-century consumerism—here understood in ideal-typical terms—lies "the desire/drive/need for the individual to act as a free agent" (Strathern 1991:594). This "desire/drive/need," moreover, comes from within the individual (however much stimulated by the world outside the individual); it is actualized through the choices that an individual makes from among the commodities that comprise the impersonal domain of the market. Choice, therefore, "creates consumption as a subjective act" (Strathern 1991:566), an expression of self-identity in which commodities are personalized through appropriation by the individual.

This vision of consumption as appropriation—whether celebrated as creative self-fashioning or derided as selfish materialism—conceives the person as a "free-standing and whole entity" (Strathern 1991:596) that makes or fails to make relationships with its environment of things (and other persons). This conception of personhood, in turn, entails a coordinate conception of the body as likewise "free-standing and whole," contained and discrete. Body and person, coterminous, comprise the individual, the locus of autonomous agency —free will, free choice, self-determination.

Individuated and "skin-bound" (Battaglia 1995a:5), the body/person is ultimately responsible for its own production and regulation, an individual responsible and accountable for its "own" conduct. This responsibility is encouraged through continuous education and persuasion, rhetorical strategies —like those of advertisements—undertaken to cause the person/body to produce, regulate, and/or reproduce itself in particular fashion. Accordingly, the ideal of individuation justifies the identification of recalcitrant and incorrigible person/bodies (and the application of force to these person/bodies when persuasion fails to elicit acceptable behavior). Failure to behave "normally" or "properly" thus becomes a matter of individual deviance, of petulance, of "not caring" or insouciance.

The edges of this ideal type of person—the individual consumer—can be and have been made sharper through contrast with another ideal type, that of the "dividual" person: not a whole entity, but a composite site of constitutive relationships (Strathern 1988:13). And this contrast, furthermore, can be and has been aligned with an opposition between the West and Melanesia (see Strathern 1988, Knauft 1989, Foster 1993).[9] Making this contrast for heuristic purposes, however, ought not to preclude recognition that in contemporary metropolitan PNG, Melanesians enact aspects of both ideal types, redefining in the process conventional possibilities for personal and collective identities. Take, for example, the "First Annual Trobriand Yam Festival," held in Port Moresby in 1985 and modeled on harvest "competitions" or *kayasa* (Battaglia 1992, 1995b). As Battaglia points out, the event, including its publicity in the national press, enabled some Trobrianders to draw on "a postcolonial rhetoric of individuality and independence to assert new versions of themselves which effectively upend power relations as structured in the Trobriand hierarchy" (1995a:10). But the event also enabled chiefly critics of the event (both in Port Moresby and the Trobriands) to assert in new ways an authority construed in terms of asymmetrical relationships—at the very same time newspaper editors were portraying the event as a colorful display of ethnic diversity within a unified national culture.

Battaglia's ethnography demonstrates how mass media can enter into and transform the contested practices and outcomes of identity construction. The media texts and images that I examine here lend themselves to another, more modest purpose: identifying some of the sources and content of a public discourse of somatic self-responsibility in PNG. This discourse of health is hardly monolithic; it is shot through with internal contradictions as well as critically engaged by its audiences. Various producers and consumers of the discourse of health might thus sometimes collude and sometimes conflict with each other in creating individuated person/bodies.

THE DISCOURSE OF HEALTH

The discourse of health recurrently evokes three different body images: athletic and "powerful" bodies; medically sound bodies; and morally acceptable bodies. These three images correspond to themes that can be labeled competitive fitness, hygiene, and temperance.

Competitive Fitness

Commercial sports imagery often suggests, in PNG as elsewhere, a complicity between state agencies and corporate sponsors in both individuating person/bodies and rendering them visible as national icons. Consider the imagery of an advertisement for Shell gasoline, the most technically sophisticated ad running on EM TV in June 1992.[10] The ad appeared almost every evening during a pause in the 6 o'clock news broadcast, directly preceding the reading of "the Shell sports report" by a man dressed in a red and yellow shirt bearing the Shell logo (figure 4.1):

> *Shell Ad.* Synchronized with the driving rhythm of a pulsating bass guitar, juxtaposed moving images of athletes, Shell corporate logos, and Shell products flash by in a fast-paced montage. All of the athletes, men and women, are dressed in uniforms of the PNG national team. Boxers, runners, tennis players, a swimmer; gas pumps and quarts of oil; a Shell flag, Shell logo, the logo for the sports report. There is neither a voice-over nor superimposed text.

The color coding of the ad effectively, if not subtly, locks nation and corporation into a relationship of mutual implication; the red, black, and gold of the athletes' uniforms blend imperceptibly into the red, black, and gold of the Shell logo. It is a relationship, moreover, connoted without words, and thus particularly apt for a multilingual, nonliterate audience. The bodies of the ath-

Figure 4.1. Frames from an EM TV advertisement for Shell gasoline.

letes, notably male and female, serve as mediators of the relationship between nation and corporation. Accordingly, the uniforms of the athletes double as national flags and corporate logos, the vestments par excellence of standardized consumer-citizenship.

Official consumer-citizenship, the assertion of national identity through the consumption of certain brands of commodities, is made possible through state-sanctioned corporate sponsorship of national sports teams. Thus, former prime minister (now Sir) Rabbie Namaliu admitted in 1992 the importance of sponsorship for financing sports programs in PNG: "Sport is becoming increasingly commercial and during these tough economic times, the Government can only do so much this year, because we gave sports some priority over the last two years, in particular because of the SP [South Pacific] Games"[11] (*Post-Courier,* 25 June 1992). He made this comment while appealing to the public to support the nationwide Fun Run, an annual event in which people, dressed in T-shirts sold at Shell gas stations to raise money for the PNG Sports Federation, run through the streets of many of the country's major towns. At 7:30 A.M. on Sunday, 28 June 1992, small groups of identically shirted runners together left starting lines in Port Moresby, Lae, Goroka, Mt. Hagen, Rabaul, Daru, and Wewak—an odd enactment of the shared space-time of an imagined national community (Anderson 1991).

The 1992 Fun Run was cosponsored by *Coca-Cola* and Shell, major contributors toward sending PNG's team to the Barcelona Olympics. *Coca-Cola* and Shell also sponsored a nationwide competition to select the Olympic torchbearer for PNG. Entry forms instructed participants to answer the question, "Why should we pick you to carry the official Olympic torch in Barcelona?" The winner of the contest was Tau John ("TJ") Tokwepota, a former boxer and marathon runner from the Trobriand Islands. To publicize his selection, TJ's picture appeared on television and in the *Post-Courier.* He was dressed in a *Coca-Cola* Fun Run T-shirt and red sweatpants stamped with the familiar *Coca-Cola* label. Corporate executives from Shell and *Coca-Cola* lifted TJ's arms over his head, thereby duplicating the image of the runner pictured on TJ's Fun Run T-shirt. A week later, TJ posed with then prime minister Namaliu in a promotional photograph for the Fun Run: two representative bodies, victors of their respective contests—prominent citizens dressed in a consumerist uniform, the permutated image of the athletes in the Shell ad and the sports reporter on EM TV (figure 4.2).

What does TJ embody? Why do the bodies of athletes often define a site where nationalist and consumerist agendas converge? Reconsider the Shell ad. It first of all depicts bodies in action—that is, bodies acting rather than being acted upon; or perhaps more precisely, bodies acting upon themselves, making themselves act. The ad also depicts bodies in competition with each other (or with themselves), bodies rendered equal by the rules of competition.

Figure 4.2. Then prime minister Rabbie Namaliu and PNG Olympic torchbearer John Tokwepota wearing Fun Run T-shirts.
Post-Courier, 25 June 1992.

Competition necessarily renders this equality axiomatic—a fundamental pre-condition of the game (and one of the differences between games and rituals that Levi-Strauss noted in *The Savage Mind*). The athletic, competitive body thus incarnates not only autonomous agency, but also jural equality—two of the defining characteristics of the "modern individual" (see Lukes 1973).

At the same time, however, competing bodies must inevitably distinguish themselves; competition ranks winners (first, second, third)—person/bodies individuated from the field of competitors made equal by the rules. Competi-tion transforms the field of anonymously homogeneous participants into an order of differentiated individuals; playing the game is a precondition of indi-viduation. Note in this regard the proliferation and apparent popularity of competitions and contests in metropolitan PNG—instant lotteries (*laki, win moni*), prize giveaways, beauty contests, and so forth. They all function as means for individuating subjects made available by a form of production that requires the mass consumption of standardized, homogeneous objects. All of these competitions are practical vehicles for becoming a certain kind of person (as well as for acquiring desirable things)—the modern individual. (Hence the moral and political entanglements that ensued from the Trobriand Yam Festival, when *kayasa* became analogized with other "competitions," thereby enabling the sponsor to promote himself as a "revolutionary" indi-vidual, an "urban cowboy" [Battaglia 1992].) Is it too implausible, then, to see international sporting events such as the Barcelona Olympics or the South Pacific Games as, among other things, mass displays of an abstract ideal, the ideal of the equally free individual that underwrites conceptions of "con-sumer" and "citizen"?

In the Shell ad, as in many other ads that exhibit athletic bodies, physical autonomy and self discipline are glossed as "power." Take, for example, this ad for a brand of rice (figure 4.3):

Power Rice Ad. The ad begins by cutting from images of an extremely mus-cular man working on a construction site to an image of several arms thrusting 1-kg bags of Power rice into the air. This power salute is synchro-nized to the soundtrack recording of "Power to the People!", with appropri-ately modified lyrics describing "the great rice revolution." Images follow of a woman's face, then of her back hurrying into a store in order to pur-chase Power rice. The ad ends with the image of the muscular man giving a thumbs-up to the camera.

The imagery here evokes power not only as the ability to make one's body more autonomous, more self-controlled, and more able to control an ex-ternal object world, but also as the ability to choose what one incorporates—that is, to choose and purchase one commodity as opposed to another. Physical or bodily autonomy implies and connotes autonomy as a consumer, autonomy to produce one's own body through freely chosen acts of consumption. The

Figure 4.3. Frames from an EM TV advertisement for Power rice.

power of the man's body is complemented by the power of the woman's [free] choice to buy/consume Power rice (rather than any other brand). The muscular male body thus instantiates the abstract ideal of autonomous agency, of the person as the cause of his or her own actions.

Powerful male bodies can also be used to evoke gendered power in perhaps a more recognizably Melanesian mode. Take, for example, this ad for utility vehicles (figure 4.4):

> *Ela Motors Ad.* The ad opens with an image of a line of men, all equipped with identical white suits and black belts, performing synchronized karate movements. Each man stands in front of a Daihatsu utility vehicle: pickups and four-wheel drives. An accompanying theme song emphasizes: "Daihatsu, Tough!" Images follow of vehicles, including a pickup truck carrying three of the karate men, moving across rough terrain. The ad closes with an aerial view of the parallel lines of karate men and utility vehicles.

The display of disciplined, self-regulating bodies intimates autonomy, as in the rice ad. But this particular public display of men—dressed identically, moving in unison—perhaps evokes other lines of power ("perhaps" marking the spot of future ethnographic research): ceremonial lines of Highlands dancers, men (sometimes women) self-decorated in spectacularly similar ways, who perforce evoke the solidary individuality of a clan. In contemporary PNG, it is not uncommon for clans to materialize as collectively purchased trucks. Here, then, the imagery of commercial mass media makes visible the syncretic tension between notions of power rooted in individual choice on the one hand, and collective action on the other.

The epitomizing combination of competition and powerful, autonomous bodies appeared in the form of the 1992 Mr. PNG Bodybuilding Contest (figure 4.5). This contest was sponsored by Trukai rice, which also sponsored a similar competition at the popular 1992 Port Moresby Show. Trukai's own advertising campaign makes heavy use of the bodybuilding motif, especially in the figure of Mr. Trukai, a peculiar hybrid with a man's muscular body and a masked head that is the registered trademark of Trukai's manufacturer, Ricegrower's Co-Operative Ltd. of Leeton, New South Wales, Australia (figure 4.6). During the South Pacific Games, which Trukai also "powered" (sponsored), rice was packaged in special commemorative bags that featured biographical blurbs about the members of the PNG Weightlifting Team. One such bag tells consumers about Pinye Malaibi, who competes in the 67.5-kg division: born in the Eastern Highlands, he now lives in Port Moresby. He has, we are told, represented PNG at the Noumea South Pacific Games, the Seoul Olympics, and the Auckland Commonwealth Games.

Pinye Malaibi is a representative Papua New Guinean in both senses of the term. Not only does he represent the nation in competitions abroad, but

Figure 4.4. Frames from an EM TV advertisement for Ela Motors.

Figure 4.5. Advertisement for bodybuilding contest sponsored by Trukai rice. *Post-Courier,* 19 March 1992.

Figure 4.6. Advertisement for Trukai rice from the program of the 1992
Port Moresby Show.

also, in the sparse specificity of his rice-bag biography, he indexes the singularity of the individual Papua New Guineans who comprise the nation. Or so, at least, seems to be the semiotic logic of the ads. Just as Trukai "powers" or sponsors the body of Pinye Malaibi in overseas contests, Trukai "powers" the bodies of individual Papua New Guineans through numerous acts of domestic consumption. Trukai thus mediates between the representative or international body of the weightlifter and the particular bodies of particular (though nameless) national consumers. Eating Trukai, or drinking *Coke*, or jogging in the Fun Run, then, links together (or incorporates) the bodies of anonymous citizens into the national community of consumption embodied by Tau John Tokwepota or Pinye Malaibi. In this regard, it is not insignificant to note that I purchased the Trukai rice bag with Pinye Malaibi's story not in a Port Moresby supermarket, but in a small village trade store in the remote Tanga Islands of New Ireland Province.

Hygiene

I turn now to the theme of hygiene, and to an image which also makes visible the syncretic tensions between different notions of persons and bodies. Consider the following ad, an explicit exhortation to adopt one type of consumption and an implicitly official injunction against another type of consumption (figure 4.7):

> *PK Ad.* The ad opens with an announcement: "This is a message from the PNG Department of Health." The narrator reminds the viewer how betel nut chewing is banned in many public places and also considered to be a cause of mouth cancer. The image of a man chewing betel nut appears; at the bottom left, a superimposed universal sign for "no betel nut chewing"; at the bottom right, an inset picture of an unidentifiable man with mouth cancer. This image gives way to one of two boys, dressed in T-shirts decorated with a picture of PK chewing gum. One of the boys addresses the camera, "When we want to chew, we chew PK." The ad closes with an image of a PK packet and words advising consumers not to pay more than ten toea for the gum.

The ad suggests to me, at least, that the state, through its agency the Department of Health, endorses the substitution of bubble gum for betel nut. This endorsement entails the supposition that chewing gum and chewing betel nut are alternative forms of chewing. The ad consequently urges consumers to choose the clean and safe PK, the more hygienic and less life-threatening alternative.

Cleanliness and freedom from disease are represented as the products of an individual's choice to replace the public act of visibly externalizing bright red spit with the private act of invisibly internalizing sweetened saliva. More

Figure 4.7. Frames from an EM TV advertisement for PK chewing gum.

precisely, the substitution defines the difference between internal and external, inside the body and outside the body. That is, in responding to the very real limitations placed by the state on one's physical capacity to project bodily fluids into and on to the landscape, the substitution redefines the body's boundaries. These boundaries are made coterminous with the skin; the body is contained, and hence individuated, separated from other similarly contained bodies. Control over these boundaries is represented as a matter of *personal* choice—that is, a matter of individual persons exercising control over themselves/their bodies.

In this particular case, however, the complicity between the state and commerce in fashioning individuals attracts far more overt resistance than in the case of competitive sports. This resistance comes about mainly because of the long-standing association of betel nut chewing with an anti-Western, pro-Melanesian argument about national cultural identity (see, for example, Bernard Narokobi's 1980 essay on this topic). One wonders, for instance, if the PK ad reminds John Kasaipwalova of the airport confrontation in his nationalistic short story from the early 1970s, "Betel Nut Is Bad Magic for Aeroplanes" (1987:72). In that quintessentially colonial scene, a white airport manager harasses a group of University of Papua New Guinea students for chewing—not spitting—betel nut outside Jackson's airport in Port Moresby. The narrator, one of the students, challenges the manager. He asks rhetorically, as a black citizen of Niugini: "Listen mate. Why aren't you arrresting those white kids inside the terminal for chewing PK? What's the difference between their PK inside the terminal and our betel-nut outside on the road pavement?" This contest over inside/outside boundaries is double, at once a struggle over the boundaries of the body and the boundaries that separate white and black bodies. It can be read as a colonial precursor to the postcolonial persuasions of EM TV.

In the same week of June 1992, two male callers voiced their refusal to accept the state's definition of "health" and its associated campaign against betel nut chewing on the radio program Talkback. Talkback is a morning phone-in show heard daily throughout metropolitan PNG on the Kalang Service of the National Broadcasting Commission. Although the program originates from Port Moresby, callers from as far away as Mount Hagen or Rabaul sometimes ring the station to speak live on the air with host Roger Hau'ofa.

The first caller, John, expressed skepticism about the connection between betel nut and mouth cancer, and wondered where the man whose cancerous mouth is featured in the PK ad came from. John argued that in his home area (Kairuku/Bereina) that people routinely swallowed their betel instead of spitting; they did not "litter." He also observed that in his home area, lime was manufactured from shells, and that this lime was probably not cancer causing, unlike alternatives made from coral or fibro (fiberboard). Furthermore, John pointed out his people's (Mekeo) practice of issuing betel nut to invite guests to a feast. He asked what would replace betel nut "as far as our culture is concerned, our custom is concerned" if the Health Department were to ban it "for the good of our health."

Roger replied by agreeing that betel spit was a major problem in Port Moresby, but he reiterated that there is a "clean way to chew betel nut," one that is "traditional and *kastam*," namely, "to swallow everything that you put in your mouth instead of spitting it out." He also agreed that John's people probably know how to chew betel nut properly, and suggested that

> Maybe the Health Department, instead of trying to discourage betel nut chewing altogether, should look at ways which are safe to chew betel nut. People have been chewing it for generations before the Health Department came into being and they knew how to chew the betel nut safely. Maybe they could recommend a certain way of chewing betel nut which will go down better because it's part of the traditional culture of the people.

Roger then claimed that "the Western culture had introduced its deadly poisons, like alcohol and cigarettes, and then tried to ban ours." John agreed enthusiastically, and asked pointedly if, after all, "we were trying to bring in the Western type of living and do away with our proper one."

Two days later, the second caller, also named John, resumed the discussion: "Betel nut is good. It's how people chew and spit, throw rubbish all over the place, that's spoiling the image of betel nut." John enlisted Roger's support as a fellow chewer, but as one who is "clean and healthy about it." The problem, as John saw it, was with people who were new to betel chewing and have only recently come across it. They are the ones who chew in an untidy, unhealthy way, spitting indiscriminately and littering the ground with betel nut skins. The answer—and here John took up Roger's earlier suggestion— was to get the Health Department to institute a chewing awareness program and to educate people about "the correct habit of chewing—getting rid of your rubbish, keeping the place clean and tidy, free from germs and things like this." Here, much like in Jack Kagoi's letter, mass media functions as a site for constructing ethnic or regional identities; for the "people who are new to betel nut" are people from the Highlands, where betel nut was not traditionally available because the areca palm does not grow at high altitudes.

The opinions of these three men hardly constitute radical liberal challenges to state authority. But they do reject the state's equation of "health" with the elimination of betel nut chewing. And they do reject this equation in part by appealing to some notion of traditional Melanesian culture. In this regard, they can be distinguished from M. Gavi of Boroko, who wrote to the *Post-Courier* (30 December 1991) in order to hold up Singapore as an example of "what a small former colony can do if it has pride, discipline and a sense of national purpose."[12] Gavi points out that, among other things, "Singapore does not tolerate the disgusting practice of spitting betel nut juice on whatever is close by (whether it is moving or not) nor does one see abandoned, burnt out vehicles littering the streets." Gavi then goes on to explain this situation as a failure on the part of both citizens and the government, a failure that is excused, moreover, "by telling the world it is the 'Melanesian Way.' " Gavi thus devalues "custom" in relation to "development" (see also the letter from "Anti-Buai Spit," *Post-Courier,* 12 February 1991).

Nevertheless, all of the Talkback interlocutors accept the state's definitions of "tidiness" and "cleanliness" with their somatic correlate of swallowing instead of spitting. And, more importantly, they do not challenge the state's power to regulate consumption by appealing to the inviolable rights of individual consumer-citizens—the relentless strategy of, say, the American Tobacco Institute. Indeed, they propose to extend the state's control over consumption practices by advocating either programs of moral education or total bans on betel nut chewing in town.

Temperance

The intervention of Christian churches such as the Seventh Day Adventist (SDA) Church in the discourse of health likewise generates tension around the ideal of autonomous consumers; for much of the SDA Church's advice about the body promotes an anticonsumption ethic—that is, abstention in a variety of forms. At the 1992 Port Moresby Show, for instance, the Narcotics Education Unit of the SDA Church distributed literature about the consumption of alcohol, tobacco, and drugs. Among the flyers was a cartoon sketch meant to be colored in by a child. At the top of the flyer is the admonition: "It's Okay to Say NO to Bia [Beer]!!" In the middle, four (nuclear) family members each extend a hand in a gesture that indicates "stop." At the bottom is the figure of an intoxicated, unkempt man, reclining on the ground. His head rests on two cartons of South Pacific Beer, proud sponsor of the South Pacific Games. With one hand he balances a short-necked bottle on his belly; with the other hand, he holds a lit cigarette.

The SDA Church's educational literature also included a pamphlet titled "God Wants You to Be Healthy!" This pamphlet was produced in Australia and is hardly local in its allusions, but it specifies clearly some of the general body precepts of Christianity that one comes across in PNG (as elsewhere). It attacks the ideal of a wholly autonomous body by suggesting that because the body is the medium through which both mind and soul are developed, it is necessary to subordinate the body's "natural tendencies" and put them in the service of a "higher power." But at the same time, the pamphlet offers another possibility for exercising autonomous agency: temperance. By acting temperately, one exerts control over one's emotions, indeed, over the physical functions of one's body. If the body must be put under the dominion of a higher power, it ought to be done so voluntarily and deliberately.

The announced point of the pamphlet is to reveal what many people overlook, "the close relationship which exists between buoyant health and a vigorous Christian experience." Because the flesh is weak, Satan takes advantage of the body. Thus, "Millions today find themselves slaves to habits which destroy health and strength. Drugs, tobacco, alcohol, overeating, lack of exercise and other misuses of the body are common." The pamphlet continues by citing a study that demonstrated the effect of poor diet on mood and attitude: "Imagine what a large number of peevish, disgruntled, mean people the devil can create just by causing them to eat incorrectly! Many people eat with no thought of whether the food is good for them or not. If it tastes good, that is all that is necessary."

In and of itself, this sort of admonition could go either way; it could support the consumption of commodities such as Trukai rice that are marketed as "healthy," or it could conflict with the consumption of commodities marketed as simply pleasurable, such as *Coca-Cola* soft drinks. Similarly, and more generally, the images and texts created by state agencies, church agencies, and commercial enterprises for producing and representing bodies and body techniques are both mutually supportive and mutually contradictory.[13] What manifestly needs further examination is the uses made of these images and texts by concrete agents in definite social circumstances. This latter consideration raises the question of "contextualization," of how agents actually use, reject, transform, or undermine the discourse of health and the blandishments of commercial mass media in general.

EXIT QUESTION: REMADE IN PNG?

It is one thing to identify the discourse of health—its images, rhetorical vehicles, and ideal practices; it is quite another thing to determine the fate of this discourse in actual practice, as the Talkback discussion of betel nut chewing attests. Here we meet the methodological limitations of textual analysis and the critique commonly leveled by anthropologists at much of the work in media studies (Spitulnik 1993). Thomas's (1991:108) comment about objects entangled in the multiple meanings of cross-cultural transfers is apposite: "To say that black bottles were given does not tell us what was received." Indeed, O'Hanlon (1995)—who cites Thomas as well—has demonstrated as much in a brilliant discussion of Wahgi battle shield designs. These designs nowadays incorporate motifs from commercial advertising for beer and cigarettes, but in ways that "re-express distinctively local issues" (1995:487) such as war histories and intergroup alliances. There is no reason, then, to suppose that the presuppositions of individualism and consumerism, including their particular definition of bodies and persons, will become routine in the lives of Papua New Guineans.

Nonetheless, it would be wrong to expect that ethnographic accounts of commercial mass media in PNG will always reveal creative appropriation of consumerist values let alone subversive resistance. Here I echo Errington and Gewertz (1996). Speaking about the efficacy and nature of Chambri cultural identity, they caution against the celebration of indigenous capacities for domesticating objects and practices of consumption emanating from exogenous sources. For example, they suggest that the endorsement by Chambri of the definition of tradition presented in the advertising of PepsiCo, Inc. and Arnott's Biscuits signals a shift in who controls or valorizes cultural identities. Indeed, they regard as likely a scenario in which "the individuating and privatizing processes of commodity consumption . . . , prompted by the purveyors of transnational capital as well as by the representatives of the state, would continue, interrupted by moments of attempted cultural reclamation in which Chambri would periodically wonder, 'What on earth is going on with us?' " (1996:123). In other words, engagements with new forms of consumer culture carry unforeseen consequences, especially, I would add, when such engagements involve remaking the physical body in conformity with new self images —for example, through beauty contests, bodybuilding, and dieting.

Joseph Tobin similarly reminds us that even the Japanese, renowned for their capacities to domesticate the foreign, have not fully escaped the consequences of "atomization" and "privatization" attendant upon the encounter with Western consumption practices: on the one hand, squid pizza; on the other, *mai puraibashii* (my privacy) (1992:22 ff.). These consumption practices, moreover, themselves advocate and promote contextualization and domestication. "Free choice," after all, promises the creation of a unique individual identity by means of idiosyncratic appropriations of mass products: the transformation of anonymous commodities into personal possessions (cf. Miller 1987). Cultural contextualization can thus quite happily coexist with or even promulgate the notion of bodies and persons that I have associated with modern individualism and consumerism.

Mass-mediated collective representations of the conflicts that ensue when different rhetorics of self-making rub up against each other, as in the Trobriand Yam Festival, already circulate in PNG (Battaglia 1995b; see also Gewertz and Errington 1991, 1996). Consider, for example, the plight of the suburban Port Moresby public servant, socially atomized in and by his wage labor, who confronts his relational personhood in the form of uninvited relatives and neighbors "from the village"—that is, his *wantoks* (extended kin). Louie Warupi, in the humorous hit pop song "There Goes My Pay," imagines the situation like this[14]:

I've got a little house out in Gerehu.
I've got a wife and a little baby too.
I've got a job, I work in Waigani.
The government, it pays my salary.

At ten past four, I catch the PMV [bus].
I find them in my house all watching EM TV.
Kids, cousins, uncles—sitting round the floor.
And some of them, I've never seen before.

I think that I'm contributing to the nation.
Cause all my money goes to my relations.
There goes my pay.

The lyrics go on to describe the tension between forms of commodity consumption associated with different schemes for organizing persons—on the one hand, a form of consumption that recognizes and develops an extensive relational matrix in terms of which persons are defined, and on the other, a form of consumption that defines the nuclear family or household as its exclusive social context. This tension is not ultimately resolved, either in the lives of contemporary Papua New Guineans or in the song. But the song unambiguously accomplishes something else. As an instance of commercial mass media that reflexively evokes an image of media consumption, the song demonstrates how commercial mass media are an increasingly salient ingredient of the "total social fact" of modern life in PNG.

5

The Commercial Construction
of "New" Nations

INTRODUCTION: FROM CITIZEN TO CONSUMER?

Almost all the questions and issues that I explore in this chapter were raised, as is often the case, by a cartoon in the *New Yorker* magazine. A man in pajamas lies propped up in bed, a companion sleeping soundly at his side. He stares ahead with glazed eyes at a television set, one finger poised on the remote control. The caption reads: "Ladies and gentlemen, our national commercial."

I read the cartoon two different ways, but to the same effect. In the first reading, the viewer is watching the start of a late-night baseball game; the stadium announcer alerts the crowd not to the singing of the national anthem, but rather to the playing of the national commercial. In the second reading, the viewer is watching *late* late-night television; the station is about to sign off, but with the national commercial instead of the national anthem. This alternative reading, however, seems less likely, or at least less available to all readers. How many young Americans, I wonder, having grown up in a world where there is no end to the broadcast day, simply do not get the reference to the old convention of opening and closing television transmission with the national anthem?

Both readings nevertheless suggest that a series of aligned shifts has taken place in contemporary American society. The substitution of advertisement for anthem implies a move from political ritual to commercial ritual that, in turn, betokens an eclipse of the state by the market as the reference point for national belonging. In other words, viewers who were once appealed to as citizens are now addressed as consumers; their sense of national belonging derives less from common membership in a polity and more from common participation in a repertoire of consumption practices. The *New Yorker* magazine, again, offers apparent confirmation. A 1997 article about marketing efforts to identify innovative trends in "cool" sneakers reports that among youngsters in Philadelphia, "Reebok Classics are so huge they are known simply as National Anthems, as in 'I'll have a pair of blue Anthems in nine and a half' " (Gladwell 1997:84).

How should we take the following claim: "We are witnessing the swift debasement of the concept of 'citizen'—the person who actively participates in shaping society's destiny—to that of 'consumer,' whose franchise has become his or her purchasing decisions" (Ewen 1992:49). What might such a displacement of agency tell us about the production of nationality as a dimension of collective and personal identity? If nation-ness and nationality no longer necessarily refer to political identities—to a state legitimated by a people—then to what sort of imagined communities, if any, do they refer?

I want to address these questions by considering the instrumental role of commodity consumption in nation making—that is, in the production of nationality. In this regard, I follow but one of the many leads offered by Benedict Anderson's (1991) discussion of print capitalism as a force that enabled, through the activity of reading, the imagination of an unseen but delimited community of fellow readers; for Anderson's discussion is first and foremost a discussion about mass consumption. Printed books were among the earliest mass-produced commodities, the purchase and consumption of which provided the vehicle for the formation of national consciousness. I want to think here in a preliminary way about how other such commodities, in their marketing and consumption, might or might not likewise enable the imagination of national community. I will use for this purpose commercial images from Papua New Guinea (PNG), the most linguistically and culturally diverse Pacific island nation-state created in the last generation—created, I reiterate, not by anticolonial revolution but rather by a ragged decolonization process instigated largely through the United Nations. In PNG, as with a slew of other nation-states from Italy to Indonesia, the independent state unambiguously preceded the nation to which it was allegedly coupled.

Accordingly, I also locate my questions about the production of nationality in the space held by the hyphen in the word "nation-state." As Arjun Appadurai (1990) has neatly remarked, this hyphen today seems to signal disjunction as much as conjunction, to separate nation from state as much as to connect them. I want to suggest, therefore, that my questions about nationality engage the issue of sovereignty—both the contested sovereignty of the nation-state and the embattled sovereignty of individual persons in the famous new world order. On the one hand, effective governmentality now emanates from agencies other than territorial nation-states—such as the complex agencies of "structural adjustment" that impinge on the daily lives of ordinary citizens in PNG as elsewhere. At the same time, global diasporas and translocal solidarities continually challenge the nation-state's capacity to mobilize, let alone monopolize, allegiance and loyalty. On the other hand, more and more people seem to be promised ever more possibilities for freedom and autonomy through their consumption choices. Global flows of media images incite people living in the most remote villages, such as those of PNG, to new and powerful fantasies of self-fashioning through consumption. The ideal of personal efficacy achieved through consumption everywhere rivals the ideal of citizens determining their collective existence.

The meaning and fate of nationality in these conflicted circumstances are, of course, uncertain. It is hardly the case, however, that nationality as a collective identity is destined to dissolve in an acid bath of global consumerism. Indeed, in some obvious instances, consumption choices appear to form the basis for nationality as a collective identity—as when an American family chooses to vacation at Colonial Williamsburg or some other outlet of the national heritage industry. Thus, even if the nation-state is no longer autonomous and self-determining, and even if the citizen's autonomy as a political subject is continually compromised, nationality is still made available to autonomous consumers: one affirms an identity as a Papua New Guinean or as an American by buying particular goods and services. Nationality, in this view, is not simply appealed to as a quality preexisting on other civic grounds and transferable to commodities; nationality emerges, if at all, as a commercial construction, a by-product of public efforts to render commodities and their use meaningful. This is particularly the case when transnational corporations conjure up "the people" to whom they attempt to legitimate themselves: witness the television advertisements for Toyota Camrys that depict the diverse American workers who build the cars; or, as I will discuss presently, the ads for *Coke* and *Pepsi* in PNG that define a "new nation" of soft drink consumers.

COMMERCIAL TECHNOLOGIES OF NATION MAKING

What would a "national commercial" of the sort evoked by the cartoon from the *New Yorker* look like? Consider this paradigmatic possibility, a World War II–era print advertisement for the soft drink *Coca-Cola* (figure 5.1). Of all the many things going on in this ad, semiotically speaking, I focus only on two: the assertion that *Coke* symbolizes an American *way of living* ("a bit of America" and "the happy symbol of a friendly way of life"), and the identification of that way of living with *modernity,* an identification made self-evident by the contrasting presence of primitive South Pacific islanders bewildered by the soldiers' radios. If we concentrate on the way in which *Coke* consumption implies participation in a distinctively American way of living—a way of living characterized by its material modernity and abundance—then we must admit that this ad exemplifies a commercial technology of nation making with a long history. Similar technologies were at work, for instance, in the early part of this century, effecting the transformation of immigrants into Americans. The historian Andrew Heinze (1990) emphasizes the way in which Eastern European Jews, in particular, were able to use consumer goods as tools for forging an American Jewish identity. Heinze writes (1990:10),

Figure 5.1. Advertisement for *Coca-Cola* soft drink, 1945.
Coca-Cola Bottler, October 1945.
Coca-Cola, Coke Always, and the Contour Bottle are registered trademarks
of The Coca-Cola Company. Used by permission.

Acquiring American speech, participating in American institutions, and making economic advances were important to the search for a new cultural identity, but vast numbers of people with little sense of the language and limited exposure to institutions were engaging, virtually from the moment they entered the streets of the city, in a new cycle of consumption that defined a uniquely American approach to life.

For these immigrants, unremarkable consumption practices—drinking Borden's condensed milk, cooking with Crisco vegetable shortening, bathing with Ivory soap—were the most easily accessible elements of the process of nationalizing themselves.

Commercial technologies of nation making, then, are not that new; there is something misleading about the suggestion of an historical trajectory from citizen to consumer, from political rituals to commercial rituals. Indeed, the familiar political technologies of American nation making—pledge of allegiance, national anthem, and Memorial Day parade—are coeval with the late nineteenth-century commercial rituals of nation making, such as shopping through nationally distributed mail-order catalogs for nationally advertised brands of products. Nor is the use of commercial technologies in identifying the nation with a modern way of life uniquely American. For instance, virtually the same effect that Heinze describes of nationalizing immigrants through consumption practices was consciously promoted by the Australian government during the 1950s and 1960s. The post–World War II influx of European immigrants was enticed with "the suburban ideal of the middle-class family with its house, garden, whitegoods and television, all fruits of the nation's industrial expansion" (MacDonald 1995:28). One telling image used to promote immigration to Australia thus depicted a bounteous Christmas Day barbecue on the shores of Sydney Harbor, complete with two "Eskys"—Australian slang for portable beer coolers.

A quick trip from Sri Lanka to Spain by way of the Cook Islands suggests some of the various ways in which consumption enables, if not enjoins, people to think the nation by, to use Steven Kemper's phrase, "blurring the line between a political act and a consumption decision" (1993:393). In the case of "new nations," where the project of the nation-state is often prominently identified with modernity, the adoption of certain consumption practices can especially function as a sign of national progress. Such is the case, Kemper argues, of the Development Lottery in Sri Lanka. Lotteries—including the same Lotto game played in the United States—began to be introduced in Sri Lanka in 1977, making the country one of seventy-nine where $154 million dollars was gambled every day (as of 1989). The Development Lottery, known for its large jackpots, is a government enterprise, the proceeds of which are used to sponsor development projects that in principle benefit the Sri Lankan citizenry. Gambling is thus by definition practical patriotism. In addition, the

Development Lottery's weekly drawings for large cash prizes are staged for television, such that viewing the lottery creates the exclusively shared space-time that Benedict Anderson—citing the daily consumption of newspapers—saw as a prerequisite for imagining the nation.

Kemper's argument about the Development Lottery in Sri Lanka capitalizes on a suggestion that I, following Appadurai, have made elsewhere, namely, to treat nations as imagined communities of consumption: "large-scale, non-intimate collectivities, unified by the ritualized fantasies of collective expenditure" (Appadurai n.d.). However, when the development that the state seeks is the development of tourism, it is not inappropriate to wonder whose fantasies and expenditures are at issue. Jeffrey Sissons (1997) has posed this question in regard to the Cook Islands, a small Pacific island nation "freely associated" with New Zealand, where since 1988 state-sponsored ethnic nationalism has stimulated and been stimulated by the expansion of a tourist economy. Through the vigorous operation of the Ministry of Cultural Development in preparing to host the 1992 Festival of Pacific Arts, Cook Islands national identity became equated with a commercially oriented cultural tradition, "an essential resource for tourism-led economic development" (Sissons 1997:184). Sissons (1997:186) goes on to say,

> The rhetoric of nationhood, which formerly emphasized the values of togetherness and progress, increasingly celebrates a more marketable ethnic pride and cultural heritage. Television advertisements encourage Cook Islanders to show friendly, smiling faces to their visitors in the national interest. National dance competitions are sponsored by international airlines. Local *vaka* [canoe] carvers are featured in tourist brochures.

Participation in nationhood has come to mean participation in the tourist industry. As a result, Sissons argues, a new sense of nationhood is emerging among Cook Islanders: "a sense of living in an increasingly commodified space, of belonging to an imagined community for others" (1997:186). An imagined community *for others,* the Cook Islands is increasingly being shaped through the consumption practices of tourists as a *desti-nation.*

Here again, we encounter a contemporary instance of a phenomenon with nineteenth-century antecedents—that is, the phenomenon of offering displays and definitions of the nation-state for public consumption by foreigners. The most striking context for such displays and definitions, judging by the amount of attention received from cultural critics of all sorts, is the world exhibition or universal exposition; the last official one of the twentieth century was held in 1992 in Seville, Spain. Penelope Harvey's intriguing meditation on the Seville exposition, *Hybrids of Modernity* (1996), suggests that the exposition was in many ways produced and received as a mass presentation of more than one hundred national commercials. That is, nation-states were objectified in a comparative and competitive environment that recalled the marketing strategies of the transnational corporations—Panasonic, Fuji, IBM—who made it financially possible for the Spanish state to host the event in the first place. I will come back to this point presently, but for now, I mention only a couple of Harvey's observations of how visitors effectively treated nations as brand name commodities.

Harvey points out that all visitors could acquire an Expo passport, which could be stamped upon exit from the different national pavilions. Some visitors apparently made the accumulation of these stamps an end in itself, entering exhibits with great speed and looking immediately for the place where they could get their passports stamped. In extreme cases, visitors collected stamps from pavilions they had not even visited. Occasionally, a distraught visitor would inquire of pavilion workers about a lost passport. One pavilion hostess reported to Harvey that a supply of found passports was kept on hand for such occasions. Thankful visitors would express great excitement if their replacement passport already had a significant number of stamps. In addition, the visitor's strategy would incorporate the recorded visits of the passport's previous owner, there being no point in visiting pavilions for which stamps had already been obtained. The transformation of citizens into consumers seems virtually complete: passports—the unique and singular validations of political identity—become rendered as transferable commodities between unknown visitors, as consumable signs detached from material referents.

Harvey also relates a story of how, in the shop at the exit from the Israeli pavilion, a box of bookmarks stood next to the cash register: "As I was casting an eye over what was on sale I noticed someone walk over and help themselves to one of these. Others immediately followed until dozens had been carried away. The shop assistant, who noticed too late what was happening, was horrified" (1996:159). Harvey's point is that the visitors were innocently, if automatically, collecting mementos, accustomed to the way pavilions often provided leaflets and paper mementos (and passport stamps) which visitors collected as they left. The difference between the national pavilion and the souvenir shop (much like the difference between national museums and their gift shops) is thus erased: visitors act as and are addressed as consumers in both spaces. Like tourists in the Cook Islands, at least some visitors to Expo'92 treated the imagined communities of others not as nation-states but rather as desti-nations—that is, as objects and experiences available for consumption.

This convenience sample—Sri Lanka, the Cook Islands, Expo'92, and turn-of-the-century America—allows me to observe three things about the place of commercial technologies and consumption practices in producing nations. First, consumption practices have the capacity to operate as powerful vehicles for materializing nationality, although with ambiguous or indeterminate consequences. On the one hand, the ordinary or mundane nature of certain consumption practices attaches nationality to everyday experience in a way that more extraordinary practices—celebrations of national holidays, occasional elections, or irregular military contests—simply do not. On the other hand, the materialization of nationality in the form of consumable objects and experiences leaves the nation vulnerable to the market. What if nobody buys? Or what if national consumer goods—take the Australian icon, Vegemite, for example—become the property of foreign corporations? Or what if mainly nonnationals buy—and so demand nationality in the forms that *they* prefer?

It is these questions that both Harvey's discussion of Expo'92 and Sissons's discussion of Cook Islands tourism pose. From this perspective, national affiliation is a matter of individual and private purchase decisions rather than an irresistible social fact. It is clear, moreover, that when these purchases are made by noncitizen tourists, the result is hardly affirmative patriotism for anyone—although, perhaps, alienated nationality for the local citizens and ironic nationality for the tourists. But even for locally based citizens, it is clear that the consumption of national brand goods or participation in national lotteries or even watching national sporting events need not produce civic consciousness. Consumption, as anthropologists such as Daniel Miller (1987) have persuasively demonstrated, is an activity through which people can appropriate and recontextualize commodities as instruments for creating differentiated, particularized, and sometimes resistant identities. At best, then, common consumption might engender a diffuse and diluted sense of collective affinity—the sort of recognition, if any, that someone affords someone else who drinks the same brand of beer or gambles at the same roulette table.

I will take up this perspective on consumption and nationality in my conclusion, but not before suggesting what this perspective marginalizes. Orvar Löfgren (1996:34), among others (see Linde-Laursen 1993), has encouraged us to pay attention to what he calls "the microphysics of learning to belong," that is, the ways in which the nationalization of routines and trivialities—including routine and trivial consumption practices—produces feelings of belonging. These feelings often only register when the routines and trivialities in question are violated or brought into juxtaposition with alternatives. Heinze (1990), for example, recounts a story from *My Mother and I,* the 1916 memoir of Elizabeth Stern, whose family came to New York City from Poland in 1891. Stern recalled the embarrassing moment when she first opened her lunch at school—a mass of fried potatoes and a crushed tomato wrapped in newspaper. By contrast, "the American students had precisely packaged meals —neat, regular-sized sandwiches, square paper napkins and lunch boxes"

(Heinze 1990:168). The fearful symmetry of these lunches, along with the criticism of her peers, shamed Stern into throwing her lunches away. Nor is it irrelevant to add that many of these students were probably using as lunch boxes the distinctive packages of Uneeda biscuits—lowly soda crackers heavily and successfully advertised by a chain of bakeries stretching from Maine to Louisiana and Colorado and incorporated in 1898 as the National Biscuit Company. Thus, the American way of presenting lunches in public made Elizabeth Stern feel, and feel deeply, that she did not belong.

Consumption practices have the capacity to link personal and collective identities in compelling fashion. It is precisely this capacity that the Sri Lankan state seeks to mobilize in its Development Lottery. As Kemper points out, the lotteries elicit the agency of the bettors, requiring bettors "to take action, make choices, and keep their eyes fixed on the prize" (1993:393). The effectiveness of the trope of development thus lies in how it connects the (modern) individual's imagined self-development with the development of a collective individual, the nation. Entering pedestrian consciousness by way of sidewalk loudspeakers and ticket booths with vivid posters, the Development Lottery makes the nation thinkable or imaginable. Buying a lottery ticket then becomes the practical means for engaging the nation with the desires and dreams of individual consumers.

Of course, like Kemper, I am not suggesting that consuming Development Lotteries or Uneeda biscuits instantly, automatically, or permanently makes Sri Lankans or Americans. But I am suggesting that we take such consumption practices seriously if we want some purchase on the way that nations become entangled with lived identities. I suggest that by doing so we are in a position to address the question about nations that Anderson raises but ultimately fails to answer in *Imagined Communities*: why do (some) people die for such limited imaginings? That is, how do nations become aspects of everyday embodied being? In this regard, I refer to the letters that American soldiers—presumably like the ones depicted in figure 5.1—wrote to their families during World War II. Selections from these letters appear in Mark Pendergrast's (1993) informative history, *For God, Country and Coca-Cola*. Here are two:

> It's the little things, not the big, that the individual soldier fights for or wants so badly when away. It's the girl friend back home in a drug store over a Coke, or the juke box and summer weather. (Pendergrast 1993:210)

> To have this drink is just like having home brought nearer to you; it's one of the little things of life that really counts. I can remember being at Ponce de Leon Park, watching the [Atlanta] Crackers play baseball as I filled up on Coca-Cola and peanuts. It's such things as this that all of us are fighting for. (Pendergrast 1993:210)

Commodity fetishism with a national inflection, perhaps. But this sort of fetishism, it seems, enabled people not only to die for, but also to kill for the nation. Pendergrast (1993:211) thus notes the delight of The Coca-Cola Company when "Colonel Robert L. Scott, in his best-seller *God Is My Co-pilot,* explained that his motivation to 'shoot down my first Jap' stemmed from thoughts of 'America, Democracy, Coca-Colas.' "

Colonel Scott's invocation of democracy leads me to a second, more straightforward observation about consumption and national identities—namely, that consumption practices offer the promise of realizing the principle of equivalence given in the idea of nationhood. This point has been made often enough, if mainly in the process of demonstrating the promise to be superficial or downright false; I merely stress here that the point has two dimensions. First, mass consumption offers to individuals the sort of agency and equality manifestly denied them in the realm of capital and labor. Certain inexpensive consumer items—Uneeda biscuits, *Coca-Cola* soft drinks, Development Lottery tickets—imply that the challenge of self-determination is open to all at the same price (or at the same cold odds). When such consumer items are nationalized, then their consumption engenders an ephemeral sort of mass enfranchisement; each consumer replicates the consumption of his or her anonymous but equal conationals.

Second, mass consumption provides a vocabulary and model for communicating the equivalence of nations, for just as each bottle of *Coke* or package of biscuits replicates every other one, so too are individuals within the nation latently alike and equal. Similarly, just as *Coke* and *Pepsi* are equivalent but different brands of colas, collective individuals or nations are equivalent polities that differ only in their constituent elements. Löfgren (1989a) has called attention to this phenomenon by identifying an internationally recognized grammar in terms of which national identity is validated and differentiated. In addition to flags, anthems, museums, and so forth, valid nations are now available for presentation through an array of national brand consumer goods. Where I live in Rochester, New York, there is a store called Beers of the World. The displays of beer, and only beer, are arranged by nation-state of origin. One can buy beers not only from Australia or France, but from their former colonies, PNG and Niger. There is a formal equivalence to these displays, much like the formal equivalence of nation-states achieved in the opening ceremony of the Olympic Games or the official self-representation of Expo'92. Indeed, as Harvey (1996:54) points out, universal exhibitions are time-tested technologies for "distinguishing nation-states through representational practices which simultaneously render them equivalent." It is not at all surprising, then, that some of the African pavilions at Expo'92 displayed their own brands of beers and soap powders.

My third, final, and briefest observation concerns the way in which consumption practices enact various relationships between tradition and modernity, relationships that figure variously in all national narratives. Elizabeth Stern, for example, yielded to her peers' classification of the lunches that her mother made as remnants of an anachronistic tradition out of place in modern America. Consumption in this case defined the split between a dead Polish past and a living American present. Almost a century later, once-novel consumption practices constitute American traditions—such as drinking *Coca-Cola Classic*—the modification of which would qualify as sacrilege. Consumption in this case allows the past to live in the present and thus to qualify the nation as both enduring and innovative. Such a resolution of past and present is particularly desirable in those "new nations" opened up to the wholesale import of modern but unmistakably foreign consumption practices. In such situations, the task of nationalizing modernity is vulnerable to criticism as selling out local traditions and heritage. The national narrative must negotiate between the twin demands of the state to represent itself as progressive and as protective of the indigenous way of life. Such a resolution, I suggest, requires the collusion of consumerism with the project of the nation-state.

COMMERCIAL CONSTRUCTIONS OF PNG

It is with these observations in mind that I now turn to the role of commercial technologies in making the nation, PNG. PNG is a place known to most Americans, if at all, through the work of anthropologists, from Bronislaw Malinowski and Margaret Mead to Marilyn Strathern and Roy Wagner. In these works, PNG emerges as the home of the authentic cultural Other, or, more precisely, the home of about 800 different authentic cultural (and linguistic) Others. Its vast diversity has delighted anthropologists with a cornucopia of myth, ritual, cosmology, and social organization, all duly made the objects of an impressive body of ethnographic analysis. What is less generally well known is the recent political history of the country and the enormous transformation of social life in the country's major cities brought about by the expansion of wage labor, commodity consumption, and mass media. Since 1975, when Australia ended its role as administrator of the United Nations Trust Territory, the independent state has deployed all available technologies for rendering PNG a *nation*-state. But the PNG state is—unlike its neighbor Indonesia, for instance—a weak state, and its capacity to impinge on the consciousness of its constituent strong societies has been limited; the results of its projects in the area of political socialization have been both uneven and tenuous. Nevertheless, certain mass-consumption practices have spread throughout the country or are accessible to anyone visiting any major town. These consumption practices now provide advertisers with vehicles for imagining the nation as the market that the advertisers aspire to address.

What, then, might a national commercial in PNG look like? Here is one possibility, a print ad for *Pepsi-Cola*. The text reads, "Pepsi. The favourite drink of the land of the unexpected. Pepsi brings out the best in Papua New Guinea's diverse culture. Pepsi. The Choice of a New Generation. The Choice of all Papua New Guineans." The accompanying image juxtaposes a product consumed by "all Papua New Guineans" with an instance of PNG's diverse culture—three young women dressed similarly in unambiguously traditional garb (see figure 2.6). Text and image thus accomplish two things. First, they suggest (to me, I want to be clear) that the *new* generation of Papua New Guineans, perhaps like PNG itself, embodies a conjunction between (local) tradition and (global) modernity. That is, tradition and modernity are represented as compatible rather than antagonistic. This compatibility is more than just posited, for the local bottlers of both *Pepsi* and *Coke* in PNG lend material and financial sponsorship support to the various cultural festivals organized around the country to celebrate PNG's cultural diversity. Such sponsorship is one of the main ways in which transnational corporations deflect criticism from themselves as foreign and exploitative (see Guss 1996). It is also one of the ways in which these corporations are complicit in the construction of PNG as a multicultural nation in which "diversity" means benign stylistic variation in dance routines and ceremonial costume.

Second, and by the same token, the *Pepsi* ad presents "the choice of all Papua New Guineans" as cutting across the diversity that *Pepsi* allegedly "brings out." Perhaps the relative uniformity of the three women's dress and the simultaneity of their drinking reinforces this claim. In any case, I infer that *Pepsi* is being likened to the nation, and vice versa, inasmuch as both encompass and transcend diversity—the diversity of individual consumers on the one hand, and the diversity of unique cultural traditions on the other. This inference is made more plausible by the following two *Coke* ads.

The first ad (figure 5.2) depicts an individual consumer whose hat marks him as *not* generic; for this particular hat is not only his favorite hat, but an article of clothing associated with a particular region of PNG (though also an item of emergent pan-PNG indigenous material culture that includes betel nut and string bags [*bilums*]). He is thus one of the diverse consumers from the diverse cultures all of whom drink *Coke* in PNG. Similarly, the second ad (figure 5.3) suggests a diversity of decoration styles and facial phenotypes encompassed within the singularity of a common commodity/brand: *Coca-Cola*.

Consumption goods that transcend diversity and perforce constitute the nation as a totality also have the capacity to link consumer-citizens and their diverse traditions to a wider world. This is the claim, at least, made by an advertisement which, although for the National Bank of Solomon Islands Limited (Solomon Islands being PNG's closest Melanesian neighbor to the east),

MY FAVOURITE HAT

MY FAVOURITE DRINK

ALWAYS MY FAVOURITE · ALWAYS COCA-COLA

Coca-Cola

Figure 5.2. Advertisement for *Coca-Cola* soft drink, 1995.
UBD Papua New Guinea Business and Trade Directory.
Coca-Cola, Coke Always, and the Contour Bottle are registered trademarks
of The Coca-Cola Company. Used by permission.

could easily run in PNG. The text of the ad, which depicts a variety of indigenous shell currencies, gives voice to an "us" and a "we" that are none other
than the nation itself:

> Money matters are nothing new to us. . . . For hundreds of years we
> Solomon Islanders have used traditional money like the examples above.
> But times do change and although the use of "Kastom Mani" is still a very
> important part of our culture, at times we need special services and exper-
> tise in our dealings with a wider world.
>
> The National Bank of Solomon Islands can provide such services and
> expertise—we know the importance of sound financial management. After
> all, we are carrying on a tradition centuries old. (*Solomons,* in-flight maga-
> zine of Solomon Airlines, circa 1995)

The services of the National Bank thus function as the means to articulate
(not to eradicate) local and ancient traditions with changing times and expanding horizons—that is, with modernity.

This same identification of consumption practices with modernity can be
achieved with less respect for or recognition of tradition or traditions. Thus,

Figure 5.3. Advertisement for *Coca-Cola* soft drink from the program of the
1992 Port Moresby Show.
Coca-Cola, Coke Always, and the Contour Bottle are registered trademarks
of The Coca-Cola Company. Used by permission.

another ad, this one for *Pepsi* (figure 5.4), suggests that the soft drink does
more than bring out the best in PNG's diverse cultures; *Pepsi* also brings out
the modern qualities of PNG's new generation. (Here I add that the models
in this ad include a former Miss PNG and two television/radio personalities;
all are recognizable as members of PNG's growing national/cosmopolitan
elite. I am uncertain, however, if consumers in PNG would recognize this
ad as related to a *Pepsi* ad of several years ago that featured the singer Ray
Charles.) A less risky way of identifying the nation with modernity through
consumption practices involves linking products with athletes and, more particularly, international sports competition. I say less risky because this strategy
usually involves, once again, corporate sponsorship of national sports teams.
This sort of sponsorship complements the sponsorship of cultural festivals, the
former promoting the nation-state's modernity while the latter affirms its traditional basis. The television ad for Shell gasoline that I analyzed in the previous chapter serves as an impressive instance not only of this strategy, but
also of the semiotic merging of nation and corporation through the fortuitous
manipulation of the colors in PNG's flag—red, black, and gold—with the colors in Shell's corporate logo.

The identification of nation and consumer product is achieved in more
homely fashion in a television ad for a brand of tinned beef called Ox and

Figure 5.4. Advertisement for *Pepsi-Cola*, 1995.
UBD Papua New Guinea Business and Trade Directory.
Pepsi, Pepsi-Cola, the Pepsi Globe design, and *The Choice of a New Generation*
are registered trademarks of PepsiCo, Inc. Used by permission.

Palm. This ad was produced by an agency located in PNG and staffed by PNG nationals, but owned and creatively managed by an Australian man. It is my candidate for the title of "National Commercial of PNG" inasmuch as it consolidates many of the general claims that I have made about the commercial construction of nations. It presents Ox and Palm tinned beef as a product whose consumption mediates geographic diversity—mountains and islands— as well as the social diversity represented by town and country. Ox and Palm is, moreover, a domestic product in both senses of the term—made in PNG and used in the homes of all Papua New Guineans—or even brought from home to school for lunch in a routine that conjures up the ghost of Elizabeth Stern. It is, like Uneeda biscuits and *Pepsi-Cola*, democratically inexpensive enough to be available at some time to almost everyone. And it is, finally, the perfect blend of tradition and modernity, an originally foreign product that arrived more than forty years ago in PNG, but has since become domesticated and familiar enough to qualify as a national tradition: Corned Beef Classic.

CONCLUSION: NATIONALITY WITHOUT NATIONALISM?

What does tinned beef have to do with nationalism? My colleague Nicholas Thomas might say that the question itself testifies to "the failure of a project of modernity in the South Pacific" (1997:211). In the introduction to their edited volume *Narratives of Nation in the South Pacific,* Otto and Thomas suggest that in places like PNG, it is not nationalism but rather nationality that develops through consumption practices: "The distinction is that between affirmative patriotism on one side and a collective imagining on the other . . . People may perceive themselves as members of a nation, and as essentially similar to other nationals, without necessarily possessing a loyal or civic consciousness" (1997:1). Drinking beer or eating corned beef that bears a national signature engenders collective affinity, perhaps, but surely an affinity too politically dilute to call nationalism.

Thomas develops this claim in part by alluding to the way in which many consumption practices relate "to non-national identities or identities that positively subvert nationality" (1997:217). Consumption practices enable people to participate in both subnational identities and international identities at the same time, thus making national identity enacted through consumption a contingent choice rather than an irresistible social fact. Furthermore, one might wonder if the attempt to identify consumer products with the nation does not have a whiff of the attic about it. The tag line "It's Pepsi in PNG" reflected a moment when transnational corporations perhaps thought it in their best interest to collude with the fledgling state's attempts to imagine a nation. That moment has passed, and PepsiCo, Inc. can now forget the nation and address the consumer directly—indeed, directly identify the consumer with the product, as in its most recent ads. The ad in figure 5.5, for example,

Figure 5.5. Advertisement for *Pepsi-Cola*, 1997.
Post-Courier, 11 April 1997.
Pepsi, Pepsi-Cola, the Pepsi Globe design, and *The Choice of a New Generation*
are registered trademarks of PepsiCo, Inc. Used by permission.

was one of the first in a coordinated worldwide campaign, the centerpiece of which was the redesign of the *Pepsi* can to emphasize the color blue. "Break Free" has replaced "It's Pepsi in PNG" as the slogan—a realization of Stuart Ewen's nightmare of consumer democracy in which freedom and autonomy refer to purchase decisions.

I am led to the conclusion that as nations are uncoupled from territorial states, nationality will live on as an idiom for some weak form of collective identity, one identity among others available in the global marketplace. If current events contradict this conclusion, it is only because, as Appadurai suggests, no other idiom "has yet emerged to capture the collective interest of many groups in translocal solidarities, cross-border mobilizations, and postnational identities" (1993:418). And this conclusion is tempting, moreover, because I could then invert the old evolutionary conceit of seeing a European past in the Melanesian present and argue that PNG anticipates Europe's future. I could suggest, with Thomas (1997:219), that while Europe struggles "to obliterate the memories that stand in the way of a posthistorical, postnational, postmodern market and superstate, Pacific societies apparently possess no national identities that need to be forgotten."

But I prefer not to conclude so for now. In March of 1997, a series of remarkable events unfolded in PNG, events that from this distance certainly look like the collective action of people in the name of a nation hitherto regarded as only weakly imagined. The revolt was triggered by the public disclosure of a deal made by high-ranking government officials, including the prime minister, to hire an outfit of South African–based mercenaries. The mercenaries were to intervene in a protracted secessionist war in Bougainville, one of PNG's island provinces. The refusal of the military to cooperate with the mercenaries, in conjunction with several days of mass protests in the capital city, led to the expulsion of the mercenaries, the stepping aside of the prime minister, and the institution of an inquiry into the multimillion-dollar deal. The PNG state was effectively charged with betraying the nation whose will it ideally expresses.

Here is one reaction to the events, a letter written to a PNG daily newspaper, the *National,* from a citizen studying in Australia:

> It's great to be Papua New Guinean.
>
> After 10 days of anxiety and distress during the Government-Defence stand-off, the final outcome makes me proud to be a Papua New Guinean. I will never compromise my nationality or pretend to be someone else which I am not.
>
> Here in Australia, the newspapers, TV programs and people enjoyed the sensationalised reports about the events in PNG. The Australian media, particularly television, were getting into each other's way in their quest for higher ratings.

> And inevitably the result is every other Australian I met felt that PNG was going down the tube and we were doomed for hell.
>
> I never lost faith and I told those Australians we could solve our problems.

I submit that these words are not a postmodern instance of what Appadurai (1993) calls "Trojan nationalisms"—nationalisms that contain transnational links and nonnational aspirations—but rather a familiar modern instance of nationalism incubated abroad. What is perhaps postmodern about the letter is the fact that it was E-mailed from Canberra to the newspaper's office in Port Moresby and made available to me through the World Wide Web on the newspaper's home page. But my point is that the author's nationalism was elicited and communicated by the same mass-mediated means through which nationality has been and continues to be disseminated in PNG. Many of these mass mediations are unambiguously commercial—advertisements for gasoline and corned beef—and many of the consumption practices that they seek to nationalize are utterly banal. Nevertheless, I submit that these images and their effects in creating personal and collective identities warrant close scrutiny before we deem the prospects of "new nations" to be closed.

PART III

Nation Making in This Era of Globalization

6

News of the World
Millenarian Christianity and
the Olympic Torch Relay

INTRODUCTION: MARGINALITY AND GLOBALIZATION

In recent years, Marshall Sahlins (1993, 1999) and Epeli Hauᶜofa (1994, 1998) have criticized scholars and policy makers alike for representing Pacific Islanders as marginal. By "marginal," Hauᶜofa and Sahlins mean primarily two things: first, isolated; and second, passive—or if not passive, then at best, re-active to the projects of alien agents and institutions. Instead, Hauᶜofa and Sahlins argue, Pacific Islanders are well connected with each other and with the so-called centers of the world system, not only now but also in the past. These connections, moreover, are self-motivated engagements in which Pacific Islanders attempt to put objects, images, and ideas of exogenous origin in the service of indigenous goals—a process that Sahlins (1992, 2000) has happily dubbed "develop-man." Develop-man—unlike development, or the globalization of Western modernity—describes the process by which people seize opportunities and resources presented by foreign encounters in order to pursue autonomously defined goals of cultural enlargement. Or, as Hauᶜofa (2000: 465) more modestly puts it, "We [Pacific Islanders] cannot do away with the global system, but we can control aspects of its encroachment and take opportunities when we see them in order to create space for ourselves."

I find these arguments compelling, not least on political grounds. Hauᶜofa thus wonders what sort of pedagogical agenda he implements by teaching Pacific Islander students at the University of the South Pacific to think of themselves—to represent themselves—as weak and dependent, inheritors of broken, inauthentic traditions on the one hand, and the straight jacket of labor-exporting, remittance-importing economies on the other. Why, Hauᶜofa asks, ought he exaggerate the helplessness of his students and inflict on them the "pathology of over-diminished expectations" (Hirst and Thompson 1996:6)? His alternative is to produce unifying, anti-insular visions of the Pacific—"our sea of islands," "the ocean in us"—visions that recast received social science wisdom by featuring the ways in which Pacific Islanders have always communicated with each other over vast distances and have met new circumstances without becoming any less themselves. Hauʿofa's point—his lesson to his students—is as important as it is urgent: if you don't represent yourselves, someone else will. And even if your representers act in sincere goodwill and declared solidarity, you might not recognize yourself in the representations that they advocate. Whether they seek to hasten your modernization or to decry your exploitation, these representers amiably insist on depicting your existence as marginal—something it probably doesn't seem like to you (see Fry 1997 for examples).

Hauʿofa's lesson makes good sense, but it apparently has not yet been taken on board by all Pacific Islanders. A quick check of the ethnographic record reveals plenty of people who profess their marginality. Right across Papua New Guinea (PNG), for instance, there seems to be a healthy competition for last place. The Miyanmin, living in the mountains of far western PNG, were said to call themselves "the last people"—that is, the last people to feel the effects of European colonization: "The Miyanmin count this as a misfortune, and are acutely aware that almost everybody else is better off than they are" (Flannery 1998:58; the "ethnographic present" here is 1981). Along the Rai Coast of northern New Guinea, villagers refer to their home in Tok Pisin as *las ples*—"the 'last place' to receive development and change" (Englund and Leach 2000:230). And way out east off the coast of New Ireland, I have heard Tangan men say that they were living on the *las ailan* ("last island"), a reference both to their physical location near the border separating PNG from the open ocean, and to a diffuse sense of remoteness exacerbated by poor transport facilities. But it is perhaps the Gapun villagers, living in the sago swamps of the lower Sepik, who best articulate the total social fact that "lastness" denotes for some Papua New Guineans. Kulick (1992:55) quotes one old Gapun man, Kruni, who contrasts his existence with that of white people in "the countries"—places like Japan, America, Germany, and Belgium (home of one former missionary)—about which Gapuners have heard:

> We're the last country. And the way of life, too. In the countries it's good. There's no work. Like what we do here —carry heavy things around on our shoulders, walk around through the jungle like pigs. No. You all just sit, drive around in cars. . . . Houses. You all live in good houses. They have rooms in them, toilets. But us here, no. We haven't come up a little bit. God papa hasn't changed us yet. We're still inside the Big Darkness. We still live the same way our fathers from a long time ago lived. Just like wild pigs.

These collective representations of marginality must not be taken only as obvious internalizations of colonialist teachings—that is, as self-loathing well learned. Professions of marginality—indeed, of moral, material, and intellectual inferiority to white people—often perform what Herzfeld (1997) calls "cultural intimacy"; they disguise not only agency, but also optimism and even a certain moral confidence (see Bashkow 2000 for a pertinent example). Papua New Guineans, for example, may be the last to hear the good news of Christianity, but unlike the apostate white people who heard it first, Papua New Guineans will take it to heart and redeem its promises. Or, somewhat differently, the coming of white people with superior technology and wealth is actually a return of some long ago departed younger brother—a reminder that stark inequality was not always the case and need not be the premise of the future. But these caveats are not to gainsay what such representations of marginality presume—dissatisfaction with the current relationship to an exogenous Other, an Other to which one is currently and ineluctably oriented (see Knauft 2002).

How do we understand this dissatisfaction? That is, how do we understand people's attempts to negotiate a perceived and sometimes deeply felt sense of marginality? Keeping in mind Sahlins and Hauᶜofa's arguments about self-determination and connection to the world, we can recognize here the long-standing problem of structure and agency, of accounting for people's actions under conditions not of their own making. This recognition in turn carries the possibility that people sometimes act as agents of their own domination, unintentionally reproducing the conditions against which they struggle (see Willis 1981, Bourgois 1995). Furthermore, how do we relate this sense of dissatisfaction and perception of marginality—if at all—to globalization? Are there forms of marginality specific to or specifically enhanced by globalization? Does globalization prompt changes in the way people experience marginality and attempt to center themselves? For, most surely, efforts at centering vis-à-vis outsiders have a long history in the Pacific, PNG not excepted. The eastern end of the small coral island where I have lived and done fieldwork is called Taonsip, a Tok Pisin twist on Townsville, the Queensland city through which many Melanesians passed in the late nineteenth century on their way to labor in the sugar fields. The name was brought back and applied by one returning laborer, Kiapsel, who subsequently brokered the official pacification of his home by the German administration and requested that a Catholic priest—not a Protestant—be sent to establish a mission (Foster 1995a; see Hirsch 1995 for a related example of topographical reinscription).[1]

I want to suggest, in the spirit of Sahlins and Hauᶜofa, that if nothing else, globalization entails an expansion of horizons, an enlargement of one's world that is not necessarily an encompassment of it by someone else's world. I want to suggest that for many Pacific Islanders, the horizons of orientation have shifted to include newly emergent regions and nation-states, transnational social categories such as "youth," and even the planet as a whole (e.g., as a single ecological system). The challenge posed by such a reorientation is one of claiming membership in this enlarged world, of finding a way to move in it. Again, I think this challenge is hardly unfamiliar to Pacific Islanders, including Papua New Guineans: recall, for example, the famous kula exchange circuit in which participants orient themselves to partners and shells located on distant islands, thereby contemplating and expanding the extent of their own renown (Munn 1990). What may or may not be new are the alleged consequences of immobility in a globalized world. Zygmunt Bauman's views on this point are extreme; for him, "being local in a globalized world is a sign of social deprivation and degradation" (1998:2). Bauman asserts that "mobility has become the most powerful and coveted stratifying factor; the stuff of which the new increasingly world-wide, social, political, economic, and cultural hierarchies are daily built and rebuilt" (1998:9). No wonder, then, that Hauᶜofa, among others, is so anxious to recover for Pacific Islanders a fluid history of long-distance canoe voyaging. In today's globalized world, immobility is an unwelcome sign of marginality.

One might be tempted to dismiss (unfairly) Bauman's obsession with mobility as the fetish of a peripatetic intellectual with too many frequent-flyer miles. But it is in any case a useful reminder of the fact that long-distance travel does not dominate the lives of the majority of people in the world today. As John Tomlinson remarks, "Although the increasing ability to move—physically and representationally—between places is a highly significant mode of connectivity, it is ultimately subordinate to—indeed derivative of—the order of location in time and space which we grasp as 'home' " (1999:9). Within the island Pacific, moreover, the frequency and scale of long-distance travel vary—greater, for example, for many Samoans and Tongans than for many Papua New Guineans. PNG, when compared to, say, the Cook Islands, is a country of stay-at-homes, relatively speaking, since besides kula exchange there is constant circulation between town and countryside. It is not now possible, however, to point to any significant overseas diaspora (neither a cadre of international jet-setters nor an army of migrant laborers)—a consequence of various colonial (and, later, national) state policies that attached rural populations to the land; limited the number of highly skilled, tertiary-school-educated graduates; and restricted immigration to the metropole (MacWilliam 1996; Scott MacWilliam, personal communication, 2001).[2] If, then, we want to talk about globalization in PNG, we might want to find other ways than to focus on flows of people. We might, for example, want to talk about the ways in which various forms or modes of connectivity affect the frames of reference "within which social agents increasingly figure their existence, identities and actions" (Tomlinson 1999:11).

Accordingly, I want to spend the rest of this chapter looking at two different projects in which people staying at home orient themselves to distant horizons. Put differently, I want to examine two instances of how people staying at home attempt to assert translocality, to participate in imagined communities of global proportion. I use the word "imagined" advisedly. Imagination might seem to be an exhausted trope. The metaphorical frenzy set off by the publication of Benedict Anderson's *Imagined Communities* in 1983 only intensified during the 1990s in the wake of Arjun Appadurai's pronouncement that "there is a peculiar new force to the imagination in social life today" (1991:197). Nevertheless, the trope still has some use, especially when thinking about the place of new forms of mass media in the lives of stay-at-homes. And it is to such boundary-breaching forms of media that I would turn in response to the question of what might be new about the present round of globalization. Thus, for example, Lila Abu-Lughod (1997) has written suggestively about how viewing televised soap operas inflects the imaginative possibilities of rural Egyptian women for participating in worlds centered in locales outside the village—in urban Egypt or "modern" Europe. The media consumption of these women, understood in the context of particular configurations of power, education, and wealth, contributes to the production of various cosmopolitanisms, various ways for claiming or disclaiming membership in translocal, even transnational, social networks—all without necessarily leaving the village (see also Schein 1998, Foster 1999b, Wardlow 1996).

The two projects of "imagined cosmopolitanism" (Schein 1998) that I will discuss involve very different sorts of institutional and individual agents. First, I want to talk about how the Urapmin, a few hundred people living in a remote area of PNG, have shaped their encounter with a millenarian version of Christianity. Second, I want to talk about how a variety of state officials and mass media personnel in both PNG and Australia contested and represented the Olympic Torch Relay which was run through Oceania en route to the 2000 Games in Sydney. I want to use these two example as vehicles for talking about the ways in which different Papua New Guineans are differently attempting to fashion themselves as subjects—to interpellate themselves—within a cosmopolitan frame of reference.

MILLENARIAN CHRISTIANITY IN URAPMIN

Urapmin social life has been described in a recent series of stimulating articles by Joel Robbins (see, e.g., 1997a, 1997b, 1998). I draw here selectively on both his original ethnography and his insightful analyses. By just about anybody's reckoning, the Urapmin fit the image of "marginality in an out-of-the-way place" (Tsing 1993). Numbering about 375 souls, they inhabit a remote part of West Sepik Province, a day's walk from the District Office; they have no airstrip and live mainly by subsistence gardening. They have been minimally engaged with the coastal world of plantation wage labor since the 1960s, and their territory is only three days' walk from the massive Ok Tedi gold mine, where many men spent short stints on construction work during the 1980s. But like the nearby Miyanmin, the Urapmin say that they live in *las Niugini* ("last New Guinea"), a phrase used to emphasize how late in time white people and Christianity came to their home, and how currently the national state ignores their needs (and better serves their neighbors).

The Urapmin nowadays look outward, toward the horizon, through the lens of millenarian Christianity. That is, they use a narrative about the rise of an evil leader, whose appearance portends the apocalypse, to orient themselves to the wider world they imagine beyond Urapmin and about which they periodically receive word. It is a narrative with exogenous origins—specifically in the nineteenth- and early twentieth-century writings of English and American dispensational premillenial Christians. In its current version, the narrative contains numerous abbreviated details about ATMs (automated teller machines), UPCs (universal product codes), and the formation of the EEC (European Economic Community)—in short, details of a world which few Urapmin know well. Nonetheless, it is this narrative that furnishes the Urapmin with the basic frame of reference for representing themselves to themselves.

Why? What makes this narrative so compelling for the Urapmin? Robbins argues that the answer must be sought more in the foreign origins of the narrative and less in its specific content, and that this answer makes sense of how Urapmin deal with a deeply felt sense of inferior racial and national identities. In fact, according to Robbins, their keen awareness of the neglect of the state has promoted among the Urapmin a strong "negative nationalism," profoundly negative feelings about being Papua New Guinean. These feelings are in turn reinforced by a sense among the Urapmin that PNG's weakness as a nation follows directly from the fact that it is a nation of black people, and that people with black skins are overwhelmingly and axiomatically inferior to those with white skins. This invidious comparison, reminiscent of Kruni's comments, whether in the form of rhetorical flourishes at public meetings or private comments among social intimates, denigrates the ability of black people to control themselves—to control their bodies, minds, and emotions. This perception of all black people/Papua New Guineans as willful and corrupt also derives support from the occasional reports that the Urapmin hear of criminal gangs (*raskols*) in the cities and dishonest politicians in the government.

Given the thrust of Urapmin racial-cum-national thinking, their Christianity, Robbins argues, is a counterdiscourse. Put simply, Christianity offers a way to transcend the limitations of perceived inferiority, to overcome these limitations by an assertion of transnational belonging; for Christianity provides Urapmin with an identity that links them to "a [white] community that they imagine is far more successful both morally and materially than their [black] national one" (Robbins 1998:113). Participation in a white religion—brought by white people from white countries—enables Urapmin to establish relations with the white Jesus and white fellow Christians, all of whom worship together on Sunday mornings in a ritual of global simultaneity.[3] Millenarian Christianity is thus the road out of negative nationalism, the promise of coming equality with whites summarized in notions of heaven as a place where, having finally mastered themselves, Urapmin will live with whites in the style of whites.

Hope has a dark side, however, as Sunday church services demonstrate. While these services performatively unite Urapmin with the global community of Christians, they also furnish powerful contexts for loud reminders about "people's lack of self control and their failure to heed God's will by avoiding sin" (Robbins 1998:115). Church services are both occasions for self-denigration and affirmations of the eventual transcendence of one's moral shortcomings. The intense promise of Urapmin millenarianism first requires Urapmin to imagine themselves intensely as sinners; that is, agency comes at a price. Paradoxically, "Urapmin point to what divides them from whites in the midst of the very ritual that most fully integrates the two groups" (Robbins 1998:115).

Robbins claims that Urapmin refer to the scraps of information that come to them from far away—information about the impending last days—as "world news." World news interpellates Urapmin as Christians, not as Papua New Guineans, and so puts Urapmin in communication with powerful members of the transnational white Christian community.[4] But world news also interpellates Urapmin as sinners, as moral deficients who must repent and prepare themselves for the time that Christ will save the worthy and only the worthy. In practice, this means that Urapmin spend lots of time confessing and cleansing themselves, sometimes to the point that they withdraw even from basic subsistence activities. Put otherwise, the price of translocal access is high—a mundane routine of self-abuse, a frequent reiteration of the view of the Urapmin Self in the eyes of the Other—superior white people from white nations. This point has been made well by Andrew Lattas, speaking of the ways in which cargo cult myths offer the Kaliai—another small group of Papua New Guineans—a narrative means of "owning the truths responsible for who they are":

> Paradoxically, the narrative re-possession of the self is realised through myths and meanings seen as not one's own but as derived from the white man's Christianity. This paradox . . . creates a divided black self whose experiences of self-alienation are often not alleviated by the fact that Christian myths are never adopted in their entirety. Indeed, in rewriting Christian myths people come to own more directly and intensely their sins. (1992: 27–28)

When I look across the contemporary PNG landscape, I see similar examples of this paradox of self-interpellation—that is, similar examples of how attempts to fashion oneself as a transnational subject exact a certain price. Or, to follow Lattas (1992) again, I see instances of how agency and constraint operate together to produce a double self: a subject that is an active agent and a subject that is subjugated; a subject with opposed positive and negative qualities; a subject as imagined by him- or herself and a subject as imagined by more powerful others. In order to explore one of these examples, and thereby to develop the idea of paradoxical self-interpellation, I turn now to a context of world news quite different from that of Urapmin Christianity.

THE OLYMPIC TORCH RELAY IN PNG

On the morning of Saturday, 27 May 2000, the prime minister of PNG, Sir Mekere Morauta, met the plane that was bringing the Olympic flame to PNG. The flame, which had traveled from its home in Greece, would be used to light the torches that 100 different runners were to carry over the course of several hours, mostly through the streets of Port Moresby. Morauta greeted the flame with a brief speech that began as follows:

> We are nearly 25 years old as an independent country, and today will go down as a day of history making. It is also a day of inspiration for us as a nation, particularly for those who have high sights as a people and particularly for the young athletes. It also marks that Papua New Guinea is no longer an island. We are caught up in the process of globalization. And I want to thank the people and government of Australia for being our friends for a long time and continuing to be our friends—for including us in its international network—a road through which this flame is traveling on its way to Australia.

Di Henry, manager of the torch relay for the Sydney Organising Committee for the Olympic Games (SOCOG), echoed Morauta's globalism with stock rhetoric about the Olympic movement:

> The Olympic Games is about being part of something bigger than yourselves. It's sharing the history, the spirit, ceremony and tradition of one of the most enduring human events of all time. The Torch Relay literally embodies this sense of sharing—from the simple connection of two individuals as the torch is passed from one to the next—to the sharing of the spirit of the relay with the people of Oceania, Australia and the entire world.

Clearly, then, there were high national stakes in the performance of the Torch Relay: the special relationship between Australia and PNG; the status of PNG as a viable nation-state twenty-five years after independence; and the place of both PNG and Australia in the inter-national order of things. Indeed, the

Torch Relay focused the efforts of Morauta to counter a growing sense among Papua New Guineans that the independent nation-state has proved itself a failure (Scott MacWilliam, personal communication, 2001; Standish 2000).

The official discourse surrounding the Torch Relay—much like Morauta and Henry's remarks—couched the event in the language of family, friendship, and sharing. But this official discourse could barely contain the struggle that unfolded during the planning stages of the Torch Relay over representations of PNG in the Australian media. This struggle, I submit, can be seen as the production of a national double self for PNG. On the one hand, PNG appeared as a nation of "fuzzy wuzzy angels," a people typified by their loyal wartime service to Australia. This identity enabled Papua New Guineans to establish a relationship with a distant ally—to assert transnational belonging—but at the price of being rendered romantically primitive—that is, innocent and childlike. On the other hand, PNG appeared as a nation of *raskols,* violent and lawless criminals—not the noble savage, but rather the plain savage. This identity recognized autonomous agency but rendered Papua New Guineans vulnerable to the same accusations of willfulness and lack of self-control that Urapmin make against themselves (and which patrol officers and other administrative agents once made), thereby putting the possibility of transnational belonging at risk. This struggle over media representations and the production of a double self crystallized around discussions of whether the Torch Relay would visit the Kokoda Trail in the mountains of the Owen Stanley Range. The infamous site of brutal World War II fighting in which Australian soldiers, with much loss of life and the assistance of local villagers, repulsed Japanese forces attacking Port Moresby, the Kokoda Trail today figures prominently in certain powerful narrations of an Australian nation.[5] Let me, then, briefly recount how the Torch Relay happened, keeping in mind Hauʻofa's most pertinent point: if you don't represent yourself, you will be represented by others.

In September 1997, Australian prime minister John Howard told South Pacific Forum leaders meeting in the Cook Islands that the Olympic Torch Relay would pass through twelve Pacific Island countries, including PNG. He pledged US$2.1 million to this end. Preliminary planning for this event by the Oceania National Olympic Committees had already been under way for some time, although details of the relay route were yet to be finalized. Consequently, when Howard's announcement was first publicized in PNG, a proposal to run the torch along the Kokoda Trail was also reported (*Post-Courier,* 22 September 1997, 25 September 1997). This proposal called for the torch to visit war memorials along the long and rugged Kokoda Trail and eventually to reach the Bomana War Cemetery outside Port Moresby.

The initial newspaper report in PNG claimed that Charlie Lynn, a Liberal Party member of the New South Wales Legislative Council, was involved in negotiating PNG's participation in the Torch Relay with the PNG Tourism Promotion Authority. Lynn was one of several Australian politicians, including the then minister for Sports and Tourism, Andrew Thomson, and National Party senator for Victoria, Julian McGauran, who, along with Returned Service League groups, strongly supported the Kokoda proposal. For Papua New Guineans, this proposal supplied a familiar script, one most recently played out in the Australia Remembers 1945–1995 program, a series of events commemorating the fiftieth anniversary of the end of World War II and highlighting Australia's involvement in the war. As Liz Reed (1999:162) has argued in her analysis of the program, Australia Remembers largely reproduced the colonialist construction of indigenous Papuans and New Guineans as "fuzzy wuzzy angels"—"as stereotypical colonial subjects who did not exercise choices in response to the war's disruption of their lives." These subjects were above all loyal subjects, "uncritical of those waging war in their country" (Reed 1999:162). In short, Papua New Guineans were being recruited once again to act a supporting role in a particular version of Australian national history, a history in which Kokoda functions as national legend. As Charlie Lynn sacramentally intoned in an address published in the conservative Christian online newspaper *Family World News,* "If Gallipoli was Australia's baptism as a nation then Kokoda was her confirmation" (April 1998).

I say "supporting role" advisedly, for not only does the script erase colonial conflict, it also assigns Papua New Guineans the permanent identity of dutiful stretcher-bearers to Australia. Hence the blatant analogy of the memorial archway erected at the Ower's Corner of the Trail, where the Torch Relay eventually visited. This archway was financed by the Kokoda Memorial Foundation, a Sydney-based nonprofit organization, and set up by sixteen Foundation volunteers who arrived in PNG with twelve tonnes of material on a Royal Australian Air Force Hercules aircraft. The archway consists of "six steel uprights to symbolise the six States of Australia with linking beams to symbolise the carriers and people of PNG" (*National,* 21 July 1999).

I should say that this sort of history making in the Pacific is not specific to PNG. Geoffrey White (1995) has written an important account of how virtually the same process of what he calls "transnational memory-making"—the construction of colonized indigenous people as loyal primitives supporting a modern war effort—unfolded around the commemoration of the fiftieth anniversary of the battle for Guadalcanal in the Solomon Islands. I should also say that these representational practices have been publicly criticized, at least in Australia. Former prime minister Paul Keating, who himself once participated vigorously in the appropriation of Kokoda for Australian nationalist purposes (see Foster 1995b), issued the following rebuke to his fellow citizens:

In the same way that Victorian England regarded the Worthy Poor, or ante-bellum American southerners felt sentimental about warm-hearted Mammies, Australians have a dangerous inclination to want our neighbors to be Little Brown Brothers—Fuzzy Wuzzy Angels who we can help and who assist us in their gratitude. (*Sydney Morning Herald,* 30 March 2000)

From the get-go, key PNG officials happily embraced both the prospect of the Torch Relay and, in particular, the Kokoda proposal. Ted Diro, then the governor of Central Province, through which the Kokoda Trail passes, and former commander of the PNG Defence Force, appreciated both the military significance of the event and its potential to aid materially his constituents living in villages along the Trail. More generally, both officials and newspaper accounts presented the relay as a rare opportunity to gain positive international media exposure and publicity for PNG. This exposure, according to Tourism Promotion Authority officials and minister for Culture and Tourism, Andrew Baing, ought to generate economic benefits. By showcasing the rich cultural diversity and natural attractions of the nation, global media exposure would draw tourists and trekkers to PNG who would provide income, especially for people living along the Kokoda Trail. PNG and the Kokoda Trail, Baing suggested, had the opportunity to be, for a short while, the focus of world attention.[6]

In April 1998, the Olympic Torch Relay Committee visited PNG to determine the route of the torch; their visit included a trip to the Kokoda Trail. Governor Diro's comments, reported in the *Post-Courier,* hinted at some of the concerns of the committee. Diro said: "As we pride ourselves in saying, this is the land of the unexpected, so do expect the unexpected." "We'll look after you," he assured the delegation. "We are not as bad as people make us to be" (*Post-Courier,* 2 April 1998). A more recent article in the Australian newspaper *The Age* was more blunt: diplomatic sources claimed that unnamed PNG officials feared that criminal gangs might try to steal the torch as it passed along the Kokoda Trail. Some places on the Trail were described as "basically lawless, no-go zones where even police don't tread" (*Age,* 31 March 2000). Here is PNG's evil twin image, the image of "fuzzy wuzzy devils" (as Suzanna Layton [1995] has referred to the image of Bougainvilleans in the PNG media during the early years of the civil war on that island). This image depicts Papua New Guineans not as once loyal subjects, now loyal allies, but rather as violent anarchists and criminals—in short, as high security risks. And indeed this issue of security shaped deliberations over the route of the relay.

No doubt there were other concerns besides security that led Kevan Gosper, senior Australian member of the International Olympic Committee (IOC), to declare in May 1998 that running the torch along the Kokoda Trail was "no longer an issue" (*Sydney Morning Herald,* 29 May 1998). Gosper pointed out that the IOC ruled out running the torch in areas unassociated with the Olympics and, furthermore, that commemorating the conflict between Australia and Japan might well offend some groups. But he also emphasized that the "physical and security risks" of Kokoda made it unacceptable, a point Phil Coles, the other Australian IOC member, had made previously (*CoolRunning Australia*, 1 June 1998). Gosper was responding to Minister Thomson's renewed suggestions to IOC president Juan Antonio Samaranch that the torch be carried between two villages on the Trail and perhaps even pass through Bougainville, the civil war–ravaged PNG province, given Australia's role in resolving the conflict there. Thomson's suggestions were reported with the claim that a favorable security assessment of the Kokoda Trail had been made to the Torch Relay organizers (*Pacific Islands Report*, 5 May 1998). Thomson also intimated that the Federal Government's funding for the Olympic Torch Relay through Oceania "might be linked with the Prime Minister's support for the torch being run along the Kokoda trail" (*CoolRunning Australia*, 1 June 2000).

In Australia, Charlie Lynn was taking SOCOG's rejection of the Kokoda proposal as treasonous proof of the indifference of the Australian people and state to the national legend of Kokoda: "They are going to take it [the Olympic Torch] to American Samoa but not across the Track . . . the subservience of our politicians has not changed" (*Family World News*, April 1998). In PNG, reaction to Gosper's comments focused on the security issue. Diro found the rejection of the Kokoda proposal to be deeply insulting to "the Australians and Papua New Guineans who gave their lives along the Trail," and John Dawanincura (now Sir John), the PNG Sports Federation secretary general, was said to be "hell-bent on getting the torch to touch base with the trail" (*National*, 17 June 1998). And, in the end, the route formally proclaimed on 25 November at the Australian High Commission chancery building in Port Moresby did make contact with the Trail—barely (*Post-Courier*, 26 November 1998). The Olympic flame was to be flown by helicopter to Ower's Corner at the southern end of the Trail, and then after a 30-minute ceremony, was to be flown to the outskirts of Port Moresby, from where it would be run into the capital city.

The security issue, however, and the troubling image of "fuzzy wuzzy devils," never fully disappeared from public view. (A major rehearsal for the relay was thus characterized in one newspaper account as "an event where PNG is expected to prove that it can host the Olympic Flame quite adequately" [*National*, 21 July 1999].) They moved quickly to the foreground after a group of Australian tourists were mugged on the Sogeri Road near the Ower's Corner on New Year's Day, 2000. This incident was widely reported in the Australian media, and its coverage prompted an angry response from Andrew Baing. A February article in *PNG Business*, "Aussie media report irks minister," quoted Baing's accusation that the Australian media (which I should make clear is easily available in PNG via radio and television broadcasts, and now the Internet), "made a feast out of an incident that should have been prevented if precautionary measures were adhered to." Baing assured SOCOG that the incident was an isolated one and not representative of the Koiari people living around Ower's Corner. Tourist Promotion Authority chairman Titus Philemon, on the other hand, directed his anger at the criminal "thugs":

> We have a lucrative tourism industry that will lure a lot of foreign exchange and lower unemployment in the country. But the acts of such ignorant tyrants only stall our efforts to develop PNG as a tourist destination on the international market. (*PNG Business,* February 2000)

Once again, PNG state officials were forced to assert an identity in response to the media images projected at them from abroad, either lashing out at the source of the image or recoiling in self-recrimination.

When the *Age* article appeared in March reporting security fears and repeating the Australian Department of Foreign Affairs advisory "not to walk the Kokoda track until further notice," Charlie Lynn again entered the media fray. His comments, reported in both PNG daily newspapers, reinvoked the image of "fuzzy wuzzy angels":

> I have trekked across the Kokoda track 22 times with Koiari guides. I have been carried off the track on a jungle stretcher after being found unconscious in a gorge. I have experienced nothing but kindness and compassion and have never felt threatened in any way.

Lynn also injected a dose of relativism into the debate by observing that "runners carrying the torch are more likely to be shot at, robbed or mugged in south-western Sydney than on the Kokoda track" (*National,* 3 April 2000; *Post-Courier,* 3 April 2000). In a tacit editorial endorsement of this observation, PNG's *The National* newspaper on the same day carried an Australian Associated Press report that vandals had again attacked a memorial in Sydney's inner western suburbs honoring the heroics of Australian soldiers on the Kokoda Trail. That memorial was officially opened about three weeks later, on ANZAC Day, with two surviving "fuzzy wuzzy angels" from the Kokoda area in attendance. Belemi Amuli, a carrier, and Clement Tanami, a scout, both aged 72, were brought to Sydney with the sponsorship of Rotary International, the Australian Government, and the government of Oro Province, PNG.

Assurances regarding the safety of the torch were being given implicitly and explicitly by PNG officials.[7] A picture of armed Mobile Squad forces appeared in the newspaper as part of the coverage of the final dress rehearsal for the relay (*National,* 16 May 2000). Australian Broadcasting Corporation radio reporter Richard Dinnen, also covering the rehearsal, noted that "Port

Moresby's reputation as a crime hot spot is well deserved. Bringing the Olympic torch through here is a risk but Sir John Dawanincura says Papua New Guineans always rise to international occasions" (19 May 2000). And as late as the morning of the event itself, Sir John was patiently telling Dinnen that "there are no great concerns or any major concerns with relation to the security of the Torch Relay. We leave to the national intelligence organisation as well as their police force to take care of day-to-day life in Port Moresby and Papua New Guinea." Dinnen then noted that Sir John had been critical of Australian media focusing on the crime risk and had urged fair and accurate reporting of the event (27 May 2000).

The focus of the Australian media on security had been given sharper definition by the actions of Sylvanus Siembo, the governor of Oro Province, through which the northern portion of the Kokoda Trail passes. About six weeks before the Torch Relay in PNG, Siembo "called upon SOCOG and the Australian government to pay A\$2 million to the Koiari people of Central Province and the Orokaiva people of Oro province for the use of the Kokoda Trail's historic name" (*National,* 17 April 2000). According to one newspaper account, the governor was responding to remarks made by Charlie Lynn, who criticized SOCOG for "the unauthorised use of the Kokoda Trail as a brand name" in commercials (*National,* 17 April 2000). Lynn, apparently upset that the commercials gave the impression that the torch would be carried along the Trail rather than merely fly in and out of Ower's Corner, called for compensation of A\$500,000 to be paid to the Koiari and Oro people. Siembo not only increased Lynn's compensation claim, but also argued that the Australian government had not assisted in bringing economic development to the Kokoda area, a fact plainly borne out by the frustrated and disgruntled locals who rob visitors to the area. In addition, Siembo brought up the issue of compensation for war service: "The famous fuzzy wuzzy angel, the late Ralph Oimbari, who is adored by Australia, and who had history books written about him, didn't receive anything better than war medals and lived in poverty in a bush material hut until his death" (*National,* 17 April 2000; for more information on Oimbari, see Reed 1999).

Compensation requests for war service by various parties, including Koiari and Orokaiva veterans themselves, are not new; they have been a continuing source of disruption to the dominant narrative of dutiful loyal subjects (see Reed 1999 for details; for a recent example of a request for "recognition," see Ricketts 2000).[8] But Siembo's demand was represented in PNG newspaper accounts as compensation for something else: the use of the name of the Kokoda Trail as a "marketing commodity" that would promote, according to Siembo, "Australia's economic and commercial gain" (*Post-Courier,* 27 April 2000; *National* 17 April 2000). By contrast, Richard Dinnen, in an Australian Broadcasting Corporation radio report, represented Siembo and his supporters as demanding A$2 million "before they'll let the Torch Relay through. A PNG version of the principle of 'user pays' " (19 May 2000). Not only did Dinnen (and subsequent Australian media reports that I've been able to track down) make no mention of Charlie Lynn, he also here apparently misunderstood Siembo's claim as something to do with local conventions of land ownership. In a later report, Dinnen clarified the matter by specifying that the claim was over the name Kokoda, but then quickly characterized the claim as "clearly opportunistic" (27 May 2000). My point is simply this: Siembo's claim has to be understood as part of the engagement by Papua New Guineans with media images originating abroad; it also has to be understood as a product of the contested engagement of Papua New Guineans with imported legal regimes over questions of copyright and intellectual property (but therein lies another essay about globalization and marginality). Representing the claims of Siembo and his supporters as either traditional or cynical grossly reduces the complexity of what "compensation" means in PNG today.

Two days before the Torch Relay, Governor Siembo announced the closure to public use of the portion of the Kokoda Trail that runs through Oro Province. The PNG newspaper *The National* reported on 1 June how *The Australian* newspaper reported on 31 May that Siembo had increased his demand to A$10 million and that "tribespeople" had cut down a cane bridge 75 km from the Trail's entrance. *The National* also paraphrased the reaction of Major-General Peter Phillips, national president of the Returned Service League: "I think it's terrible . . . sure, we had a debt from World War II, but that debt has been paid, and I can't condone this sort of thuggery." It did not, as far as I know, report *The Australian*'s statement, under the heading "Rogue Kokoda governor a drop-out," that Siembo "is a former bus driver" facing charges of misappropriating government funds (1 June 2000).

The domestic response to Siembo's demands, as registered in newspaper editorials and letters to the editor, indicate the sensitivity of at least some Papua New Guineans to how they were appearing in the eyes of others. Peter Wangi of East Sepik Province wrote that "as a Papua New Guinean I bow my head in shame, especially over how low the MP [Siembo] is stooping and dragging the world famous 'good name' of Kokoda" (*National,* 1 June 2000). A letter in the *Post-Courier* (6 June 2000) said of Siembo's demand that "it has virtually been laughed off by folk overseas." John Otage of Oro Province took the opportunity to criticize his Member's demand as one more instance of what stands in the way of PNG's development: "Siembo, in his right mind, should not be encouraging the hand-out mentality among his people while the rest of the country under the captaincy of Sir Mekere Morauta are moving towards a self-help ethos" (*Post-Courier,* 31 May 2000). And Lai Namona of Port Moresby likewise wrote, "So instead of baying for compensation all the time and looking for reward by taking short cuts, let's see some good honest hard work and some good, hard-thought, honest decision-making just for a change" (*Post-Courier,* 31 May 2000). These sorts of criticisms of the "hand-out mentality," Gewertz and Errington (1999) have noted, are increasingly common rhetorical devices by which the emerging middle class in PNG both distinguishes itself from the less affluent mass of so-called grassroots and expresses frustration with official corruption.

Much more could be said about the Trail's closure: the threats of landowners to invite logging companies into the area if their demand was not met; the tensions between Central Province Koiari and Oro Province Orokaiva over the distribution of development aid along the Trail; dissension among the Koiari themselves over the work of provincial and local level governments as well as the Koiari Development Authority. Indeed, the whole issue of whether there can in practice be such a thing as "national cultural property" in PNG merits more attention. But for now, I note only that as of July 2000, the PNG Tourism Promotion Authority was no longer promoting the Trail to the international tourists who were supposed to be drawn there as a result of the exposure gained through the Olympic Torch Relay. The Authority, according to an article in the *Age* (14 July 2000), as if in self-fulfilling prophecy, declared the area a "no-go zone" for tourists. Peter Barter, acting chairman of the Authority, was quoted as saying,

> Political leaders are trying to use this as a blackmail tactic to get development. They should be capitalizing on the name Kokoda, which is so famous, and not using it as a means to pressure governments to put more money into it. This is a bad mistake. (Sustainable Tourism Newswire Mailing List, Year 2000: Pacific: K)

As for the actual Torch Relay, it went off without a hitch. Large crowds lined the streets to witness and cheer the torchbearers—politicians, athletes, and representatives of provinces, youth groups, and PNG Olympic Team sponsors. Community groups of dancers, dressed in splendid traditional *bilas* (decoration), and choruses of schoolchildren greeted the Torch at several points along the route. National radio and EM TV, PNG's commercial television station, broadcast live updates on the Torch's progress through the city. A large crowd packed Sir John Guise Stadium to see the Torch handed to the last bearer, prime minister Sir Mekere Morauta himself, who lit the small cauldron presented to the people of PNG by SOCOG. The Monday-morning newspapers devoted several pages and triumphant editorials to the event, including generous color-photo spreads.

The very success of the event perhaps allowed some expression of the resentment that PNG officials were harboring at the narrow focus of the Australian media and even SOCOG officials on security. Much like the reactions to

Sylvanus Siembo's demands, these expressions reveal the consciousness of the gaze of others with which some Papua New Guineans went about trying to represent themselves to an international audience.[9] National Capital District Central Police commander, assistant commissioner Raphael Huafolo, called "disheartening" the calls placed by SOCOG members to high-ranking police officials seeking assurances of the torch's safety (*National,* 31 May 2000). And Sir John Dawinincura revealed in the moments after the Relay ended that "as late as 9 o'clock last night, certain Australian officials still doubted our capacity to stage this event. To the extent that the comment was made that pressure may be brought to bear on Canberra to cancel (?) our Torch Relay" (EM TV news broadcast, 28 May 2000). But these expressions only heightened the sense of national pride and accomplishment with which some commentators looked on the successfully completed Torch Relay. Thus John Eaggins, a veteran EM TV journalist, reflected on Sir John's revelation (EM TV news broadcast, 28 May 2000),

> That is indeed sad. But yesterday Port Moresby and parts of the Central Province dispelled the misconceptions—misconceptions drawn from allegations and promoted by people who have never set foot in PNG. Those who flew in the Mother Flame saw a very different group of people here—in organisation, in generousness, and in sincerity, as they came together to give the Olympic spirit significance. . . . For once adverse publicity belonged to the back pages.

For some PNG citizens—not including Siembo and his unhappy supporters—the Olympic Torch Relay was (as perhaps Prime Minister Morauta hoped) an effective, almost moving rite of national identity and unity—a demonstration that Papua New Guineans are "one people, one country, one nation" (*Post-Courier,* 31 May 2000). For other people, the highlight of the event was elsewhere, in the intense excitement surrounding the participation of Marcus Bai in the Relay. Bai, a well-known Papua New Guinean who plays winger for the Melbourne Storm, a professional Australian rugby team, missed a game to fly back home for the Relay. As the ninety-ninth torchbearer, Bai carried the flame around the oval of the Sir John Guise Stadium to thunderous applause, especially from a huge section of male supporters who seemed to be there expressly to see him. For these men, and many others, I dare say, Bai was a tangible vehicle for asserting translocality. And I suggest that he has a real, if strongly gendered, efficacy in this role, for he represented—interpellated—Papua New Guineans neither as loyal natives nor demonic *raskols.* Instead, Bai stood for PNG's participation as an equal competitor in the highest level of rugby on an international stage. Here was an imaginative form of translocal access where the steep price of a split double self need not be paid. Indeed, it is the sort of imagined cosmopolitanism that Bai provokes which perhaps explains why the biggest popular event in PNG in the year 2000 was probably not the Torch Relay or the twenty-fifth anniversary of PNG's independence. It was probably, as in years past, the State of Origin rugby series, in which Papua New Guineans, men and women, like and with Australians, fashion themselves as Maroons or Blues, supporting either the Queensland team or the New South Wales team by donning caps, T-shirts, and (in PNG) *laplaps* (sarongs) of appropriate color. Thus the fantastic enthusiasm (or enthusiastic fantasy, as Appadurai might say) with which some Tangan men—residents of the last island—will hire speedboats to take them northwest over treacherous open sea to Lihir, site of an enormous gold mine and numerous television monitors on which to view the satellite broadcast of State of Origin rugby.

CONCLUDING REMARKS

Urapmin Christianity and the Olympic Torch Relay differently illustrate "complex connectivity" (Tomlinson 1999), the linkages of Papua New Guineans to global media circuits and the ways in which Papua New Guineans produce and consume world news. Urapmin Christianity and the Olympic Torch Relay thus also illustrate different ways in which Papua New Guineans assert their agency—that is, their desire and capacity to fashion themselves as cosmopolitan subjects. My discussion therefore avoids, I hope, the pitfall identified by Sahlins and Hauᶜofa—of representing Pacific Islanders as isolated and passive.

I have also tried to suggest, however, with the loose idea of self-interpellation—and with apologies to Althusser—that the self-fashioning efforts of Papua New Guineans unfold within a certain set of discursive constraints. Papua New Guineans such as the Urapmin or Sir Mekere Morauta hail themselves as the kind of subjects that they aspire to recognize themselves as. But the terms in which they hail themselves—whether the terms of millenarian Christianity or of nationalist history—are not entirely of their own authorship. They are terms entangled in colonial histories which exert their effects in the postcolonial present. Geoff White has made this point in his discussion of the 1992 Guadalcanal commemorations, and his comments apply equally to the Olympic battle over Kokoda:

> War histories and memorials are part of a global vocabulary of nationhood —a repertoire of symbols, narratives and ritual practices readily deployed in the service of national identity projects. But in large measure the terms of this vocabulary are established by world powers who, victorious in war, use it to write chapters of their own histories. As such, transnational practices of recalling war easily override or transform other, local meanings and histories, including dissonant memories within dominant nations. This tension between the global and the local in the production of national histo-

ries is particularly acute for newly independent states who remain closely entangled, culturally, economically and politically with former colonial powers. (1995:552)

Put differently, for many Papua New Guineans, the attempt to speak in a global vocabulary and perforce to assert belonging in a transnational community often entails the creation of a double self. Admission to the transnational community first requires a recognition of the self through the eyes of a more powerful other, a recognition of the self as something less than what one aspires to be.

In making this suggestion, I do not wish to counter the optimism of Hauᶜofa and Sahlins with the pessimism of "despondency theory" (Sahlins 1999). I want only to highlight, as do Hauᶜofa and Sahlins, how the struggle over representation of and by Pacific Islanders—a struggle in which anthropologists and historians, indigenous and otherwise, are of course implicated—turns on the rapid and widespread dissemination of competing points of view. This is especially true in circumstances of globalized media flows. And although the concentration of corporate power in this area gives justifiable cause for alarm—one of the PNG newspapers that I have quoted from extensively here is owned by Rupert Murdoch's News Corporation—there are also new possibilities emerging for criticism and self-representation. In his commentary on the Torch Relay, John Eaggins thus noted that EM TV's satellite-broadcast live coverage "importantly showed countries which could pick up its signal that PNG is a great country and has people just like themselves." And journalist Kevin Pamba, in a Focus piece for *The National* newspaper (15 June 2000), reminded readers how wrong international media coverage proved to be not only in the case of the Olympic Torch Relay, but also in the case of the crisis over state-sponsored mercenary intervention in Bougainville a few years back. I was one of Pamba's readers, logged onto the Internet in Rochester, New York, considering an item of world news that originated in PNG.

CODA

The National edition of 15 June 2001 reported that after almost one year, the Kokoda Trail has been reopened to tourists. Governor Siembo and the governor of Central Province, Opa Taureka, announced a plan in which incoming tourists, both foreign and Papua New Guinean, would deposit fees in a trust account for local landowners before visiting the Trail.

The same edition of *The National* also reported that the U.S. volunteer service, the Peace Corps, was closing down its operations in PNG after twenty years for reasons of deteriorating security. In a separate report, the PNG Tourism Promotion Authority chairman, Sir Peter Barter, expressed his anger and disappointment that the Peace Corps described PNG as a "dangerous country." Sir Peter noted the adverse effect on tourist bookings of a "high security risk" travel alert posted on the Peace Corps Web site. Several days later, the head of the PNG Tourism Association registered similar sentiments: "We are of the opinion that most of these volunteers would be experiencing worse problems in their own home towns in the US if the statements attributed to US national newspapers can be believed" (*National,* 21 June 2001). On the other hand, the PNG ambassador to the United States, Sir Nagora Bogan, while acknowledging Sir Peter Barter's comments, emphasized that "it is also important for us in Papua New Guinea to take the cue and reflect where things have gone wrong. . . . No matter how hard we try to rebut the negative press vibes on Papua New Guinea in the international media, the problem of law and order will still be there" (*National,* 21 June 2001).

7

Globalization
A Soft Drink Perspective

INTRODUCTION: COMMODITY CONNECTIONS

I have appropriated the title of this chapter from Roberto C. Goizueta, the fabulously successful chairman and CEO of The Coca-Cola Company from 1981 until his death in 1997. Goizueta used the title for an address to the Town Hall of California in Los Angeles in 1989. In that address, he listed some of the reasons why companies such as his own ought to think in terms of a single global marketplace: rising disposable income around the world; the decreasing average age of the world's population outside the United States and Europe; and the increasing ease with which the world's markets could now be reached. Most importantly, Goizueta noted, contrary to critics of Coca-Colonization and American cultural hegemony, the world's consumers have taken advantage of their new-found economic and political freedom to pick and choose the products that *they* find most appealing. In so doing, Goizueta suggested, consumers themselves have internationalized certain products— above all, *Coca-Cola.*

Goizueta's point was in many ways my point—namely, "that people around the world are today connected to each other by brand-name consumer products as much as by anything else" (1989:361). But whereas I regard the nature and significance of these connections as an open question, Goizueta already saw them as plain evidence of what Theodore Levitt—an influential Harvard business professor—described as the tendency "towards global commonality and modernity, cosmopolizing preferences and homogenizing consumption" (quoted in Goizueta 1989:361). Levitt argued that such "homogenizing consumption," driven largely by the globalization of media, produces in effect "heteroconsumers": "People who've become increasingly alike and indistinct from one another, and yet have simultaneously varied and multiple preferences" (1988:8). To Roberto Goizueta (1989:361), this argument made good sense of the big brute fact with which he impressed his Town Hall audience:

Nearly half of all soft drinks sold around the world are our products. 560 million times a day, consumers in more than 160 countries refresh themselves with Coca-Cola, diet Coke, Fanta, Sprite and our other soft drinks. No other company sells half as much.

Such was, in part, Roberto Goizueta's soft drink perspective on globalization. Here is another perspective, that of Elizabeth Solomon (a pseudonym), a 54-year-old Papua New Guinean, a former teacher at a Christian mission-run elementary school. Solomon grew up and now lives again in rural Morobe Province. But she came in April of 1997 to Port Moresby, the capital city of Papua New Guinea (PNG), to provide day care for her daughter and son-in-law's children. Participating in a pilot survey on soft drink consumption that I organized, Elizabeth Solomon reported that

> I encourage my grandchildren, 5 and 4 years old, to drink fruit juice. I don't think Coke and Pepsi are good for the children's health. It contains acid which is not good.
> I'm an ALANON member and I think that Coke gives out bubbles like that of beer (SP) [South Pacific brand lager]. So, I think it contains some alcoholic acid. . . . If I list all the soft drinks, I would put Coke last [among her favorites]. I do not like Coke because Coke makes you burp like beer the men drink. Coke has the same colour as beer and some spirits . . . Coke is associated with men, and men are usually drunkards.[1]

For Elizabeth Solomon, thinking about soft drinks is bound up with thinking about the uncertain future of her family and former students. Asked what came to mind when she heard the word "*Pepsi*," she replied,

> I usually imagine how my children are getting on. This is especially for young people who will get hooked with white man's culture and forget what and how I taught them to be. Simply—how my children will survive trying to imitate a white man's culture.

No one will confuse Elizabeth Solomon's soft drink perspective on globalization with that of Roberto Goizueta, despite a shared concern with the convergence of tastes among the world's young consumers. What strikes me, however, is not so much the difference in perspective as its presupposition: both Roberto Goizueta in Atlanta or Los Angeles and Elizabeth Solomon in Port Moresby or Morobe occupy positions within the same commodityscape. That is, these two individuals are indeed connected by a brand-name consumer commodity, though each imagines or envisions both these connections and the commodity itself in radically discordant ways. Their different locations within the global soft drink commodityscape clearly afford different perspectives. My two main questions follow accordingly: what conceptual tools are available to us as anthropologists in trying to trace and understand multiple perspectives within a global commodityscape? And how are we to accomplish the task as ethnographers in the field?

AN ANTHROPOLOGY OF GLOBALIZATION: NETWORKS, PERSPECTIVES, HORIZONS, CHAINS

I will return to the methodological question in my conclusion. For now, I want to address the question about conceptual tools—even if only in brief and schematic fashion—by taking up some of the suggestions put forward in several publications by Ulf Hannerz (e.g., 1987, 1989, 1992a, 1992b). I single out Hannerz's work because it resolutely refuses to reinvent the wheel and instead encourages us to find a useful past in the history of social and cultural anthropology. It is from this history that Hannerz has recovered the concepts of ecumenes and networks. Hannerz (1989:215), heeding Igor Kopytoff, advises us to think of the world as an ecumene—"a region of persistent cultural interaction and exchange." Cultural interaction and exchange in the global ecumene are loosely structured by center–periphery relations; that is, the flow of meanings and meaningful forms enabled by, for example, mass media and labor migration is asymmetrical in both scale and direction. "Global culture" is therefore, contrary to Levitt, hardly uniform and homogeneous; it is necessarily diverse and heterogeneous inasmuch as it is distributed differentially through asymmetrically organized channels of flow.

Hannerz has suggested, furthermore, that we use the metaphor of networks to grasp intellectually the processes of cultural flow within the global ecumene—in other words, that we create a sociology of diffusion by tracing the various chains of relationships—or networks—through which ideas and images (meaning) circulate. These networks include not only enduring personal relationships sustained through new non–mass media technologies such as fax and E-mail, but also impersonal encounters with mass media, commoditized popular culture, and educational systems, and fleeting interactions with sundry transnationally mobile individuals—tourists, migrants, and even anthropologists. We might thus think of the global ecumene as either a single large and complex network or, perhaps, a network of networks. The latter possibility makes it clearer how the differential distribution of culture in the global ecumene takes shape as lived experience. I quote Hannerz at length on this point:

> it becomes increasingly obvious that the individual's perspective, the individual's share or version of socially organized meaning, is in large part a product of his network experience, and that the greater variety and the less density there is in ego-centred networks, the more different perspectives will be.... Individuals' perspectives, then, come to consist of the concep-

tions which they have come to construct or appropriate for their own use, as it were, but also of their perspectives on other perspectives—*their approximate mappings of other people's meanings.* (1989:42–43, my emphasis)

Under such conditions, people—like Roberto Goizueta—are aware of others —like Elizabeth Solomon—whose perspectives they do not share, and know they do not share. This is one way to describe the phenomenon of relativized consciousness frequently associated with globalization.

Hannerz's invocation of ecumenes and networks has the virtue of uncoupling culture from bounded territories—locales, regions, nation-states— such that we must recognize the horizons of people in, say, a provincial Nigerian town to include London and Mecca as well as Lagos and "the bush." In this regard, Hannerz's formulation of the global ecumene resonates with George Marcus's (1995) call for the deployment of tracking strategies in constructing multisited ethnographies. For example, although Hannerz suggests that the networks drawing people into a more globalized existence may vary almost randomly within a local population, he also suggests that such variation is ordered by center–periphery relations. Accordingly, he invites us "to trace how culture makes its way through network links of different kinds" from centers to peripheries, and sometimes back again. This strategy has the virtue of drawing our attention to the "creolized and creolizing cultural forms which grow between center and periphery" (1989:213). It also has the virtue of providing a framework for specific strategies—devised for other purposes —that document the social life of things in the capitalist world system, strategies such as tracking the circulation of material objects in and out of various contexts as gift, commodity, or resource (Appadurai 1986), or such as identifying the links in a commodity chain that bring together land, labor, and machinery in the production of some consumable good (Wallerstein 1991, cited in Marcus 1995; Haugerud et al. 2000).

Daniel Miller (1997) has published an ethnographic study of a commodity chain that engages Hannerz's concern with the flow of meaning through network links of different kinds; for Miller attends to the institutional contexts in which commodities such as soft drinks are produced as complex symbolic formations—that is, given complex symbolic attributes through processes such as branding, marketing, advertising, and retailing. The method here is one of self-conscious fetishism—a sustained focus on commodities rather than on people or, more precisely, a focus on people—marketing managers, advertising agents, diverse consumers—whose own orientation is to commodities as meaningful forms.

Miller's overall aim is to expose the articulations among the production, distribution, and consumption of specific commodities within a single site— Trinidad—but he recognizes the obvious applicability of his approach to multisited research on the transnationally extensive commodity chains characteristic of contemporary capitalism. Miller's approach strikes me as particularly suited to the study of marketing intensive industries such as soft drinks and to commodity chains that move images and meanings—that is, brands—rather than component parts or outsourced finished products over long distances. Miller, however, also recognizes the prematurity of such multisited research, given how much ethnographic work needs to be done on capitalism as a practice subject to local and regional difference. This chapter, then, is admittedly premature. It is a first attempt to delineate the perspectives of people located differently in a transnational soft drink commodityscape: corporate executives attempting to enlarge their business and increase their profits; advertising agents plotting global marketing strategies for local execution; university students and office workers negotiating soft drinks within their own changing routines of consumption.

In one sense, these perspectives open out from locations that can be aligned with specific geographical locales: Atlanta, headquarters of The Coca-Cola Company; New York, headquarters of advertising agencies that coordinate global marketing campaigns; and Port Moresby, where the consumers with whom I am most immediately concerned reside. In another sense, these perspectives mark locations that can be identified with specific economic functions in the commodity chain that connects people like Roberto Goizueta at one end and Elizabeth Solomon's grandchildren at the other. These functions include the strategic planning of soft drink corporations, as well as the consumption and marketing of soft drinks. In any case, it is neither necessary nor advisable to elide these two senses of location—nor, of course, to restrict our understanding of "location" to either sense. Indeed, by making geographical locale only one possible sense of location, we broach the question of what constitutes a fieldsite and hence what constitutes fieldwork.

I will begin, then, with a discussion of the perspectives of some people engaged in strategic planning. I then move on to discuss perspectives of a few of the many people who consume and market soft drinks. In each case—planning, consuming, marketing—I am concerned to demonstrate how people produce what Hannerz called "approximate mappings of other people's meanings"— that is, how a network of perspectives on perspectives takes shape around the movement of a particular category of global commodities: branded soft drinks, or more precisely, *Coca-Cola* and *Pepsi-Cola*.

STRATEGIC PLANNING: IMAGINED MARKETS (OR INTIMATIONS OF INFINITY)

In May 1991, Coca-Cola Amatil (CCA) announced the signing of contracts for the acquisition of the two major *Coca-Cola* bottling operations in

PNG at a price of 27 million kina (A$36 million). The operations were acquired from Steamships Trading Company, which in 1969 became the first "local" company licensed to market *Coca-Cola* in what was then the Trust Territory of Papua and New Guinea. Fifty-one percent owned by the U.S.-based Coca-Cola Company, CCA was at the time Australia's dominant producer of soft drinks and snack foods, with market shares of 60 percent in each of these categories.[2] It was also, until its division in 1998, The Coca-Cola Company's second largest "anchor bottler."[3] CCA operates throughout Asia as well as elsewhere in the South Pacific (the 1998 division assigned CCA's European operations to a new bottler, Coca-Cola Beverages, based in Vienna [*New York Times,* 5 February 1998]). At the time of CCA's purchase, one generous estimate attributed 56 percent of the PNG share market to *Coca-Cola* and 44 percent to *Pepsi-Cola*; by 1997, CCA claimed two-thirds of PNG's entire soft drink market (*Post-Courier,* 8 August 1997).

Until recently, the *Pepsi* franchise in PNG belonged to South Pacific Holdings Ltd., which also owns South Pacific Brewery, the one and only producer of beer in PNG.[4] South Pacific Holdings is itself owned by Singapore-based Asia-Pacific Breweries Ltd., a joint venture of the Heineken NV international brewing group.

One might reasonably ask just what sort of potential such transnational corporations see in the PNG market for soft drinks. (PNG has a population of about 4.6 million, of which CCA estimates that it services 3.8 million [CCA Annual Report 1999].) Soft drink executives have a compelling and distinctive way of answering this question. When, for example, CCA acquired the bottling operations in PNG, its director of overseas operations, Russel Phillips, said, "The acquisition presents us with a further opportunity to grow our bottling business. On a per capita basis, consumption of soft drinks in PNG is just 10 litres per year, compared with Australia's per capita consumption of 98 litres per annum" (CCA news release, 21 May 1991). The implication, then, is that there is a potential 88 liters (at least) of *Coca-Cola* consumption per person per year that has not been tapped in PNG. Indeed, CCA executives seemed to imagine all the markets that it was moving into in 1991 in much the same way. Consider, for example, the comments of Dean Wills, who in 1991 was chairman and managing director of CCA, regarding joint ventures that enabled CCA to capture 40 percent of Indonesia's soft drink market: "While the per capita consumption of Indonesia . . . is a far cry from Australia, it has a 7 per cent growth in gross domestic product and, with a population of 180 million, that represents excellent opportunities during the next few years" (*Australian,* 22 May 1991). From Wills's point of view, the consumption gap between Indonesia and Australia—much like the gap between Australia and Eastern European countries where CCA has operated—would inevitably close with increasing "economic and political sophistication": "When countries emerge from such controlled backgrounds they start getting the taste for all things Western and while the cars and houses come much later, a can of Coke is a cheaper, more easily identifiable and accessible status symbol" (*Australian*, 22 May 1991). This is a conceit—an approximate mapping of other people's meanings—that I'll return to consider presently.

It is not so surprising to learn that Roberto Goizueta, doing the math of per-capita consumption and total population, imagined Indonesia as "soft drink paradise"—"200 million people, nearly all of them Muslims forbidden to drink alcohol," exclaimed one *Business Week* article ("Coke pours into Asia," 28 October 1996). It is perhaps more surprising to learn that Goizueta applied the same calculations to the U.S. market. Consider the following anecdote that Goizueta used to open his 1996 address to share owners (posted on The Coca-Cola Company's home page on the World Wide Web):

> The other day, after I spoke to a group of engineering students at my alma mater, one of them asked me a simple question: "Which area of the world offers The Coca-Cola Company its greatest growth potential?"
>
> Without hesitation, I replied, "Southern California."
>
> They all laughed, thinking I was trying to be funny.
>
> So to drive home the point, I shared with them one very interesting fact. The per capita consumption of bottles and cans of *Coca-Cola* is actually lower in the southern part of California than it is in Hungary, a country which is one of our supposedly "emerging" markets, while the U.S. is supposedly a "matured" soft drink market.
>
> The students went silent for several seconds. I'm sure they had never before pondered our virtually *infinite* opportunity for growth.

The universe of his company's business as imagined by Goizueta is limitless—at least for all practical purposes. And it was this vision of potential infinite growth that drove the company's massive capital investments in new Asian markets, including the relatively small market in PNG. But even with this investment, The Coca-Cola Company is merely getting started on a very long road, for as Goizueta informed his fellow share owners,

> we have become increasingly mindful of one undeniable fact—the average human body requires at least 64 ounces of liquid every day just to survive, and our beverages account for not even 2 of those ounces. For every person on this planet, consuming at least 64 ounces is not an option; but choosing where those ounces come from is.

The Coca-Cola Company, Goizueta assured his fellow share owners, is "resolutely focused on going after the other 62."

It would be wrong to dismiss Goizueta's pronouncement as simply the overblown rhetoric of annual corporate reporting. *U.S. News and World Report* could point out that in 1985, Americans drank more soft drinks than tap water—43 gallons per person as opposed to 39 gallons (cited in Clairmonte and Cavanagh 1988:137). Indeed, per capita consumption of tap water in the United States dropped from 269 liters in 1965 to 178 liters in 1982 (Clairmonte and Cavanagh 1988:27). Clairmonte and Cavanagh, in their book *Merchants of Drink: Transnational Control of World Beverages,* claim that "an unalterable feature of corporate beverage strategy is and will remain the sustained campaign against tap water," the only beverage still overwhelmingly within the public sector (1988:138). Hence, they imagine the potentially infinite growth in soft drink markets in terms that Goizueta would no doubt have eschewed:

> Whereas tap water constitutes only a quarter of US liquid consumption, it still embraces more than four-fifths in the periphery. This gigantic economic divide between developed and developing world highlights the vast potential market that is up for grabs by the TBCs [Transnational Beverage Corporations]. (1988:27)

From this perspective, the global expansion of soft drink consumption is a war against tap water—or, more accurately, the transformation of tap water from an end product to an ingredient, a "wholly subordinated input" into higher-priced commercial beverage product lines. From this perspective, then, it comes as little surprise that in 1999, it was not Americans who led the world in annual per capita consumption of The Coca-Cola Company's products, but rather Mexicans—at 431 8-oz servings per person (The Coca-Cola Company Annual Report 1999).[5]

CONSUMPTION: NEW COMMODITIES FOR NEW CONTEXTS?

If soft drink executives imagine people like Elizabeth Solomon as vessels to be filled with more and more ounces of cola, we might well ask what relationship their imagination bears to actual social behavior. When CCA acquired the bottling operations in PNG, a spokesman explained that the reason behind the low consumption rate in PNG (10 liters per capita) "had been nonavailability more than anything" (*Herald-Sun,* 21 May 1991). In fact, CCA fully expected to return a profit in its first year of business in PNG. In other words, it was taken for granted that the desire for *Coca-Cola* was already in place; what was missing were the conditions that put *Coca-Cola* "always within an arm's length of desire," as an old piece of company wisdom advised.

Here, manifestly, is another conceit. For anthropologists, of course, desire for *Coca-Cola* can hardly be taken for granted, perhaps especially in settings such as PNG, where experiences of commodity consumption are relatively new and uneven. Such desire must rather be the object of historical ethnography, an historical ethnography that locates changing patterns of consumption in the context of both the specific strategies of TBCs and the more general encounter of Melanesians with modernity. While that task is beyond the scope of this chapter, it is possible to address briefly the related question posed by Sidney Mintz (1996:17): "How does a society learn to consume food [including beverages] differently: to eat more food (or less), to eat different food, differently prepared, in different contexts; to revise or modify the social (and perhaps even the nutritive) purpose of the consumption itself?" Or, more particularly, what *does* soft drink consumption in contemporary PNG look like?

I should say at the outset that Papua New Guineans are apparently consuming more and more soft drinks, at least in aggregate. In its 1995 annual report, CCA described PNG as "a great success story," noting a 13 percent increase in sales volume and 16 percent increase in trading profit. Halfway through 1996, CCA reported itself extremely pleased with "strong double digit growth in sales volume" and a 20 percent increase in trading profit, which doubled the following year. Similarly, SP Holdings announced in April 1997 a before-tax profit of 25 million kina (approximately US$18.5 million). The company's general manager, Tan Ang Meng, explained the 8.9 percent increase in profits over the previous year despite the liquor bans declared in many provinces of the country: "Our result of the last financial year was affected by the ongoing prohibition in the Highlands. However, growth in soft drinks is very encouraging and managed to offset the downturn in beer sales" (*National*, 1 April 1997). In a very short period of time, it seems, Papua New Guineans—aside from the Elizabeth Solomons of the country—have learned to drink soft drinks in increasing quantities. Although it is difficult to measure this increase accurately, urban household surveys carried out in the 1980s suggest that expenditures on soft drinks already then accounted for as much as 7% of all food and beverage purchases (Gibson 1995).

My own survey suggests that growth in soft drink consumption accompanies the proliferation of new contexts for food and beverage consumption outside the home. That is, soft drink consumption is part of a whole range of social transformations that involve the emergence of scheduled consumption contexts associated with wage labor—contexts such as "lunch" or "work break." More generally, soft drink consumption is one dimension of a new urban lifestyle that routinizes the consumption of food outside the home—in restaurants or snack bars, at school or in the marketplace. Participants in my pilot survey infrequently indicated that they drank soft drinks at home, where many said they preferred to drink water. Instead, soft drink consumption occurred in the context of shopping, lunching with fellow workers or students, "spinning" (pleasure outings), or attending sporting events. Most soft drink consumption therefore occurred in the presence of others—with others also consuming—as a manifestly extra-household social activity.

None of this will come as unexpected to readers of Mintz's 1976 book,

Sweetness and Power. Mintz described therein how the eating habits of the working poor in eighteenth- and nineteenth-century Britain were transformed by increasing sucrose consumption (especially in the form of stimulating beverages such as sweetened tea). Much of his description seems directly pertinent to contemporary soft drink consumption in PNG, including the way in which soft drink consumption is often seen as the natural complement of sugary fast food consumption (the equivalent of an English worker's jam on bread). Thus the justification given by one 25-year-old woman, a secretary at Telikom, for her preference for *Coke*: "Coke is more preferable because it helps to dissolve unnecessary fat in the body. After taking greasy and fatty food, I take Coke, coz it helps break down the fat. That's why I like Coke [more] than other drinks. Other drinks are too soft for me." Or, as another 26-year-old woman answered the question of when she usually drank soft drinks: "When I am having Big Rooster"—Port Moresby's answer to Kentucky Fried Chicken. No wonder, then, that CCA's chairman could proclaim about its new Asian markets: "The potential in the region is enormous and when we have established our beverage division, snack food will undoubtedly follow" (*Australian*, 22 May 1991).

I must point out that many Papua New Guineans involved in the survey emphasized that they consumed soft drinks in contexts in which no other choice was available to them: away from home in public spaces devoid of drinking fountains. But much like the people Mintz wrote about, many Papua New Guineans explicitly described soft drinks as a cheap food substitute: "I can just drink Coke and go without food for lunch," or "It makes me feel full when I'm hungry." There is no denying, then, that certain material constraints are shaping the emerging patterns of soft drink consumption in Port Moresby. Yet at the same time, there is no denying that urban Papua New Guineans are using soft drinks as material supports for the creation and recreation of social intimacy (especially intimacy among men). Responses to my question "When was the very last time you had a soft drink?" often took the form of this one from a 42-year-old unemployed man from Bundi:

> The last time I had a soft drink was 2 days ago. I drank a bottle of Coke. I drank it at the bus stop at 6 mile while waiting for the bus. I was standing with one of the guys whom I used to work with. He had bet on a winning horse. So, when he saw me, he went into the shop, bought two bottles of Coke, and came and gave one to me.

Or this one, from a 20-year-old anthropology student from Koroba, in the southern highlands:

> The last time I had a soft drink was on 27-07-97 [3 days earlier]. I had a Coke. It was for lunch. At about 1 P.M. at Erima [a settlement in Port

Moresby]. I wasn't alone. I was with 2 other boys who bought me the Coke and others attending a funeral were there as well. Actually, the guys bought the Cokes. I had half of each bottle.

I had half of each bottle. Similar instances of sharing soft drinks, as well as buying them for others, were common enough that some survey participants explained why they acted otherwise. Thus, an anthropology student from Manus reported that she had yesterday drunk one of the newly introduced 500-mL bottles of *Coke* at lunchtime: "I had it all and I was definitely alone coz I didn't want to share." And a 23-year-old arts student from Madang confessed that

> When I'm drinking Coke, I hate to share my drink, because I always have this fear of my colleague/friend could use it to make *puripuri* [sorcery]. If a friend buys a drink, I buy it for him if I have enough. Otherwise I say, sorry I can't share my drink. I'm thirsty. Really, [inside of me] I'm scared to death of *puripuri*.

Here, then, is the Melanesia we all know and love: land of compulsive reciprocity and body fluid transfers. Or, put differently, here is the Melanesia in which foreign imports are revalued in terms of domestic agendas, where within the material constraints of budgets stretched by the cheap calories of a *Coke*, other projects are accomplished. But in an important way, this is not the Melanesia we all know and love; for the sociocultural contexts in which urban Papua New Guineans appropriate a foreign import such as *Coke* or *Pepsi* differ from the contexts in which Papua New Guinean villagers appropriate such imports. In Port Moresby, the context in which *Coke* is consumed is often, like the *Coke* itself—indeed, like the very space of the city (or of a rural plantation)—an artifact of the spread of capitalism and its temporal routines: "lunch" or "snack time" or "weekend." In other words, the orientation of consumers to the commodity in Port Moresby is likely to differ from orientations held by other differently located consumers in PNG; for these orientations or perspectives emerge at specific points in the networked flow of meanings between center and periphery.

Let me elaborate by moving quickly to another point in the network. Consider figure 7.1, a picture of a Huli woman from the Southern Highlands eating a can of rice. According to Holly Wardlow, Huli women fill empty soft drink cans with rice and water, stop up the opening, and carry the cans when visiting other women. The cans are thrown on a fire and the rice cooks, providing a quick meal while away from home. Thus Huli women have analogically extended a cooking technique once widespread in island Melanesia, but rarer since the displacement of bamboo tubes by aluminum pots; they have appropriated the can for use within a familiar social context. That is, and more

Figure 7.1. Agnes, a Huli woman from the Southern Highlands, poses with a can of cooked rice.
Photo by Holly Wardlow. Reproduced with permission.

generally, the *Coke* can is appropriated into a set of cultural dispositions and practices that preexist and even shape the spread of capitalism. If Mintz has his moment in Port Moresby, then Sahlins has his in Huliland, for there foreign imports are seen to be put in the service of a locally defined sociality—an instance of what Sahlins (1992) calls "develop-man"—not development—in order to highlight its positive human potential.

I can make my point clearer with someone else's ethnography. Figure 7.2 is a picture of Kaipel Ka, a sign painter who lives in the Wahgi Valley of Highlands PNG, standing next to a war shield that he decorated with the handsome logo of South Pacific Export Lager and the more modest logo of SP Bia (South Pacific Beer), the domestic brew. A similar image appears in Michael O'Hanlon's remarkable book *Paradise: Portraying the New Guinea Highlands* (1993), a catalog published by the British Museum in conjunction with an exhibit that O'Hanlon curated. The caption next to that image says, "Kaipel Ka sometimes fought alongside his maternal kin and so decorated his own shield with the South Pacific beer logo otherwise used on theirs" (O'Hanlon 1993, plate 14).

Kaipel Ka's shield reminds us how juxtapositions we regard as unexpected point to another reality, another set of cultural principles at work. Here is O'Hanlon's (1993:68) account:

Figure 7.2. Kaipel Ka posing with a war shield that he painted.
Photo by Michael O'Hanlon (see O'Hanlon 1995). Reproduced with permission.

Kaipel's own explanation of his use of the SP design was that he had been asked by senior men to incorporate a representation of a beer bottle on the shield, to make the point that "it was beer alone which had precipitated this fighting." (The war followed the breakdown of negotiations for compensation after an inebriated Senglap [clan] man had fallen from a Dange [clan]-owned vehicle.) Rather than including a picture of a beer bottle, Kaipel decided instead to make the point by using the SP design as a whole.

O'Hanlon continues with his own exegesis:

At one level, then, this design parallels those that express regret. At another level, there is also something appropriate in the use of beer. Beer drinking is often a "group" matter, just as warfare is. As Marie Reay observed.... "Clansmen fight together; they also drink together."

Thus O'Hanlon makes the point that the shield design signals another reality, a set of alternative principles for thinking about and representing corporate associations.

My point is that this "other reality" is the sociocultural context into which both the general activity of beer drinking and the specific image of the SP Export logo are appropriated. Neither the activity nor the image here—at this point in the network flow—comprise intrinsic features of wholly new contexts; they are instead adapted to familiar and prior contexts of warfare, as close inspection of Kaipel Ka's design suggests. The original logo of SP Export features only one bird of paradise; Kaipel Ka's shield depicts two. O'Hanlon again:

> "Raggiana bird of paradise war" is the term for the most bitter type of conflict. The fact that a pair of birds . . . was represented . . . was also suggestive, since pairing is a characteristic Wahgi practice, and the groups who fight "Raggiana bird of paradise" war are listed in pairs. (O'Hanlon 1993:69)

Thus, one of O'Hanlon's friends interpreted the shield in intelligible local terms as a warning that the war between Senglap and Dange clans was in danger of escalating to bird of paradise proportions.

MARKETING: INFINITE DESIRE

It's unlikely that the use to which Huli women put *Coke* cans is what CCA officials have in mind when they talk about "the development of a soft drink culture." Such development requires "establishing the basics of acceptability," and this, they imagine, is achieved through an effort called "community based marketing": "a host of grassroots promotional and marketing activities including market impact teams . . . , sampling, door to door selling, special events sponsorships such as regional fairs, sporting and music sponsorships and consumer promotions and contests" (CCA Annual Report 1994). It is through sponsorships in particular that CCA discharges its "responsibility as a good corporate citizen." As the CEO of operations put it: "We strive not only to earn the respect of customers and consumers, but of governments, authorities and communities where we operate. That is, we involve ourselves in a range of activities over and above those dictated by our operational imperatives" (CCA Annual Report 1995).

In PNG, these activities are anything but ancillary to CCA's operational imperatives, for they are among the principal means through which new soft drink consumers are made. Both SP Holdings and CCA, for example, regularly and with great publicity stage promotions in the elementary schools of Port Moresby, distributing T-shirts or athletic equipment emblazoned with logos. In 1996, the Australian pop group Hot Hot Hot—a sort of Spice Girls act—toured primary schools promoting both *Fanta* Orange and a "say no to drugs" message—a deeply ironic message given Mintz's history of the narcotic effects of sugar in making the English working class work. Community-based marketing, moreover, creates more new contexts for soft drink consumption. That is, CCA and SP Holdings are official sponsors of the emergent urban public culture with which soft drink consumption is widely associated in PNG. Through their sponsorship of major sporting events and holiday celebrations such as Remembrance Day, soft drink companies insinuate their products into the life of the nation, effecting thereby a convergence between consumption and citizenship (see chapters 3 and 5). Through their sponsorship of annual cultural events, soft drink corporations identify their products not only with the multicultural nation(-state), but also with modernity itself, for it is in this context that soft drinks are represented (not to mention sold and consumed) as the modern complements of indigenous tradition. That is, it is in these contexts that soft drink companies bring their unambiguously foreign products within the same frame as products defined, by contrast, as unambiguously domestic.

This move is not, however, the same as that effected by the Huli women or by Kaipel Ka; for it is a move that remains forever incomplete. It generates a composite of discrete heterogeneous elements—a juxtaposition, not a blending—as figure 2.6 illustrates. Here, then, is a projection of Papua New Guineans—a mapping of other people's meanings—as a new generation of people whose collective identity derives from the ever present, infinitely repeatable encounter of tradition and modernity. The national Us that crystallizes from this imagery is a composite of past and present, indigenous and exogenous, tradition and modernity. The nation of PNG embodies, now and forever, an encounter between radically heterogeneous elements—much like, as William Pietz would remind us, a fetish (see chapter 2).

The reconciliation of the foreign with the domestic is one of the main concerns of advertising agents and marketing managers charged with the responsibility of selling global commodities like *Coke* and *Pepsi*. What this means, in the words of Marcio Moreira—former creative team leader and director for Coca-Cola International at McCann Erickson in New York—is that "it's more important to communicate a common viewpoint than to use a common execution" (O'Barr 1989:2). That is, Moriera strove to produce *Coca-Cola* advertising with a "common idiom," but not necessarily a "common look," let alone a common advertisement for all of *Coca-Cola*'s different markets. Locally made executions of a single global marketing campaign are intended to produce a sense of familiarity such that one would recognize a *Coke* commercial in Colombia and a *Coke* commercial in Holland as variations on a single theme. As Moreira put it, "Becoming part of people's lives, belonging, is the name of the game" (O'Barr 1989:5).

What does such a strategy look like in contemporary PNG? In answering this question, we meet again the twin conceits of soft drink executives operating in the Asia–Pacific region—namely, that soft drinks are affordable items of Western provenance, and that the desire for "*all* things Western" is itself to be taken for granted. Now this first conceit has some merit to it; for as Sidney Mintz (personal communication, 1997) notes, products like *Coke* and *Pepsi* are notably "democratic" in character; that is, they combine recognizability as specific trademarked forms of sweetness with relatively low price (at least until the devaluation and collapse of the PNG kina). Andy Warhol was, somewhat earlier, also keenly aware of this aspect of consumer democracy:

> What's great about this country is that America started the tradition where the richest consumers buy essentially the same things as the poorest. You can be watching TV and see Coca-Cola, and you can know that the President drinks Coke, Liz Taylor drinks Coke, and just think, you can drink Coke, too. A Coke is a Coke and no amount of money can get you a better Coke than the one the bum on the corner is drinking. (1975:100–101)

The second conceit, however, has dubious merit, despite its infiltration of Melanesianist anthropology through the post–World War II fascination with cargo cults. As Lamont Lindstrom suggests, writings about cargo cults are allegories that effectively normalize a definition of desire as unremitting and never fully satisfied—the sort of desire appropriate to Goizueta's vision of infinity (see chapter 2). This normalization subverts the manifest effect of cargo writings in depicting cargo cultists as radically alien. It is, in fact, just the opposite: "we are all cargo cultists in that we wait eternally for an end to desire that will not end. The Melanesian cultist merely reads our lines" (Lindstrom 1995:56). And today, these lines include "*Olgeta Taim Coca-Cola*" ("Always *Coca-Cola*" in Tok Pisin).

Let us consider two television commercials, one for *Pepsi* and one for *Coke*, that both ran in PNG in 1997 (the *Coke* ad was still running three years later). These commercials project different but related versions of modern materialism in which the identity of individuals (singular or collective) is constructed through the consumption of trademarked or brand-name commodities. The commercial for *Coke* was filmed in PNG but produced by personnel from the Sydney office of McCann Erickson's global network of advertising agencies. The commercial for *Pepsi* was filmed in Queensland and produced by Savi (now HRD-Savi), a PNG-based advertising agency that handles advertising for global commodities such as Shell gasoline and Benson and Hedges cigarettes. It ran as a "locally" executed version of a global *Pepsi* campaign known as "Change the Script" (forerunner to "Generation Next")—a campaign theme which the *Pepsi* marketing manager in PNG thought necessary to revise on the assumption that not many Papua New Guineans would be familiar with the concept of "the Script." Both 30-second commercials were made by non–Papua New Guinean creative directors in accordance with the client's brief and global marketing strategy; both are slickly produced.

First the *Pepsi* commercial (see figure 5.5):

Pepsi Ad. To a pulsating bass sound, a red balloon rises in the air. A young man pops the balloon and many blue balloons rise up instead. The lyrics chime: "Do what you wanna do. Be what you wanna be. *Pepsi.* Break free." A series of images follows quickly: A young woman's smiling red lipstick changes to blue. Youthful rollerbladers swirl in a discolike blue haze. The camera pans over a blue can of *Pepsi-Cola*, its surface beaded with small drops of sweat. A platform diver flips languorously into a pool. The lyrics repeat, more passionately. A man and women walk across a street; their formal attire (long-sleeve white shirt and tie for the man; a miniskirt suit for the woman) change into leisurewear, and they begin to dance in the crosswalk. The camera returns to the can of *Pepsi*. A can of blue paint splatters against a red brick wall. Red paint oozing down some stairs turns blue. A woman paints over her red fingernails with blue polish. Red balls bouncing down concrete steps turn blue; a young man in a blue T-shirt and sunglasses lounges on the steps as the balls bounce by. The camera returns again to the can of *Pepsi*, which then rolls forward toward the viewer. "Break Free," written in white script, appears across the television screen.

The lyrics of the jingle accompanying this ad explicitly peddle consumer agency, a hallmark promise of modern materialism: "Do what you wanna do. Be what you wanna be." This invitation to exercise individual self-determination exhorts a break from convention—not only the conventional red of rival *Coca-Cola*, but the conventions of work clothes and perhaps even work itself. All the images evoke youthful leisure and play, including (fantastically, for PNG) rollerblading and platform diving. Here, then, we encounter one of the themes of cargoism—Our projection on to Them of a deep longing for a pre-Fall world without work (see chapter 2). In addition, the appearance of women's painted lips and nails tinge the ads with sexual highlights. The slogan "Break Free" thus suggests the emancipatory and eroticized potential of self-construction through commodity consumption. All this is very much in keeping with a marketing theory of global youth culture that recommends universal appeals to autonomy, anti-authoritarianism and refusal to conform.

Responses to these ads from Papua New Guinean university students and other young to middle-aged adults tended to be negative. Three interrelated objections were made to the images in *Pepsi*'s "Break Free" ads. First, the people depicted in the ads were described as "show-offs" or as "pretending to be somebody while they're not." This association of *Pepsi* with social pretension even came from a 34-year-old Milne Bay man who enjoyed the Break Free ads and endorsed the message of the lyrics: "I think Pepsi is drunk by people who just pretend to be different."

Second, the images in the ad were interpreted as being exclusionist and discriminatory—that is, as including only teenagers and young adults. Put differently, the images associated with *Pepsi* denied the democratic potential of soft drinks as accessible mass commodities. One 35-year-old man claimed that *Pepsi* is "only for the new generation"—a sign of the dubious success of *Pepsi*'s previous ad campaign—while another older man from Bougainville claimed that *Pepsi* "is only for people in the towns. The youth of the life in town." Other respondents associated *Pepsi* with "rich people" and "superstar" endorsers, such as Cindy Crawford—an association maybe strengthened by *Pepsi*'s sponsorship of a television show devoted to glitzy, foreign music videos.

Third, the Break Free images associated *Pepsi* in some people's view with a morally disreputable kind of person—"fancy people," "dancers," and "party-goers." (One student similarly linked *Pepsi* to the morally objectionable activities of one of its past spokespersons, Michael Jackson.) Several respondents commented unfavorably on the "sexual connotations" of *Pepsi*, specifically objecting to the image of the young woman in "tight jeans" as demeaning to PNG women and "irrelevant" to the context of PNG society. Elizabeth Solomon, sounding very much like an ex–school teacher, said that she associated the very sound of the word "*Pepsi*" with the hissing noises that young people use in public to attract each other's attention from afar. A 23-year-old young man wondered about what the couple crossing the street in the ad were trying to break free from: "Is it telling us to break our marriages by going out to have fun with Pepsi? . . . I don't know."

Now the *Coke* commercial (figure 7.3):

Coca-Cola Ad: To the strains of a few tentatively plucked guitar strings, a man emerges onto a porch from inside a house; a tropical bird perches on the porch railing. He nervously scans the horizon.

A *Coca-Cola* delivery truck rolls to a stop in front of a tree fallen across the road.

A young man, shirtless in a red *laplap* [sarong], opens a red cooler and rakes his fingers through the ice cubes; the cooler is empty. In the background, villagers prepare for a *singsing* [song/dance performance]; a man wipes his brow.

Back at the truck, the red-shirted driver waves at a passing airplane; he shouts into his radio. "Take it through!" The music quickens, and the guitars screech and grind.

An aerial shot of the village below with its thatched houses. A small child points at the plane. From the side of the plane, two red-shirted *Coca-Cola* employees drop a large red cooler, with the famous *Coca-Cola* script in white on its sides. The cooler parachutes downwards while a group of young boys, all in red shorts, run to collect it. The cooler gently splashes into a stream. The young boys merrily slide down the muddy bank of the stream into the water. They retrieve the cooler and haul it up the bank.

Back in the village, the cooler is now full of bottles of *Coca-Cola*. The

Figure 7.3. Newspaper circular advertising *Coca-Cola* soft drink, Port Moresby, Papua New Guinea, 1997.
Coca-Cola, Coke Always, and the Contour Bottle are registered trademarks of The Coca-Cola Company. Used by permission.

singsing proceeds, with traditionally decorated men pounding hourglass drums. The man who was first awaiting the delivery at the start of the commercial quaffs a bottle of *Coke*. An older man congratulates the young man who had worriedly inspected the empty cooler, both drinking thirstily from bottles of *Coke*. The *Coca-Cola* logo appears on the screen, encircled with the words, "Fun bilong yu, fun bilong *Coca-Cola*."

Like the *Pepsi* ad, this *Coke* ad projects an image of the product consistent with its globally asserted associations—in this case, associations with inclusive sociability, good times, and the celebration of tradition. Unlike the *Pepsi* ad, the *Coke* ad includes children, young adults, and, in its closing frame, an older adult. And unlike the *Pepsi* ad, the exclusion of girls and women from the foreground of the action obviates certain messages of sexual impropriety.[6] Indeed, the overt message of this *Coke* ad appears to be summarized in the mixed English/Tok Pisin of the logo: "Fun bilong yu, fun bilong *Coca-Cola*." In other words, *Coca-Cola* is easily incorporated into local traditions—a piece of modernity entirely compatible with valued ancestral customs. Here, then, is the modernity of certain anticolonial nationalisms as sold by a transnational corporation: the material and technological wonders of modernity can be happily married to the spiritual and moral values of indigenous traditional culture. The cargo has, at last, arrived. Papua New Guineans can determine themselves collectively—as a collective individual—not by breaking free from tradition and joining an international youth culture, but rather by staying put, incorporating and domesticating the material culture brought in—no matter what the obstacle—from the outside.

One respondent who participated in the survey—an anthropology student at the University of Papua New Guinea—criticized this *Coke* ad because it "demeans/exploits traditional dancing." Another student remarked: "They shouldn't use traditional clothes when advertising Coke. Coke is not part of our tradition and it should not interfere with our traditions." Opinions of this sort, advocating a clear separation between commercial enterprises and traditional or customary practices are not uncommon in PNG (see chapter 4 for an example). But on the whole, participants in the survey approved of this *Coke* ad. Several people recalled it without prompting as their favorite advertisement, and the reasons given for approving the ad generally invert the objections to the *Pepsi* ad. Simply put, respondents saw the ad as "more Papua New Guinean" because of its recognizably local setting. The village setting, moreover, evoked the democratic character of *Coke*. As one 26-year-old male art student put it: "[The ad] says that Coke is not for white men only but blacks can drink it too. With/without clothes in villages/towns—anywhere." Similarly, the village setting communicated an inclusive and uncomplicated kind of sociality, in which children and adults both participated. At least one respondent claimed that watching the ad made her happy. Even Elizabeth Solomon, who associated *Pepsi* with hissing adolescents and decried soft drinks as bad for one's health, yielded to the memories that the ad provoked for her. This 54-year-old grandmother, who had come to town only several months earlier to baby-sit, confessed that "I like village situations. [The ad] reminds me of home. I want to go back quickly."

*   *   *

The terms in which university students and other urban Papua New Guineans talk about *Coke* and *Pepsi* ads are the organizing terms of the ads themselves. These terms include a familiar litany of dichotomies: modernity/tradition; present/past; foreign/local; town/village; and elders/youth—such that a 26-year-old secretary from New Ireland can devise her own marketing analysis of the *Pepsi* campaign as follows: "For us the civilized, educated people in towns, I don't think the lady in the mini-top is insulting. Let's face it, it's today's fashion, but I guess those in the villages and elders will disapprove and say it's sexist." "But," she concludes in a way that echoes the *Pepsi* ad's lyrics, "like I said, people are different and have their own opinions." Here is an unambiguous example of the complexity involved in a network of perspectives: one perspective—a mapping of other people's meanings in the form of an ad—incites a woman's awareness of/construction of a perspective that she knows she does not share—that of the less civilized and less educated —but which she knows impinges uncomfortably on her own perspective. Or conversely, in the case of Elizabeth Solomon: an ad for *Coca-Cola* made by a transnational agency incites her construction of a perspective in which she does not feel at home—that of the white man's world entangling her children and grandchildren in urban Port Moresby.

In sum, contemporary advertisements for *Coke* and *Pepsi* in PNG improvise on a narrative tradition established with the very coming of carbonated soft drinks to the South Pacific during World War II. Consider figure 5.1, a 1945 print advertisement for *Coca-Cola*. Muscular male American soldiers, bottles of *Coca-Cola* in hand, watch a group of Admiralty Islands men, without bottles of *Coca-Cola*, stare in pop-eyed wonder at a shortwave radio. Soft drinks and shortwaves are both tokens of the modernity that separates the soldiers from the natives. Today, of course, the Admiralty Islanders have their own shortwave radios, and *Coke* too is not just for white men. The promise of modern materialism has been redeemed in the pause that refreshes.

CONCLUSION: ETHNOGRAPHIC PRACTICE IN THIS ERA OF GLOBALIZATION

Let me conclude briefly by raising again the question I posed earlier about ethnographic practice in this era of globalization: how do we do it? In this question we confront what has taken shape as the problem of globalizing fieldwork methods—the concern, as Gupta and Ferguson (1997:3) put it, "about the lack of fit between the problems raised by a mobile, changing, globalizing world, on the one hand, and the resources provided by a method originally developed for studying supposedly small-scale societies, on the other." Appadurai (1997:118) surely is correct in suggesting that fieldwork in this era of globalization "is not ultimately a problem of technique, either for anthropologists or anybody else. It is a challenge to the imagination and our ethical selves." But the penultimate question is not, after all, trivial: what techniques and tactics are available to fieldworking anthropologists for apprehending the sociocultural complexity of global flows of objects and images, capital and people? And what might be the consequence of adopting such techniques and tactics for the conventional disciplinary validation of anthropologists by—when all else fails—the practice of fieldwork?

The sort of ethnographic project entailed in a soft drink perspective on globalization involves a revisioning of fieldwork methods along the lines proposed by several anthropologists in the last few years. Some, like Gupta and Ferguson, have suggested that participant observation will need to take its place alongside "reading newspapers, analyzing government documents, observing the activities of governing elites, and tracking the internal logic of transnational development agencies and corporations" (1997:37). Other anthropologists, such as George Marcus (1995), have suggested that ethnography move from its conventional single-site location to multiple sites, deploying as it does so a variety of "tracking" strategies in which ethnographers follow people (such as scientists) or things (such as cans of *Coke*) through and across diverse and discontinuous social and cultural contexts.

I find little to argue with in these suggestions, although I recognize that there is plenty to discuss about negotiating the demands of intensive ethnography with mobile ethnography, as well as the practical logistics of multisited fieldwork. What strikes me in this connection is how infrequently one seemingly sensible suggestion is made: collaborative fieldwork—by which I mean not the sort of collaboration all ethnographers enter into (acknowledged or not) with informants or interlocutors. Nor do I mean the sort of multidisciplinary teamwork that Paul Stoller (1997) advocates on the basis of his study with a legal scholar of West African traders in New York City—teamwork with urban geographers, political scientists, and so forth. What I have in mind is collaboration among anthropologists—more-than-one-person fieldwork designed, to cite Marcus, "around chains, paths, threads, conjunctions or juxtapositions of locations in which the ethnographer [I suggest the plural, ethnographers] establishes some form of literal, physical presence with an explicit, posited logic of association or connection among sites that in fact defines the argument of the ethnography" (1995:105). It is this sort of collaboration, pressed on us by the realities of globalization, that might force anthropologists to drop what Appadurai (1997:118) calls "a crucial conceit of classical ethnography—its image of the self sufficiency of the ethnographer" (a conceit sustained even in Marcus's idea that multisited ethnographers think of themselves as artists—Russian constructivists, to be exact). Dropping this conceit would not mark the end of fieldwork, but perhaps the end of fieldwork as the heroic individual rite of passage that marks disciplinary legitimacy—which would in turn imply a revisioning of institutional practices. What would it take for a graduate student contemplating fieldwork to consider a project of collaborative, multisited research as academically viable? Or is it perhaps the case that collaborative multisited research must build on the prior experiences of intensive and individual single-site research if it is not to forfeit the insights of an ethnographic approach? What can we, wary of reinventing the wheel, learn from anthropology's own history of collaborative field projects?

The question of how merges into the question of why or for what stakes. Gupta and Ferguson encourage us to think of "shifting locations" rather than "bounded fields"—that is, not geographical locales, but rather "sites constructed in fields of unequal power relations" (1997:35). Sometimes these social sites do align with geographical locales: marginal in both senses, as in the case of the "out-of-the-way places" particularly associated with Melanesianist anthropology. But not always. Hence the sort of fieldwork that self-consciously shifts both geographical locale and/or social site potentially exposes phenomena that would otherwise remain invisible. What phenomena, and why should we care?

I would say first and foremost, again citing Gupta and Ferguson (1997:38), that this sort of fieldwork exposes "the ways in which we anthropologists are historically and socially (not just biographically) linked with the areas we study." (I would prefer to say "with the people we study.") This lesson has still not been fully acknowledged by Melanesianist anthropology which—more than any other regional subfield of anthropology—has taken furthest the methodological strategy of sustaining radical alterity in Us/Them terms. My own ethnographic analyses have been at times conducted in these terms. And, make no mistake, I do not wish to repudiate these terms here or to deny the critical insights they afford. But I do wish to claim that these terms and the fieldwork practices these terms underwrite do not accomplish what fieldwork attuned to shifting locations might accomplish; for this latter sort of fieldwork brings "our here and their there [into] a common ethical space" (Appadurai 1997:118).

Imagining "the field" as a network of interlocked perspectives potentially transforms not only the practice but also the politics of ethnography in an era of globalization. The political challenge, then, becomes one of how to connect and act on the different insights made possible from different perspectives—

how to trace "lines of possible alliance and common purpose between them" (Gupta and Ferguson 1997:39). The simple, almost banal observation that both Elizabeth Solomon and I worry about our children's consumption of soft drinks thus relocates Melanesia at the same time that it defines possible grounds for joint action—as consumers linked in a global commodityscape.

Notes

INTRODUCTION

1. See Harper (1999) for a discussion of how Hungarian environmental activists have resisted the postsocialist enticement of consumer identities by protesting the commercialization of public space.

2. Danforth (2001) has similarly extended the approach to the nation as narrative in his analysis of Australian soccer.

3. Australia ruled Papua (formerly British New Guinea) as a territory from 1906; from 1921, Australia ruled the Territory of New Guinea (formerly German New Guinea) by mandate of the League of Nations. The two territories were first jointly administered by Australia in 1949 as the United Nations Trust Territory of Papua and New Guinea; a legislative council was established in 1951. In 1964, the legislative council was replaced by a house of assembly with an elected indigenous majority. The territories were renamed "Papua New Guinea" in July 1971. Self-government was granted in December 1973, and full independence followed on 16 September 1975.

4. Tok Pisin, which originated as a trade jargon, is now the major lingua franca in PNG and one of the country's three official languages, along with English and Motu.

5. Similarly, it is frustration over the failure of development in PNG that often renders the turn of many people to millenarian Christianity as a potent form of "negative nationalism" (see chapter 6).

6. In Melanesia, only New Caledonia (Kanaky) and Irian Jaya (West Papua) remain colonies of France and Indonesia, respectively.

7. See Bodnar (1992) for a discussion of how monument making in the United States once entailed a set of contested meanings about local and ethnic identities largely irrelevant today.

8. Miller (1987, 1988) suggests that such domestication or "appropriation" is a mundane feature of all consumption in industrial societies in which almost everything one consumes has been anonymously produced by other people.

9. The competition/pageant form, however, generates its own instabilities. Consider the item in a recent *New York Times* (23 August 2001), "Multicultural Bronx stars strike nationalistic chord." The item reports how fans of the Rolando Paulino All-Stars from the Bronx, New York, waved flags of the Dominican Republic and Puerto Rico during the team's appearance at the Little League World Series. Many team members and their parents were born in the Dominican Re-

public and Puerto Rico. One of the Bronx team coaches, and Rolando Paulino himself, a league official, expressed concern about the appropriateness of waving anything but the American flag; some supporters of other American teams, according to the report, regard the Bronx players as foreigners.

10. Thus the most striking example of contesting the PNG flag reviewed by Strathern and Stewart: the flag's original designer, Susan K. Huhume, demanded in 1998 that if the state did not materially compensate her for her work (as the winner of a design competition when she was a 17-year-old high school student in 1970), then she would reclaim the flag on the grounds that it was her property (2000:28). Incidentally, Huhume reportedly chose the color white in the flag to represent the lime with which many Papua New Guineans chew betel nut, and red and yellow to represent PNG's splendid tropical flowers (*Pacific Islands Monthly,* February 1991).

11. Weber defined "the nation" as "a community of sentiment" but observed that "an unbroken scale of quite varied and highly changeable attitudes toward the idea of the 'nation' is to be found among social strata and also within single groups to whom language usage ascribes the quality of 'nations.' The scale extends from emphatic affirmation to emphatic negation and finally complete indifference" (1958:174).

1. TAKE CARE OF PUBLIC TELEPHONES

1. There is some evidence that the National Law Week Committee defined the PNG state in very similar terms. One of the prize-winning essays selected by the committee claims, "Since the people in the government are well educated, they can make laws and then pass these laws and expect the people in the country to follow these rules for the betterment of their lives, as well as for the development and the betterment of the country" (Wallace 1985:30).

2. It is worth noting that the universalist discourse of Christianity, pervasive in public affairs and enshrined in the preamble to the constitution of PNG, often reinforces this conception of a modern world inhabited by generic individuals. In some instances, however, this same universalism comes into conflict with state projects. Consider, for instance, the opposition of many church leaders to the introduction of capital punishment in PNG on the grounds that no one has the right to take another person's life.

3. I suggest in passing that this formulation of "caring" foregrounds what indigenous Melanesian views of personhood relegate to the background. Strathern (1988) has argued that the Melanesian person is relational—the precipitate or node of multiple and particular social relations. This particularity is irreducible, such that the concept of generically identical persons (whose identity is the basis for mutual care) is, while recognized, hardly taken for granted, let alone considered natural.

4. Several days later, a parody of Kapun's suggestion appeared in the form of an editorial cartoon depicting new requirements for Australian citizenship: "Applicants for Australian citizenship must demonstrate ability to consume 4 cans of Fosters plus 2 pies and sauce in 30 minutes flat" (*Post-Courier,* 3 August 1973).

5. The ban proved ineffective. See the *Times of Papua New Guinea,* 25 Janu-

ary 1985, "Buai ban loses its bite." See also the comments of Frank Senge, reporting in *Pacific Islands Monthly* on crackdowns on betel nut chewing in Port Moresby and Lae: "Only one other town authority—Goroka—was crazy enough to impose a buai [betel nut] ban in 1985. It was a disaster: instead of officers chasing buai chewers, the chewers almost mugged the officers" (July 1988).

6. One author's account of his participation in National Law Week attributed the idea to "the American institution of Law Day proclaimed by President Eisenhower in 1968 [*sic*]" (Wallace 1985:39).

2. YOUR MONEY, OUR MONEY, THE GOVERNMENT'S MONEY

1. The term "cargo cult" usually refers to the millenarian movements that occurred throughout Melanesia during the early period of European colonization and in the wake of World War II: "Charismatic cult leaders emerged among the native population, claiming that European trade goods (cargo) would arrive in the near future and be delivered to the natives in large quantities, heralding the dawn of a new era of plenty in which the 'cargo' would be controlled by natives and not by white men" (Seymour-Smith 1986:31).

3. PRINT ADVERTISEMENTS AND NATION MAKING

1. Diro, then a backbencher member of parliament from Central Province, was both deputy prime minister and head of the People's Action Party until a scandal over corruption forced his resignation in 1991. He subsequently returned to public politics as the governor of Central Province (see chapter 6).

2. The government delayed the enforcement of the Commercial Advertising Act as the result of requests presented by local business executives to Karl Stack, then the minister for industrial development, at a public meeting organized by the Chamber of Commerce in July 1985 (*Post-Courier,* 29 July 1985). A grace period of 540 days, into 1987, was subsequently approved by Parliament (*Post-Courier,* 19 November 1985). In 1990, then communications minister Brown Sinamoi announced that he would use the provisions of the act to stop the overseas production of company and annual reports (*Pacific Islands Monthly,* February 1990).

3. Thus, for example, the inclusion of a picture of a jar of Vegemite in the video that introduces visitors to the mission of the National Museum of Australia in Canberra, and the postcard reproduction of a Sunlight soap advertisement from the 1920s on sale at the souvenir stand.

4. This approach converges at points with the approach taken by Karl Deutsch in *Nationalism and Social Communication* (1966 [originally published 1953]). Deutsch argues that the ability to communicate effectively defines membership in a *people* or *nation* (terms that are not synonymous for Deutsch). He stresses, moreover, that such communicative ability does not require a shared language. Alternative "facilities," including, I suggest, primarily visual advertisements and shared consumption practices, equally enable social communication— mutual understanding of memories, associations, habits, and preferences. I emphasize, however, that shared "language" for communication does not imply social

solidarity; shared languages facilitate arguments and disagreements as well as consensus.

5. If consumers do not recognize this by no means self-evident rhetoric, then they will not be able to decode the message of an ad—that is, to recognize the ad *as an ad*. While this might seem a moot point in, say, the contemporary United States, it is particularly germane in contemporary PNG, especially rural PNG. However, note that consumers who contest, reject, or obviate the message of an ad nonetheless respond to the ad's rhetorical devices.

6. Consider in this regard Deutsch's (1966:172) definition of national consciousness: "National consciousness . . . is the attachment of secondary symbols of nationality to primary items of information moving through channels of social communication. Not wit, but 'French wit'; not thoroughness, but 'German thoroughness'; not ingenuity, but 'American ingenuity.' "

7. See Filer (1985) for some informed speculation on the identity of the readership of the *Post-Courier*. I would emphasize that although the newspaper reaches only 3 to 4 percent of the total population, its main constituency includes the urban-dwelling politicians, bureaucrats, and business people with most access to the financial and technical means for nation making in PNG (see, for example, figure 3.5; cf. Anderson's 1991 remarks about the "reading classes" of nineteenth-century Europe, 75 ff.). Put differently, its main constituency is the emerging middle class of urban PNG—the population of main concern in this chapter.

8. Both ads seem to have been produced by the same firm, Samuelson Talbot.

9. I would suggest that many Papua New Guineans sense these borders despite never having physically crossed them. Their intuition takes the often-reported form of stories about the unease people felt at the time of independence when it became necessary to convert Australian dollars into PNG kina (see chapter 2). Village men in New Ireland would often ask me if there were a different kind of money in America, or comment ironically when I informed them that PNG currency and coinage are produced abroad.

10. The tradition versus modernity contrast appeared more explicitly in other cigarette ads from the same period that juxtaposed pictures of Highlands-style round houses with the Port Moresby skyline.

11. This motif was used more recently in Toyota's "Wheels for the Nation" campaign, in which ads picture different types of Toyota trucks in various locales.

12. In this regard, it possible to compare the pilgrimages of colonial administrators (from province X to capital to province Y) that Anderson (1991) interprets as a potent force in first making a national community imaginable to the journey of Jumbo, the elephant sponsored by South Pacific beer. Jumbo traveled from Lae to the Mount Hagen show, stopping at various towns along the way, in a procession that linked communities through reference to the beer. Jumbo's movements were regularly reported in the *Post-Courier*, thus linking newspaper readers throughout the country to the elephant's progress (*Post-Courier*, 31 July 1973, 1 August 1973).

13. James Carrier has reminded me that the introduction of Ramu raw mill sugar and the disappearance of CSR (Australian made) refined sugar were not greeted happily by many Papua New Guineans, who thought the more expensive domestic product compared unfavorably with its foreign predecessor. These con-

sumers might well reject the message about enjoyment communicated in the ad. But—and this is my point more generally—to reject the message about enjoyment is not necessarily to reject the implicit message about Ramu sugar being a commodity owned by the nation; indeed, it could be because a consumer has accepted the implicit message that the person is aggravated by the claims of the explicit message—that is, Ramu sugar might be perceived as an inferior national commodity and hence a poor reflection on "the nation." This perception of Ramu as a national commodity was in any case evinced in some of the letters to the *Post-Courier* that expressed support for the product.

4. COMMERCIAL MASS MEDIA

1. For PNG, see, e.g., Battaglia 1992, 1995b, Errington and Gewertz 1995a, Gewertz and Errington 1991, Hirsch 1990, 1995, Kulick and Willson 1992, 1994, O'Hanlon 1993, 1995.

2. In 1994, a new commercial FM station, NauFM, began broadcasting nationwide. Based in Port Moresby, NauFM features American and Australian pop music and English-speaking disc jockeys. NauFM is part of PNG FM Ltd., which is 80 percent PNG owned; Communications Fiji Ltd., which has the management contract, owns the remaining 20 percent (Semel 1996). In 1997, PNG FM Ltd. launched a new station, Yumi ("You and me") FM. YumiFM is aimed at middle-aged listeners and broadcasts exclusively in Tok Pisin.

3. There is not now, nor has there ever been, a state-operated television network in PNG.

4. EM TV currently broadcasts via the Russian-owned Gorizont satellite, the footprint of which extends from New Zealand through Australia and Southeast Asia into India (John Taylor, personal communication, 1996).

5. Pacific View Productions is foreign owned, but local or "national" staff occupy important positions in the multiauthor production process, such as producer, director, and editor (see Sullivan n.d.).

6. *Mekim Musik,* renamed *Golden Mekim Musik,* is now sponsored by Benson and Hedges cigarettes.

7. For more on advertisements in PNG, see Errington and Gewertz 1996, Franklin 1990, Romaine 1990. For analyses of letters to PNG newspapers, see Cooper 1994, Filer 1985, Hogan 1985, and Lindstrom 1998. For an account that also draws on other materials from PNG newspapers, see Battaglia 1995b.

8. See note 5. Papua New Guinean actors also travel the country in theater groups that perform humorous instructional skits promoting new and unfamiliar products such as *Coca-Cola* soft drinks, Colgate toothpaste, and Omo washing powder (see the film *Advertising Missionaries,* directed by Chris Hilton and Gauthier Flauder [1996, Aspire Films]).

9. Recent uses of this contrast extend discussions of Melanesian personhood that date back to the work of Marcel Mauss and Maurice Leenhardt and that include the original ethnographic work of Kenneth Read.

10. This ad, according to EM TV station manager and chief executive John Taylor (personal communication, 1992), was filmed in Brisbane—rather than videotaped locally—using facilities unavailable in PNG.

11. The South Pacific Games, held in September 1991 in Port Moresby, are a kind of regional olympiad, complete with pomp and ceremony, souvenir caps and cassettes, and so forth. They were at the time probably the most expensive and dramatic project of official nationalism undertaken in postindependence PNG, a deliberate and concerted effort to market PNG to an international audience.

12. My thanks to the late Jeffrey Clark for bringing this letter to my attention.

13. For example, the image of the family in the SDA flyer—mom, dad (note "papa is tops" on the smaller child's T-shirt), and two children—is anything but an entrenched archetype in the collective representations of most Papua New Guineans. But this image of the family frequently appears in commercial advertising, especially for household cleaning products such as laundry detergent (see Foster 1993). This sort of advertising circulates not only images of new commodities, but also images of the proper social context of commodity consumption. To the extent that nuclear families serve as the units of consumption in highly commoditized societies, nuclear family imagery and ideology reinforces consumerist discourses. I thank Ranajit Guha for drawing my attention to this point.

14. "There Goes My Pay," written, produced and recorded by Richard Dellman, Last Card Studios (trading as Advantage), Boroko, PNG. The accompanying notes to this cassette describe Louie Warupi as a Yule Islander and lead guitarist for Tar Bar: "Through his work at Advantage, he has played and sung on more Radio and TV ads than any other Papua New Guinean."

6. NEWS OF THE WORLD

1. Of course, too, the experience of marginality does not require or imply the presence of Europeans on the scene. Thus, for example, Min/Mountain Ok groups such as the Asabano regarded themselves as remote from and peripheral to the more populated ritual center at Telefolmin.

2. Papua New Guineans, and perhaps Melanesians more generally, were arguably more internationally mobile as laborers in the nineteenth century than the twentieth century.

3. On a recent trip to the Tanga Islands, I observed the activity of multiple chapters of the Legion of Mary, small groups of Catholic men and women who meet regularly, sometimes at village shrines, to pray to the Virgin Mary. One woman explained to me that the Legion was brought to Tanga by a Filipina nun; moreover, she continued, the Legion ultimately originated in Ireland, where white people like myself come from ("*ples bilong yupela*" in Tok Pisin).

4. See the related discussion of apocalpyticism and globalization by Richard Eves, who points out that while Christianity in PNG always had a supralocal dimension, "What is new is that these [premillennial] discourses about the end of the world have brought the global horizon into prominence in a way that the previous more orthodox Christianity did not, so that local events take on significances that they did not have in the past" (2000:73).

5. See Kapferer (1988) for a discussion of the importance of legends of war and death, especially the legends of Gallipoli, in Australian nation making.

6. John MacAloon, who has studied the Olympic Torch Relay in other settings (see MacAloon and Kang 1990), notes that "world attention," far from fo-

cusing on the torch relay, is "a shared illusion of marginals and globalized elites alike" (personal communication, 2001).

7. MacAloon rightly points out that "safety of the flame" is a rhetorical feature of all torch relays, a cause and consequence of the flame's symbolic power (personal communication, 2001).

8. Siembo also mentioned seeking redress for the alleged wartime beheading of Orokaivas without a proper trial, thus further disrupting the dominant narrative (*Post-Courier,* 26 May 2000). For more on this allegation, and on the execution of Orokaivas charged with treason and murder by the Australian Army, see Newton (1996).

9. Of course, SOCOG officials themselves acutely felt the gaze of Euro-international media and the IOC, mindful that any trouble with the Torch Relay would be attributed to *Australian* mismanagement (MacAloon, personal communication, 2001). A May coup in Fiji—where the Torch Relay was ultimately canceled—and intensifying ethnic fighting in the Solomons—where the Torch Relay stopped before moving on to PNG—also fueled Australian media perceptions of Melanesia as a region spiraling downward into chaos and turmoil.

7. GLOBALIZATION

1. This survey was carried out with the assistance of students in the journalism program at the University of Papua New Guinea. Sixty-seven people, all living in Port Moresby during July 1997, were interviewed about their soft drink consumption practices and responses to soft drink advertising.

2. By the end of 1999, The Coca-Cola Company had reduced its holdings in CCA to about 37 percent of all ordinary shares (CCA Annual Report 1999). CCA sold its Snack Food Division in 1992 to United Biscuits of the United Kingdom.

3. "We designate certain bottling operations in which we have a noncontrolling ownership interest as 'anchor bottlers' due to their level of responsibility and performance. The strong commitment of anchor bottlers to their own profitable volume growth helps us meet our strategic goals and furthers the interests of our worldwide production, distribution and marketing systems. Anchor bottlers tend to be large and geographically diverse, with strong financial resources for long-term investment and strong management resources. In 1998, our anchor bottlers produced and distributed approximately 43 percent of our total worldwide unit case volume" (The Coca-Cola Company Annual Report 1998).

4. SP Holdings relinquished its *Pepsi* franchise and withdrew from the soft drink business in early 2000 when The Coca-Cola Company acquired bottling rights to all Schweppes brands in PNG; SP Holdings had previously bottled these products. By mid-2000, no PepsiCo, Inc. brands (such as *Pepsi-Cola* and *Mirinda*) were being bottled in PNG, although supermarkets in Port Moresby carried cans of *Pepsi-Cola* imported from Queensland, Australia.

5. According to one estimate, 58 percent of Papua New Guineans are without reasonable access to an adequate amount of drinking water from improved sources (United Nations Development Programme 2001:150). "Reasonable access is defined as the availability of at least 20 litres per person per day from a source within one kilometre of the user's dwelling. Improved sources include household

connections, public standpipes, boreholes with handpumps, protected dug wells, protected springs and rainwater collection" (United Nations Development Programme 2001:256).

6. Some respondents, however, commented on the masculine inflection of this ad. A 42-year-old man from Bundi who grew up in Kudiawa wrote, "I think [the] Coke advertisement shows *'em man tru ya'* [here's a real man]. It shows a man's sweat on his skin after a *singsing*, therefore, what makes a man a man."

References

Abu-Lughod, Lila. 1997. The interpretation of culture(s) after television. *Representations* 59:109–34.

Anderson, Benedict. 1991 [1983]. *Imagined Communities: Reflections on the Origins and Spread of Nationalism*. Rev. ed. London: Verso.

———. 1998. Nationalism, identity and the logic of seriality. Chap. 1 in *The Spectre of Comparisons: Nationalism, Southeast Asia and the World*, 29–45. New York: Verso.

Appadurai, Arjun. n.d. Communities of consumption: Public life in contemporary India. Typescript.

———. 1990. Disjuncture and difference in the global cultural economy. *Public Culture* 2(2):1–24.

———. 1991. Global ethnoscapes: Notes and queries for a transnational anthropology. In *Recapturing Anthropology: Working in the Present*, edited by Richard G. Fox, 191–210. Santa Fe, N.M.: School of American Research Press.

———. 1993. Patriotism and its futures. *Public Culture* 5(3):411–29.

———. 1997. Discussion: Fieldwork in the era of globalization. *Anthropology and Humanism Quarterly* 22:115–18. (Special issue, *Fieldwork Revisited: Changing Contexts of Ethnographic Practice in the Era of Globalization*, edited by Joel Robbins and Sandra Bamford.)

Appadurai, Arjun, ed. 1986. *The Social Life of Things: Commodities in Cultural Perspective*. Cambridge: Cambridge University Press.

Australia. 1962. Banks aid education drive. *Australian Territories* 2(5):34–35.

Babadzan, Alain. 1988. *Kastom* and nation building in the South Pacific. *Ethnicities and Nations: Processes of Interethnic Relations in Latin America, Southeast Asia, and the Pacific*, edited by R. Guidieri, F. Pellizi, and S. J. Tambiah, 199–228. Austin: University of Texas Press.

Balibar, Etienne. 1990. The nation-form: History and ideology. *Review* 13:329–61.

Bashkow, Ira. 2000. "Whitemen" are good to think with: How Orokaiva morality is reflected on whitemen's skin. *Identities* 7(3):281–332.

Battaglia, Debbora. 1992. Displacing culture: A joke of significance in urban Papua New Guinea. *New Literary History* 23:1003–17.

———. 1995a. Problematizing the self: A thematic introduction. In *Rhetorics of Self-Making*, edited by Debbora Battaglia, 1–15. Berkeley: University of California Press.

———. 1995b. On practical nostalgia: Self prospecting among urban Trobrianders. In *Rhetorics of Self-Making*, edited by Debbora Battaglia, 77–96. Berkeley: University of California Press.

Bauman, Zygmunt. 1998. *Globalization: The Human Consequences.* New York: Columbia University Press.

Bhabha, Homi K., ed. 1990. *Nation and Narration.* New York: Routledge.

Billig, Michael. 1995. *Banal Nationalism.* London: Sage.

Bodnar, John. 1992. *Remaking America: Public Memory, Commemoration, and Patriotism in the Twentieth Century.* Princeton, N.J.: Princeton University Press.

Boorstin, Daniel. 1973. *The Americans: The Democratic Experience.* New York: Random House.

Bourgois, Philippe. 1995. *In Search of Respect: Selling Crack in El Barrio.* Cambridge: Cambridge University Press.

Bronner, Simon J., ed. 1989. *Consuming Visions: Accumulation and Display of Goods in America, 1880–1920.* New York: W. W. Norton.

Carrier, James G. 1990a. The symbolism of possession in commodity advertising. *Man,* n.s., 25:693–706.

———. 1990b. Reconciling commodities and personal relations in industrial society. *Theory and Society* 19:579–98.

———. 1991. Gifts, commodities, and social relations: A Maussian view of exchange. *Sociological Forum* 6:119–36.

Carrier, James G., ed. 1995. *Occidentalism: Images of the West.* Oxford: Oxford University Press.

Cass, Philip. 2000. "*Yu mas kamap wan nesen*": The mainstream churches, Tok Pisin, and national identity in Papua New Guinea. *Paideuma* 46:253–66.

Clairmonte, Frederick, and John Cavanagh. 1988. *Merchants of Drink: Transnational Control of World Beverages.* Penang, Malaysia: Third World Network.

Clark, Jeffrey. 1997. Imagining the state, or tribalism and the arts of memory in the Highlands of Papua New Guinea. In *Narratives of Nation in the South Pacific,* edited by T. Otto and N. Thomas, 65–90. Amsterdam: Harwood Academic Publishers.

Cohen, Colleen Ballerino, Richard Wilk, and Beverly Stoeltje, eds. 1996. *Beauty Queens on the Global Stage: Gender, Contests and Power.* New York: Routledge.

Comaroff, Jean, and John L. Comaroff. 2000. Millennial capitalism: First thoughts on a second coming. *Public Culture* 12(2): 291–343. (Special Issue, *Millennial Capitalism and the Culture of Neoliberalism,* edited by Jean Comaroff and John L. Comaroff.)

Comaroff, John L. 1987. Of totemism and ethnicity: Consciousness, practice, and the signs of inequality. *Ethnos* 52(3–4):301–23.

Connell, John. 1984. Betel-mania in PNG. *Islands Business,* October, 57–58.

Cooper, David. 1994. Reading a public culture: Letters to the editor in a pidgin language newspaper. Master's thesis. Department of Anthropology, University of Western Ontario.

Corrigan, Philip. 1981. On moral regulation: Some preliminary remarks. *Sociological Review* 29(2):313–37.

Corrigan, Philip, and Derek Sayer. 1985. *The Great Arch: English State Formation as Cultural Revolution.* Oxford: Basil Blackwell.

Danforth, Loring M. 2001. Is the "world game" an "ethnic game" or an "Aussie game"? Narrating the nation in Australian soccer. *American Ethnologist* 28(2):363–87.

Dávila, Arlene. 1998. El Kiosko Budweiser: The making of a "national" television show in Puerto Rico. *American Ethnologist* 25(3):452–70.

Deutsch, Karl. 1966 [1953]. *Nationalism and Social Communication: An Inquiry into the Foundations of Nationality.* 2nd ed. Cambridge, Mass.: MIT Press.

Dinnen, Sinclair. 1986. Perspectives on law and order. In *Law and Order in a Changing Society,* edited by Louise Morauta, 76–89. Canberra: Department of Political and Social Change, Research School of Pacific Studies, Australian National University.

———. 2001. *Law and Order in a Weak State: Crime and Politics in Papua New Guinea.* Honolulu: University of Hawai'i Press.

Dundon, Alison. 1998. Sitting in canoes: Knowing places and imagining spaces among the Gogodala of Papua New Guinea. Ph.D. diss. Department of Archeology and Anthropology, Australian National University, Canberra.

Englund, Harri, and James Leach. 2000. Ethnography and the meta-narratives of modernity. *Current Anthropology* 41(2):225–48.

Epstein, A. L. 1992. *In the Midst of Life: Affect and Ideation in the World of the Tolai.* Berkeley: University of California Press.

Errington, Frederick K., and Deborah B. Gewertz. 1995a. *Articulating Change in the "Last Unknown."* Boulder, Colo.: Westview Press.

———. 1995b. Duelling currencies in East New Britain: The construction of shell money as national cultural property. Chap. 2 in *Articulating Change in the "Last Unknown,"* 49–76. Boulder, Colo.: Westview Press.

———. 1995c. From darkness to light in the George Brown Jubilee: The invention of nontradition and the inscription of national history in East New Britain. Chap. 3 in *Articulating Change in the "Last Unknown,"* 77–106. Boulder, Colo.: Westview Press.

———. 1996. The individuation of tradition in a Papua New Guinean modernity. *American Anthropologist* 98(1):114–26.

Eves, Richard. 2000. Waiting for the day: Globalisation and apocalypticism in central New Ireland, Papua New Guinea. *Oceania* 71(2):73–91.

Ewen, Stuart. 1992. Pragmatism's postmodern poltergeist. *New Perspectives Quarterly* 9(2):46–51.

Ewen, Stuart, and Elizabeth Ewen. 1982. *Channels of Desire: Mass Images and the Shaping of American Consciousness.* New York: McGraw-Hill.

Filer, Colin. 1985. What is this thing called "brideprice"? *Mankind* 15:163–83. (Special Issue, *Recent Studies in the Political Economy of Papua New Guinea,* edited by Don Gardner and Nicholas Modjeska.)

———. 1992. The escalation of disintegration and reinvention of authority. In *The Bougainville Crisis: 1991 Update,* edited by M. Spriggs and D. Denoon, 112–40. Department of Political and Social Change Monograph 16. Canberra: Australian National University.

Flannery, Tim. 1998. *Throwim Away Leg: Tree Kangaroos, Possums and Penis Gourds— On the Track of Unknown Mammals in Wildest New Guinea.* New York: Grove Press.

Foster, Robert J. 1991. Making national cultures in the global ecumene. *Annual Review of Anthropology.* 20:235–60.

———. 1993. Bodies, commodities and the nation-state in Papua New Guinea. Paper presented at the Association for Social Anthropology in Oceania Meeting, Kona, Hawai'i.

———. 1995a. *Social Reproduction and History in Melanesia: Mortuary Ritual, Gift Exchange and Custom in the Tanga Islands.* Cambridge: Cambridge University Press.

———. 1995b. Introduction: The work of nation making. In *Nation Making: Emergent Identities in Postcolonial Melanesia,* edited by Robert J. Foster, 1–30. Ann Arbor: University of Michigan Press.

———. 1999a. TV talk in Papua New Guinea: A search for policy in a weak state. *Pacific Journalism Review* 5(1):52–79.

———. 1999b. Marginal modernities: Identity and locality, mass media and commodity consumption. Paper presented at the German–American Frontiers of the Social and Behavioral Sciences Symposium, Dölln, Germany, March 25–28.

———. 2001. Unvarnished truths: Maslyn Williams and Australian government film in Papua and New Guinea. In *In Colonial New Guinea: Anthropological Perspectives,* edited by Naomi McPherson, 64–81. Pittsburgh: University of Pittsburgh Press.

———. 2002. Bargains with modernity in Papua New Guinea and elsewhere. In *Critically Modern: Alterities, Alternatives, Anthropologies,* edited by Bruce M. Knauft, 57–81. Bloomington: Indiana University Press.

Fox, Richard G., ed. 1990. *Nationalist Ideologies and the Production of National Cultures.* American Ethnological Society Monograph Series, No. 2. Washington, D.C.: American Anthropological Association.

Fox, Richard Wightman, and T. J. Jackson Lears, eds. 1983. *The Culture of Consumption: Critical Essays in American History 1880–1980.* New York: Pantheon Books.

Franklin, Karl. 1990. Cross-Cultural advertising: Tok Pisin and English in Papua New Guinea. *Language and Linguistics in Melanesia* 21:71–97.

Fry, Greg. 1997. Framing the islands: Knowledge and power in changing Australian images of "the South Pacific." *Contemporary Pacific* 9(2):305–44.

Frykman, Jonas. 1993. Becoming the perfect Swede: Modernity, body politics, and national processes in 20th century Sweden. *Ethnos* 58(3–4):259–74.

Gell, Alfred. 1986. Newcomers to the world of goods: Consumption among the Muria Gonds. In *The Social Life of Things,* edited by Arjun Appadurai, 110–38. Cambridge: Cambridge University Press.

Gewertz, Deborah B., and Frederick K. Errington. 1991. *Twisted Histories, Altered Contexts: Representing the Chambri in a World System.* Cambridge: Cambridge University Press.

———. 1996. On piety and PepsiCo in a Papua New Guinea "modernity." *American Ethnologist* 23(3):476–93.

———. 1999. *Emerging Class in Papua New Guinea: The Telling of Difference.* Cambridge: Cambridge University Press.

Gibson, John. 1995. *Food Consumption and Food Policy in Papua New Guinea.* Port Moresby, Papua New Guinea: Institute of National Affairs.

Giddens, Anthony, ed. 1986. *Durkheim on Politics and the State.* Translated by W. D. Halls. Stanford, Calif.: Stanford University Press.

Gladwell, Malcolm. 1997. The coolhunt. *New Yorker,* 17 March, 78–88.

Goizueta, Roberto C. 1989. Globalization: A soft drink perspective. *Vital Speeches of the Day,* 1 April, 360–62.

Grant, Bruce. 2001. New Moscow monuments, or, states of innocence. *American Ethnologist* 28(2):332–62.

Gregory, C. A. 1980. Gifts to men and gifts to God: Gift exchange and capital accumulation in contemporary Papua. *Man,* n.s., 15:626–52.

Gupta, Akhil. 1995. Blurred boundaries: The discourse of corruption, the culture of politics, and the imagined state. *American Ethnologist* 22(2):375–401.

Gupta, Akhil, and James Ferguson. 1997. Discipline and practice: "The field" as site, method and location in anthropology. In *Anthropological Locations: Boundaries and Grounds of a Field Science,* edited by A. Gupta and J. Ferguson, 1–46. Berkeley: University of California Press.

Guss, David. 1996. "Full speed ahead with Venezuela": The tobacco industry, nationalism, and the business of popular culture. *Public Culture* 9(1):33–54.

Handler, Richard. 1985. On having a culture: Nationalism and the preservation of Quebec's *patrimoine.* In *Objects and Others: Essays on Museums and Material Culture,* edited by G. W. Stocking Jr., 192–207. Madison: University of Wisconsin Press.

———. 1988. *Nationalism and the Politics of Culture in Quebec.* Madison: University of Wisconsin Press.

Hannerz, Ulf. 1987. The world in creolisation. *Africa* 57(4):546–59.

———. 1989. Culture between center and periphery: Toward a macroanthropology. *Ethnos* 54(3–4): 200–21.

———. 1992a. The global ecumene as a network of networks. In *Conceptualizing Society,* edited by Adam Kuper, 34–56. New York: Routledge.

———. 1992b. *Cultural Complexity: Studies in the Social Organization of Meaning.* New York: Columbia University Press.

Hansen, Karen. 1994. Dealing with used clothing: *Salaula* and the construction of identity in Zambia's third republic. *Public Culture* 6(3):503–23.

Harper, Krista. 1999. Citizens or consumers? Environmentalism and the public sphere in postsocialist Hungary. *Radical History Review* 74:96–111.

Harvey, Penelope. 1996. *Hybrids of Modernity: Anthropology, the Nation State and the Universal Exhibition.* New York: Routledge.

Hassall, Graham Hume. 1990. Religion and nation-state formation in Melanesia: 1945 to independence. Ph.D. diss. Australian National University, Canberra. Ann Arbor: University Microfilms International.

Haugerud, Angelique, M. Priscilla Stone, and Peter D. Little, eds. 2000. *Commodities and Globalization: Anthropological Perspectives.* New York: Rowman and Littlefield.

Hau'ofa, Epeli. 1994. Our sea of islands. *Contemporary Pacific* 6(1):148–61.

———. 1998. The ocean in us. *Contemporary Pacific* 10(2):392–410.

———. 2000. Epilogue: Pasts to remember. In *Remembrance of Pacific Pasts: An Invitation to Remake History,* edited by Robert Borofsky, 453–71. Honolulu: University of Hawai'i Press.

Heinze, Andrew R. 1990. *Adapting to Abundance: Jewish Immigrants, Mass Consumption and the Search for American Identity.* New York: Columbia University Press.

Herzfeld, Michael. 1997. *Cultural Intimacy: Social Poetics in the Nation-State.* New York: Routledge.

Hirsch, Eric. 1990. From bones to betelnuts: Processes of ritual transformation and the development of "national culture" in Papua New Guinea. *Man,* n.s., 25:18–34.

———. 1995. Local persons, metropolitan names: Contending forms of simultaneity among the Fuyuge, Papua New Guinea. In *Nation Making: Emergent Identities in Postcolonial Melanesia,* edited by Robert J. Foster, 185–206. Ann Arbor: University of Michigan Press.

Hirst, Paul Q., and Grahame Thompson. 1996. *Globalization in Question: The International Economy and the Possibilities of Governance.* Cambridge, Mass.: Blackwell Publishers.

Hobsbawm, Eric, and Terence Ranger, eds. 1983. *The Invention of Tradition.* Cambridge: Cambridge University Press.

Hogan, Evelyn. 1985. Controlling the bodies of women: Reading gender ideologies in Papua New Guinea. In *Women and Politics in Papua New Guinea.* Working Paper No. 6, Department of Political and Social Change, Research School of Pacific Studies, Australian National University, Canberra.

Jacobsen, Michael. 1995. Vanishing nations and the infiltration of nationalism: The case of Papua New Guinea. In *Nation Making: Emergent Identities in Postcolonial Melanesia,* edited by Robert J. Foster, 227–49. Ann Arbor: University of Michigan Press.

Jolly, Margaret. 1992. Specters of inauthenticity. *Contemporary Pacific* 4(1):49–72.

Jourdan, Christine. 1995. Stepping-stones to national consciousness: The Solomon Islands case. In *Nation Making: Emergent Identities in Postcolonial Melanesia,* edited by Robert J. Foster, 127–49. Ann Arbor: University of Michigan Press.

Kapferer, Bruce. 1988. *Legends of People, Myths of State: Violence, Intolerance and Political Culture in Sri Lanka and Australia.* Washington, D.C.: Smithsonian Institution Press.

Kasaipwalova, John. 1987. Betel-nut is bad magic for aeroplanes. Reprinted in *Through Melanesian Eyes: An Anthology of Papua New Guinean Writing,* compiled by Ganga Powell, 69–77. Melbourne: Macmillan.

Keesing, Roger M. 1989. Creating the past: Custom and identity in the contemporary Pacific. *Contemporary Pacific* 1(1–2):19–42.

Kelly, John D. 1995. The privileges of citizenship: Nations, states, markets and narratives. In *Nation Making: Emergent Identities in Postcolonial Melanesia,* edited by Robert J. Foster, 253–73. Ann Arbor: University of Michigan Press.

Kemper, Steven. 1993. The nation consumed: Buying and believing in Sri Lanka. *Public Culture* 5(3):377–93.

Knauft, Bruce M. 1989. Bodily images in Melanesia: Cultural substances and natural metaphors. In *Fragments for a History of the Human Body, Part 3,* edited by M. Feher with R. Naddaff and N. Tazi, 198–279. New York: Zone Publications.

———. 2002. Trials of the oxymodern: Public practice at Nomad Station. In *Critically Modern: Alterities, Alternatives, Anthropologies,* edited by Bruce M. Knauft, 105–143. Bloomington: Indiana University Press.

Kulick, Don. 1992. *Language Shift and Cultural Reproduction: Socialization, Self and Syncretism in a Papua New Guinean Village.* Cambridge: Cambridge University Press.

Kulick, Don, and Margaret Willson. 1992. Echoing images: The construction of savagery among Papua New Guinean villagers. *Visual Anthropology* 5(2):143–52.

———. 1994. Rambo's wife saves the day: Subjugating the gaze and subverting the narrative in a Papua New Guinean swamp. *Visual Anthropology Review* 10(2):1–13.

Larmour, Peter. 1996. Research on governance in weak states in Melanesia. State, society and governance in Melanesia. Discussion Paper 96/1. Research School of Pacific and Asian Studies, Australian National University, Canberra.

Lattas, Andrew. 1992. Skin, personhood and redemption: The double self in West New Britain cargo cults. *Oceania* 63(1):27–54.

Lātūkefu, Sione. 1988. Noble traditions and Christian principles as national ideology in Papua New Guinea: Do their philosophies complement or contradict each other? *Pacific Studies* 11(2):83–96.

Layton, Suzanna. 1995. Fuzzy-wuzzy devils: Mass media and the Bougainville crisis. *Contemporary Pacific* 4(2): 299–323.

Leiss, William, Stephen Kline, and Sut Jhally. 1990. *Social Communication in Advertising: Persons, Products, and Images of Well Being.* New York: Routledge.

Lepowsky, Maria. 1982. A comparison of alcohol and betelnut use on Vanatinai (Sudest Island). In *Through a Glass Darkly: Beer and Modernization in Papua New Guinea,* edited by Mac Marshall, 325–42. Boroko, Papua New Guinea: Institute of Applied Social and Economic Research.

Levitt, Theodore. 1988. The pluralization of consumption. *Harvard Business Review,* May–June, 7–8.

Linde-Laursen, Anders. 1993. The nationalization of trivialities: How cleaning becomes an identity marker in the encounter of Swedes and Danes. *Ethnos* 58(3–4):275–93.

Lindstrom, Lamont. 1993. *Cargo Cult: Strange Stories of Desire from Melanesia and Beyond.* Honolulu: University of Hawaii Press.

———. 1995. Cargoism and occidentalism. In *Occidentalism: Images of the West,* edited by James G. Carrier, 33–60. New York: Oxford University Press.

———. 1998. *Pasin tumbuna:* Culture and nationalism in Papua New Guinea. In *From Beijing to Port Moresby: The Politics of National Identity in Cultural Policies,* edited by Virginia Dominguez and David Wu, 141–88. Amsterdam: Gordon and Breach.

Linnekin, Jocelyn. 1990. The politics of culture in the Pacific. In *Cultural Identity and Ethnicity in the Pacific,* edited by Jocelyn Linnekin and Lin Poyer, 149–73. Honolulu: University of Hawaii Press.

Linnekin, Jocelyn, and Lin Poyer. 1990. Introduction. In *Cultural Identity and Ethnicity in the Pacific,* edited by Jocelyn Linnekin and Lin Poyer, 1–16. Honolulu: University of Hawaii Press.

LiPuma, Edward. 1995. The formation of nation-states and national cultures in Oceania. In *Nation Making: Emergent Identities in Postcolonial Melanesia,* edited by Robert J. Foster, 33–68. Ann Arbor: University of Michigan Press.

———. 2000. *Encompassing Others: The Magic of Modernity in Melanesia.* Ann Arbor: University of Michigan Press.

Löfgren, Orvar. 1989a. The nationalization of culture. *Ethnologia Europaea* 19(1):5–24.

———. 1989b. Anthropologizing America (review essay). *American Ethnologist* 16(2): 366–74.

———. 1993. Materializing the nation in Sweden and America. *Ethnos* 58(3–4):161–96.

———. 1996. The nation as home or motel? On the ethnography of belonging. *Anthropology Newsletter,* October, 33–34.

Lukes, Steven. 1973. *Individualism.* Oxford: Basil Blackwell.

MacAloon, John J., and Kang Shin-pyo. 1990. Uri Nara: Korean nationalism, the Seoul

Olympics, and contemporary anthropology. In *Toward One World, Beyond All Barriers,* vol. 1, edited by Koh Byong-ik et al., 117–60. Seoul: Poong Nam Publishing.

MacDonald, R. 1995. Selling a dream. *Australian Magazine,* 4–5 November, 25–28.

MacWilliam, Scott. 1996. "Just like working for the dole": Rural households, export crops and state subsidies in Papua New Guinea. *Journal of Peasant Studies* 23(4): 40–78

McDannell, Colleen. 1995. *Material Christianity: Religion and Popular Culture in America.* New Haven, Conn.: Yale University Press.

Marcus, George. 1995. Ethnography in/of the world system: The emergence of multi-sited ethnography. *Annual Review of Anthropology* 24:95–117.

Mauss, Marcel. 1990 [1925]. *The Gift: The Form and Reason for Exchange in Archaic Societies.* Translated by W. D. Halls. New York: W. W. Norton.

Mbembe, Achille. 1991. The banality of power and the aesthetics of vulgarity in the postcolony. *Public Culture* 4(2):1–30.

Merlan, Francesca, and Alan Rumsey. 1991. *Ku Waru: Language and Segmentary Politics in the Western Nebilyer Valley, Papua New Guinea.* Cambridge: Cambridge University Press.

Michaels, Walter Benn. 1987. *The Gold Standard and the Logic of Naturalism: American Literature at the Turn of the Century.* Berkeley: University of California Press.

Migdal, Joel S. 1988. *Strong Societies and Weak States: State–Society Relations and State Capabilities in the Third World.* Princeton, N.J.: Princeton University Press.

Mihalic, F. *The Jacaranda Dictionary and Grammar of Melanesian Pidgin.* Milton, Australia: Jacaranda Press.

Miller, Daniel. 1987. *Material Culture and Mass Consumption.* Oxford: Basil Blackwell.

———. 1988. Appropriating the state on the council estate. *Man,* n.s., 23:353–72.

———. 1997. *Capitalism: An Ethnographic Approach.* Oxford: Berg.

Mintz, Sidney. 1976. *Sweetness and Power: The Place of Sugar in Modern History.* New York: Penguin Books.

———. 1996. Food and its relationship to concepts of power. Chap. 2 in *Tasting Food, Tasting Freedom: Excursions into Eating, Culture and the Past,* 17–32. Boston: Beacon Press.

Mira, William J. D. 1986. *From Cowrie to Kina: The Coinages, Currencies, Badges, Medals, Awards and Decorations of Papua New Guinea.* Sydney: Spink and Son.

Morauta, Louise, ed. 1986a. *Law and Order in a Changing Society.* Canberra: Department of Political and Social Change, Research School of Pacific Studies, Australian National University.

———. 1986b. Law and order: A tenth anniversary report. In *Law and Order in a Changing Society,* edited by Louise Morauta, 7–19. Canberra: Department of Political and Social Change, Research School of Pacific Studies, Australian National University.

Munn, Nancy D. 1990. Constructing regional worlds in experience: Kula exchange, witchcraft and Gawan local events. *Man,* n.s., 25:1–17.

Narokobi, Bernard. 1980. Take another bite of the betel nut. In *The Melanesian Way,* edited by H. Olela, 49–52. Boroko, Papua New Guinea: Institute of Papua New Guinea Studies.

Nash, Sorariba. 1995. National radio and development. In *Nius Bilong Pasifik: Mass Me-*

dia in the Pacific, edited by David Robie, 35–46. Port Moresby: University of Papua New Guinea Press.

Nelson, Hank. 2000. Liberation: The end of Australian rule in Papua New Guinea. *Journal of Pacific History* 35(3):269–80.

Neumann, Klaus. 1992. *Not the Way It Really Was: Constructing the Tolai Past.* Honolulu: University of Hawaii Press.

Newton, Janice. 1996. Angels, heroes and traitors: Images of some Papuans in the second world war. *Research in Melanesia* 20:141–56.

Nihill, Michael. 1989. The new pearlshells: Aspects of money and meaning in Anganen exchange. *Canberra Anthropology* 12 (1–2):144–59.

O'Barr, William. 1989. The airbrushing of culture: An insider looks at global advertising. *Public Culture* 2(1):1–19.

O'Hanlon, Michael. 1993. *Paradise: Portraying the New Guinea Highlands.* London: British Museum Press.

———. 1995. Modernity and the "graphicalization" of meaning: New Guinea Highland shield design in historical perspective. *Journal of the Royal Anthropological Institute* 1(3):469–93.

Otto, Ton. 1997. After the "tidal wave": Bernard Narokobi and the creation of a Melanesian way. In *Narratives of Nation in the South Pacific,* edited by T. Otto and N. Thomas, 33–64. Amsterdam: Harwood Academic Publishers.

Otto, Ton, and Nicholas Thomas. 1997. Narratives of nation in the South Pacific. In *Narratives of Nation in the South Pacific,* edited by T. Otto and N. Thomas, 1–13. Amsterdam: Harwood Academic Publishers.

Papua New Guinea. 1987a. *Money: Community Life Pupil Book.* Port Moresby, Papua New Guinea: Department of Education.

———. 1987b. The report of the board of inquiry into broadcasting (including television) in Papua New Guinea. Port Moresby, Papua New Guinea: Government Printing Office.

———. 1993. National policy on information and communication of Papua New Guinea. Division of Policy and Research, Department of Information and Communication. Port Moresby, Papua New Guinea: Government Printing Office.

———. 1994. TV impact study on Pari and Hanuabada villages, Papua New Guinea. Division of Policy and Research, Department of Information and Communication. Port Moresby, Papua New Guinea: K. Kaiah, Acting Government Printer.

Parry, Jonathan, and Maurice Bloch, eds. 1989. *Money and the Morality of Exchange.* Cambridge: Cambridge University Press.

Pendergrast, Mark. 1993. *For God, Country and Coca-Cola: The Unauthorized History of the Great American Soft Drink and the Company That Makes It.* New York: Macmillan.

Pietz, William. 1985. The problem of the fetish, I. *Res* 9:5–17.

———. 1987. The problem of the fetish, II. *Res* 13:23–45.

———. 1988. The problem of the fetish, IIIa. *Res* 16:105–23.

Powdermaker, Hortense. 1950. *Hollywood: The Dream Factory.* Boston: Little, Brown.

Project Liberty. 1993. Why a bankrupt America? Arvada, Colo.: Project Liberty.

Reed, Liz. 1999. "Part of our own story": Representations of indigenous Australians and Papua New Guineans within Australia Remembers 1945–1995; The continuing desire for a homogeneous national identity. *Oceania* 69(3):157–70.

Reilly, Benjamin. 2000–2001. Democracy, ethnic fragmentation, and internal conflict: Confused theories, faulty data, and the "crucial case" of Papua New Guinea. *International Security* 25(3):162–85.

Reserve Bank of Australia. 1961a. Your money. Sydney: Reserve Bank of Australia.

——. 1961b. What is wealth? Sydney: Reserve Bank of Australia.

——. 1962a. Your money [film version]. Sydney: Reserve Bank of Australia.

——. 1962b. What is wealth? [film version]. Sydney: Reserve Bank of Australia.

Ricketts, Kevin. 2000. Fuzzy wuzzies still await recognition. *Post-Courier*, 25 April, p. 11.

Robbins, Joel. 1997a. "When do you think the world will end?": Globalization, apocalypticism, and the moral perils of fieldwork in "last New Guinea." *Anthropology and Humanism* 22:6–30.

——. 1997b. 666, or Why is the millennium on the skin? Morality, the state and the epistemology of apocalypticism among the Urapmin of Papua New Guinea. In *Millennial Markers*, edited by Pamela Stewart and Andrew Strathern, 35–58. Townsville, Australia: Centre for Pacific Studies, James Cook University.

——. 1998. On reading "world news": Apocalyptic narrative, negative nationalism and transnational Christianity in a Papua New Guinea society. *Social Analysis* 42(2):103–30.

Robie, David. 1995. Ownership and control in the Pacific. In *Nius Bilong Pasifik: Mass Media in the Pacific*, edited by David Robie, 5–15. Port Moresby: University of Papua New Guinea Press.

Romaine, Suzanne. 1990. Pidgin English advertising. In *The State of the Language*, edited by C. Ricks and L. Michaels, 195–203. Berkeley: University of California Press.

Rosi, Pamela. 1991. Papua New Guinea's new Parliament House: A contested national symbol. *Contemporary Pacific* 3(2):289–324.

Sack, Peter, and Dymphna Clark, ed. and trans. 1979. *German New Guinea: The Annual Reports.* Canberra: Australian National University Press.

Sahlins, Marshall. 1992. The economics of develop-man in the Pacific. *Res* 21:3–25.

——. 1993. Goodbye to *Tristes Tropes:* Ethnography in the context of modern world history. *Journal of Modern History* 65:1–25.

——. 1999. What is anthropological enlightenment? Some lessons of the twentieth century. *Annual Review of Anthropology* 28:i–xxiii.

——. 2000. "Sentimental pessimism" and ethnographic experience; or, Why culture is not a disappearing "object." In *Biographies of Scientific Objects*, edited by Lorraine Daston, 158–202. Chicago: University of Chicago Press.

Schein, Louisa. 1998. Of cargo and satellites: Imagined cosmopolitanism. Typescript.

Semel, Raphael. 1996. Radio wars: NauFM's tough struggle. *Pacific Journalism Review* 3(2):112–15.

Seymour-Smith, Charlotte. 1986. *Dictionary of Anthropology.* New York: G. K. Hall.

Shell, Marc. 1982. The gold bug. Chap. 1 in *Money, Language, and Thought: Literary and Philosophical Economies from the Medieval to the Modern Era*, 5–23. Berkeley: University of California Press.

Sissons, Jeffrey. 1997. Nation or desti-nation? Cook Islands nationalism since 1965. In *Narratives of Nation in the South Pacific*, edited by T. Otto and N. Thomas, 163–88. Amsterdam: Harwood Academic Publishers.

Spitulnik, Debra. 1993. Anthropology and mass media. *Annual Review of Anthropology* 22:293–315.

Standish, Bill. 1994. Papua New Guinea: The search for security in a weak state. In *Papua New Guinea: Issues for Australian Security Planners,* edited by Alan Thompson, 51–97. Canberra: Australian Defence Studies Centre.

———. 2000. Papua New Guinea reflects. *Journal of the Pacific Society* 23(3–4):76–84.

Stoller, Paul. 1997. Globalizing method: The problems of doing ethnography in transnational spaces. *Anthropology and Humanism Quarterly* 22:81–94. (Special Issue, *Fieldwork Revisited: Changing Contexts of Ethnographic Practice in the Era of Globalization,* edited by Joel Robbins and Sandra Bamford.)

Strathern, Andrew J. 1993. Violence and political change in Papua New Guinea. *Pacific Studies* 16(4):41–60.

Strathern, Andrew J., and Pamela J. Stewart. 2000. *"Mi les long yupela usim flag bilong mi":* Symbols and identity in Papua New Guinea. *Pacific Studies* 23(1–2):21–49.

Strathern, Marilyn. 1988. *The Gender of the Gift: Problems with Women and Problems with Society in Melanesia.* Berkeley: University of California Press.

———. 1991. Partners and consumers: Making relations visible. *New Literary History* 22:581–601.

Sullivan, Nancy. n.d. MTV for PNG: Music video production in Papua New Guinea. Typescript.

———. 1993. Television and video production in Papua New Guinea: How media become the message. *Public Culture* 5(3):533–55.

Taussig, Michael. 1992. Maleficium: State fetishism. Chap. 7 in *The Nervous System,* 111–40. New York: Routledge.

Thomas, Nicholas. 1991. *Entangled Objects: Exchange, Material Culture and Colonialism in the Pacific.* Cambridge, Mass.: Harvard University Press.

———. 1997. Nations' endings: From citizenship to shopping? In *Narratives of Nation in the South Pacific,* edited by T. Otto and N. Thomas, 211–19. Amsterdam: Harwood Academic Publishers.

Tobin, Joseph. 1992. Introduction: Domesticating the West. In *Re-Made in Japan: Everyday Life and Consumer Taste in a Changing Society,* edited by Joseph Tobin, 1–41. New Haven, Conn.: Yale University Press.

Tomlinson, John. 1999. *Globalization and Culture.* Chicago: University of Chicago Press.

Tsing, Anna Lowenhaupt. 1993. *In the Realm of the Diamond Queen: Marginality in an Out-of-the-Way Place.* Princeton, N.J.: Princeton University Press.

United Nations Development Programme. 2001. *Human Development Report 2001.* New York: Oxford University Press.

Wallace, I. M., ed. 1985. *Papua New Guinea National Law Week 1984: A Record of the Events and Activities Organised by the National Law Week Committee.* Department of Justice, Executive Branch, Central Government Office, Waigani, Port Moresby, Papua New Guinea.

Wallerstein, Immanuel. 1991. *Report on an Intellectual Project: The Fernand Braudel Center, 1976–1991.* Binghamton, N.Y.: Fernand Braudel Center.

Wanek, Alexander. 1995. *The State and Its Enemies in Papua New Guinea.* Richmond, UK: Curzon Press.

Wardlow, Holly. 1996. *Bobby Teardrops:* A Turkish video in Papua New Guinea: Reflections on cultural studies, feminism, and the anthropology of mass media. *Visual Anthropology Review* 12(1):30–45.

Warhol, Andy. 1975. *The Philosophy of Andy Warhol: From A to B and Back Again.* New York: Harcourt Brace Jovanovich.

Webb, Michael. 1993. *Lokal Musik: Lingua Franca Song and Identity in Papua New Guinea.* Port Moresby, Papua New Guinea: Cultural Studies Division, National Research Institute.

Weber, Max. 1958. Structures of power. Chap. 6 in *From Max Weber: Essays in Sociology,* translated and edited by H. Gerth and C. Wright Mills, 159–79. New York: Oxford University Press.

White, Geoffrey M. 1995. Remembering Guadalcanal: National identity and transnational memory-making. *Public Culture* 7(3):529–55.

Wilk, Richard. 1995. Learning to be local in Belize: Global systems of common difference. In *Worlds Apart: Modernity through the Prism of the Local,* edited by Daniel Miller, 110–33. London: Routledge.

Williams, Maslyn. 1970. *In One Lifetime.* Melbourne: Cheshire.

Williamson, Judith. 1978. *Decoding Advertisements: Ideology and Meaning in Advertisements.* New York: Marion Boyars.

Willis, Paul. 1981 [1977]. *Learning to Labor: How Working Class Kids Get Working Class Jobs.* New York: Columbia University Press.

Young, Michael. 1997. Commemorating missionary heroes: Local Christianity and narratives of nationalism. In *Narratives of Nation in the South Pacific,* edited by T. Otto and N. Thomas, 91–132. Amsterdam: Harwood Academic Publishers.

Index

Robert J. Foster is Associate Professor and Chair of Anthropology at the University of Rochester. He is author of *Social Reproduction and History in Melanesia* and editor of *Nation Making: Emergent Identities in Postcolonial Melanesia.*

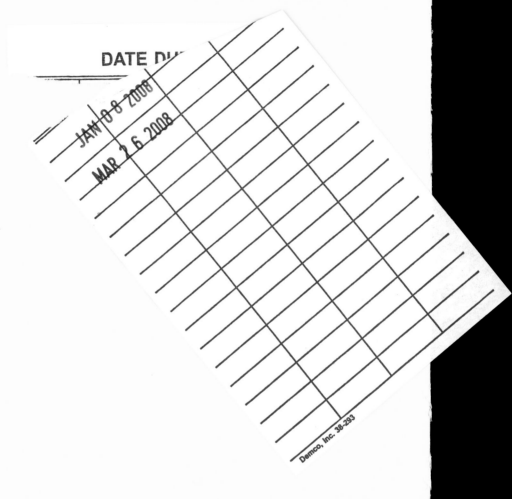